THE
IT W
THE G
BO
REGRETTABLE
QUOTATIONS

THEY GOT IT WRONG!

THE GUINNESS BOOK OF REGRETTABLE QUOTATIONS

COMPILED BY

DAVID MILSTED

GUINNESS PUBLISHING

For my family and friends
and for Jan, as always.

33 London Road, Enfield, Middlesex.

Reprint 10 9 8 7 6 5 4 3 2 1 0

Cover and book design by John Rivers

Typeset by Ace Filmsetting Ltd., Frome, Somerset.
Printed and bound in Great Britain by Cox & Wyman, Reading.

A catalogue record for this book is available from the British Library.

ISBN 0–85112–660–X

Contents

ACKNOWLEDGEMENTS

My thanks are due – and readily given – to the following books, whose authors have previously ploughed over, or around, the field of my investigations. They are recommended reading for anyone who would like to explore the arcana of Regrettability in depth. Alternatively, you could try locking yourself in a padded cell for a month to read the collected prose works of George Bernard Shaw.

Christopher Cerf and Victor S. Navasky: *The Experts Speak: the definitive compendium of authentic misinformation*, Pantheon Books (New York), 1984.

Brian J. Ford: *The Cult of the Expert*, Hamish Hamilton, 1982.

Don Atyeo and Jonathon Green: *Don't Quote Me*, Hamlyn p/back, 1981.

Graham Nown: *The World's Worst Predictions*, Arrow p/back, 1985.

Ronald Duncan with Melvyn Harris, *Critics' Gaffes*, Futura p/back, 1983.

R. L. Weber and E. Mendoza, *A Random Walk in Science*, Institute of Physics, 1973.

André Bernard (Ed.), *Rotten Rejections*, Robson Books, 1991.

Chris Morgan and David Langford, *Facts and Fallacies*, Webb & Bower, 1981.

This book has been written with the active help of many people, most of whom I have never met. For assistance far above and beyond the bounds of helpful curiosity – or even friendship – I wish to thank especially Charles Fyffe, Bernard Langley, Annette Lobb, Professor Garry Tee (University of Auckland) and Francis Wheen. Few acts are nobler than that of lending a book, by post, to a complete stranger. You know who you are, Bernard.

The following people sent me material without which this book would be the poorer. Thank you all for your help.

J. Bradley, Glen Chilton (University of Calgary), R. A. Collinssplatt, Mrs E. Cook, C. B. Cooper, Michael Cross, Manny Curtiss, Dr Bill Duffin, Geoff Edgington, Alan Edwards, Breda Egan, C. Frank Fischl, Professor Antony Flew, Brian Franklin, Naomi Goldblum, Rabia Harris, Professor John Hibbs, Bill High, Wing Commander T. F. G. Hudson, Maurice Jay, J. Jocelyn, Colin Jordan, N. G. van Kampen (University of Utrecht), Joan F. Lafferty, Mrs Ursula E. K. Light, Andrew Lobb, C. Lynch, Roy Maxwell, Alex Milne, John N. G. Pisani, Roderick Ramage, Michael Rubinstein, Richard Smith, J. C. Stewart, Mark Terrell, David Wilson, Christopher Yates.

I am grateful to Max Davidson and the *Sunday Express* for running a feature on the book's preparation, and to the Letters Editors of the following publications for allowing me to appeal for help to their readers:

The Connoisseur, *Doctor*, *The Independent*, *The Literary Review*, *New Scientist*, and *The Spectator*. Thanks also to *Private Eye* for being there every fortnight.

Finally, I'm happy to thank my editor, Richard Milbank, for saying 'yes' in the first place – and for quite a lot else.

I think that's it; my apologies if it isn't.

THE ART OF REGRETTABILITY

Next to being right in this world, the best of all things is to be clearly and definitely wrong.
T. H. Huxley.

There is more to achieving Regrettability than being merely wrong. Millions of us get it wrong every time we buy a ticket for the National Lottery, but we don't expect to be known for the rest of our lives as the person who wasted a whole pound, or even a million pounds, on six useless numbers. Wrongness of this sort, even on a grand scale, does not achieve the special quality of Regrettability.

Nor is it necessarily even a matter of publicity. You could go out and buy yourself a million Lottery tickets, and be quoted in a mass-circulation newspaper prophesying huge winnings, and end up winning nothing at all, and still not be Regrettable. You'd just be a perfectly ordinary and sadly unremarkable monumental idiot . . .

Unless, that is, you happened to be an eminent professor of Mathematics, one of the foremost authorities of your generation on Probability Theory and the author of a well-known work on the futility of betting systems and the gullibility of those who are taken in by them. You'd become Regrettable then, all right: in fact, you would be in a very similar situation to the one Lord Dacre found himself in after he pronounced on the authenticity of the 'Hitler Diaries'. Your name would feature in subsequent editions of this book.

This would, of course, be a great honour. Even so, £1m seems rather a high price to pay for it. It's not recommended. And in any case, for each person who goes out of his (or, I need surely not add again, her) way to achieve such immortality there are bound to be dozens more who have it, so to speak, thrust upon them simply as a reward for being their own very special and wonderful selves.

These are the people who are quoted in this book: the professionals, people who, in the chosen courses of their lives, have talked or written themselves into the halls of cherished incorrectitude: people who ought to have known better. . . .

People such as the critics, for instance. Criticism, in its purest form, is simply an argued opinion on a subject about which a final, objective, right-or-wrong answer will never be found. Criticism in its purest form, then, is incapable of being Regrettable. But when the form is corrupted – as it so often is – Regrettability is the inevitable consequence. The critic who strays from the simple path of saying 'I like/don't like this, and now I'll try to explain why' is bound to write himself into a hole, sooner or later; he becomes a victim of his own self-esteem, a believer in his own infallibility. The critic who can make or break a show – or a book, or film, or painting – with one review has certainly existed, from time to time, but he is the exception, not the rule, and he's bound to come a cropper in the end. As in the case – to take a topical example – of the stock market gambler who tries to push the market up to recoup the disastrous losses of his earlier betting, real life always breaks in eventually. And a good thing, too.

Then there is the critic's close cousin, the pundit. We are all, of course, amateur pundits. We all make confident predictions about elections, wars, the economy, football matches and so on, in the comfort of our own homes, or pubs, or bus queues. But we're not Regrettable, because we don't do it for money. We don't take ourselves seriously enough. We don't believe our special wisdom gives us revelations that lesser mortals are too stupid to see or understand for themselves. Pundits do. Day in, day out, week after week in newspapers and magazines, like saloon-bar bores from hell, they tell us what is fit for us to think, believe and know. Often they do it with great condescension. Since they presumably regard being colossally wrong from time to time as an acceptable occupational hazard, it surely won't hurt them to be reminded of it now and again. If being wrong was a sackable offence for pundits, they'd all be unemployed – and, after all, they don't do any real harm.

Politicians do, though. Politicians are a special case: we expect them to talk rubbish, most of the time. It's their job to tell us things are getting better when we know they're getting worse (or vice-versa) – that, after all, is politics. And politicians, like weather forecasters, are usually adept at couching their assertions and prognostications in terms that are so vague, so hedged about with ifs and buts and maybes and small-print escape clauses, as to be irrefutable even when they turn out to be balderdash. But sometimes they slip up. They say what they really think or show themselves as they really are – or they promise us jam, not at some unspecified future date (and only then if we really deserve it) but by next Tuesday week at the latest, without fail. Politicians will say today the exact opposite of what they said the day before yesterday, in the confident expectation that we've all forgotten what it was. Usually they get away with it, but there are exceptions to this dismal rule. Some of them are in these pages. Being wrong, or two-faced – even being caught out as liars – doesn't seem to damage their careers – more's the pity, we might think. Richard Milhous Nixon didn't get away with it, in the end, it's true – but then, he *was* Richard Milhous Nixon. That explains everything, really.

Politicians can start wars but they don't fight them, which is just as well. And it's just as well, if this collection is anything to go by, that generals don't, as a rule, run governments. Heaven only knows what some of them might do for the balance of payments or the conservation of white fish stocks, if their capacity for military foresight and strategy is anything to go by. Still, there is a refreshing directness about their wrongness that is oddly comforting, particularly for those of us who are in no danger of winding up horribly dead as a consequence of it. The observant reader will note that the seam of Military Regrettability more or less peters out after Vietnam – the last big conflict during which military men put their foot in it in terms we could all understand. Stormin' Norman Schwarzkopf had a reputation for talking straight from the shoulder, and straight from the shoulder was, indeed, where the talk came from – but most of it was verbal blancmange. Contemporary military persons (particularly in America, which is pretty well the only place left in the civilized world where military persons are still taken seriously) speak a private, largely acronymic gobbledegook that is so convoluted and syntactically scrambled that one wonders if they even understand each other. Perhaps they don't – in which case there may be grounds to hope that the goal of World Peace has crept a few inches closer. They shall beat their swords into In-Scabbard Offense/Defense Capabilities, and won't understand what to do with them.

Speaking of private languages brings us to Science, and to the interesting question, *Why?* Why do these people, who really ought to know better, come out with this sort of thing? What demon sat on Lord Kelvin's shoulder and muttered in his ear the words, 'X-rays will prove to be a hoax'? Lord Kelvin had, after all, been one of the foremost and most successful scientific innovators of his century, a man who was not afraid to take risks with his imagination. Why did he suddenly turn into the crusty old reactionary who said radio had no future and that alternating current was lethal – a piece of advice that was acted on by Britain's Royal Family, whose official residences were until comparatively recently wired up for the much riskier DC system? The answer, perhaps, lies ironically in the fact that Kelvin *had been* such an imaginative innovator. He got old, he got tired; he wanted, not unreasonably, to bask in the afterglow of his achievements. But things went on happening without him; the standards and horizons he had helped to set in place were altered, redefined, in some cases even abolished. He resented it. One can imagine even more readily that a working scientist would be tempted to use all his authority to denigrate a theory that threatened to put hard-won work – not to mention reputation and funding – at peril. Such a scientist – Thomas Edison is one name that springs to mind – may be so tempted without even knowing it, and yield to it in the sincere belief that he is acting according to strict scientific principles.

The case of Technology, which I have treated as a separate subject from Science and Health, gives many illustrations of what Arthur C. Clarke has memorably defined as 'a failure of the imagination'. Very often it is not the purely scientific basis of the innovation that is in dispute: it is merely that the nay-sayer simply cannot imagine, as the inventor can, that it could ever be put to practical and popular use. In extreme cases, such as rocket technology, this imaginative sclerosis leads otherwise knowledgeable and sensible people to come out with the most appalling rubbish.

The quotations in the Technology section are, for the most part, self-explanatory, whereas many of the purely scientific ones have required a little in the way of commentary. I have tried to keep this as brief as possible, both for the sake of lucidity and readability and out of consideration for the regrettable (but not, I hope, Regrettable) shakiness of my own scientific understanding. I stand corrected in advance for any howlers I've committed.

The sections on Business and Race & Gender speak for themselves, I think. I have tried to confine myself to the most catastrophically memorable of all the quotations on offer, and to stick to my own self-imposed rule of quoting only those people who ought at least to have stood a fair chance of knowing better. Alert readers will notice a sprinkling of quotations which do not conform to my own definitions of Regrettability; some are *double entendres*, some are just plain mistakes, and some are apocryphal. The reason they are included is because I am very fond of them and I could not bear to leave them out, and that's that; no correspondence will be entered into!

The titanic figure of Robert Maxwell – regrettable in life, in death Regrettable – looms large in no fewer than three chapters. In his case I have tried to keep my own comments to the barest factual minimum. It seemed the kindest, and most damning, thing to do.

There are gaps, of course: Sport in particular, and the wacky world of horoscopes. One of each is all you get here. I don't much care for

Sport – unless you count supporting Brighton and Hove Albion F.C. – and in any case, most sporting howlers are of the 'Don't waste your money on Foinavon' sort – a perfectly reasonable thing to say in all but one of the foreseeable circumstances. Only the 1994 Foreman-Moorer fight gets a mention here: it was reasonable to say Foreman would almost certainly lose, and fair enough to deplore the circumstances which led to the contest. But it was unwise to detail in advance the hideous punishment he was to undergo, and even more Regrettable to forecast the round he'd be knocked out in. In the end I put all the boxing pundits in together – I thought it might be comforting for them. Similarly – and because horoscopes are always wrong anyway, except on the rare occasions when they're accidentally right – I have quoted only one sayer of supernatural sooth, Mr Barry Fantoni, whose toes must surely only now be beginning to uncurl from the region of his ears. I'm sure he'll forgive me, just as I'm sure Terry Waite has forgiven him.

Once again, my thanks to all the people who have, knowingly or unknowingly, helped me compile this selection. I've had tremendous fun doing it, and I hope you enjoy browsing through the book.

Oh – and good luck with the Lottery!

David Milsted.
Dorset, 1995.

REGRETTABLE
PRONOUNCEMENTS
OF OUR POLITICAL
MASTERS AND MISTRESSES

The wrong sort of people, as Jon Wynne Tyson observed, are always in power because they would not be in power if they were not the wrong sort of people. Here is a selection of soundbites that prove him right.

1600–1900

The Lord Mayor of London

Pish! A woman might piss it out.

On being roused from his bed – to which he immediately returned – at 2 am on September 13th 1666, to see a small fire in a bakery in Pudding Lane. The ensuing blaze destroyed 13,000 houses and 87 churches.

George III

Once vigorous measures appear to be the only means left of bringing the Americans to a due submission to the mother country, the colonies will submit.

Letter, February 15th 1775. After eight years of vigorous measures, the mother country submitted in 1783.

Alexander Hamilton

A shilly-shally thing of milk and water, which could not last.

The great statesman's verdict on the US Constitution of 1787, still quite robust in its third century.

Louis XVI

The French people are incapable of regicide.

1789. They proved him wrong with the guillotine in 1793.

Andrew Jackson

The policy of the general government toward the red man is not only liberal, but generous.

The US President comments on Native Americans' objections to his plan to clear them off all land east of the Mississippi River, 1830.

Abraham Lincoln

Negro equality? Fudge! How long, in the Government of a God great enough to make and rule the universe, shall there continue knaves to vend, and fools to quip, so low a piece of demagogism as this?

1859. *See* **They're not like us** *for the reasoning behind this remark.*

The South has too much commonsense and good temper to break up the Union.

1860: the eve of the American Civil War.

The world will little note nor long remember what we say here.
Oration at the dedication of the National Cemetery in . . . Gettysburg, November 19th 1863. If true, his prophecy would have spared the world the agony of hearing the rest of his address performed by Margaret Thatcher.

Benjamin Disraeli

Prussia is a country without any bottom, and in my opinion could not maintain a war for six weeks.
1864. Six years later Prussia's bottom was substantial enough to crush France, Napoleon III being captured after six weeks' fighting.

Theodore Roosevelt

I don't go so far as to think that the only good Indians are the dead Indians, but I believe nine out of every ten are, and I shouldn't inquire too closely into the case of the tenth.
Writing in The Winning of the West, *1889–1896.*

Her Majesty Queen Victoria

Why should women be included in this Act? It is surely impossible for them.
The Queen ensures the exclusion of lesbians from the Criminal Law (Amendment) Act of 1886 prohibiting 'indecency' between members of the same sex.

1900–1945

Louis Mouttet

The safety of St Pierre is absolutely assured. Do not allow yourselves to fall victims to groundless panic. Please allow us to advise you to return to your normal occupations.
The Governor of Martinique reassures his citizens, shortly before perishing along with 30,000 of them in the eruption of Mt Pelée on May 8th 1902.

Grover Cleveland

Sensible and responsible women do not want to vote. The relative positions to be assumed by man and woman in the working out of our civilization were assigned long ago by a higher intelligence than ours.
The US President settles the question once and for all, 1905.

Kaiser Wilhelm

You will be home before the leaves have fallen from the trees.
Addressing German troops in August 1914. The survivors returned, defeated, in November 1918.

Woodrow Wilson

He Kept Us Out Of War!
1916 campaign slogan of the US President who declared war on Germany in 1917.

Prince Kropotkin

In my opinion the attempt to build up a Communist republic on the lines of strongly centralised State Communism, under the iron rule of the dictatorship of the party, is ending in failure.
The Russian revolutionary anarchist is seventy years early in his prediction of 1920.

David Lloyd George

This solemn moment of triumph . . . is going to lift up humanity to a higher plane of existence for all the ages of the future.
The Prime Minister's thoughts on Armistice Day, November 11th 1918.

Democracy cannot survive another world war.
Interviewed in the News Chronicle, *1936.*

Leon Trotsky

England is at last ripe for revolution.
Wishful thinking in 1925.

General Smuts

We are all satisfied in South Africa now.
The Golden Age of 1926.

Herbert Hoover

We shall soon be in sight of the day when poverty will be banished from this nation.
The Republican candidate for the US Presidency makes a pledge in 1928.

Gentlemen, you have come sixty days too late. The depression is over.
The US President rejects appeals for a reflationary policy at the start of the Great Depression in June 1930. Recovery began a decade later.

George Lansbury MP

It is certain as the day that a Labour town council, a Socialist or Communist government, would not for a day tolerate strikes in social or other services necessary for the life of the nation.
The leader of the Labour Party gives a firm commitment in 1934. He was right about the Communists.

Joseph Stalin

Gaiety is the most outstanding feature of the Soviet Union.
1935

Leslie Hore-Belisha MP

If cars continue to be made at the same rate as now and with increasing cheapness, there will soon be no pedestrians left.

The Minister of Transport who introduced driving tests and gave his name to flashing orange lights on zebra crossings, 1935.

Sir Oswald Mosley

Before the organisation of the Blackshirt movement free speech did not exist in this country . . . We shall reach the helm within five years.

The leader of the British Union of Fascists in 1938.

I am not, and never have been, a man of the right. My position was on the left and is now in the centre of politics.

The ex-leader of the British Union of Fascists, thirty years later.

Lord Lugard

The cession of any Colony or Protectorate – save as the result of a crushing defeat in war – is simply unthinkable and would never be accepted by the nation.

An ex-colonial governor speaks in 1938.

Sir Thomas Inskip MP

War today is not only not inevitable, but it is unlikely. The Government have good reason for saying that.

Soothing words from the Minister for Co-ordination of Defence, August 1939.

Neville Chamberlain

For the second time on our history, a British Prime Minister has returned from Germany bringing peace with honour. I believe it is peace for our time. Go home and get a nice quiet sleep.

Addressing cheering crowds in Downing Street, September 30th 1938.

One thing is certain: he missed the bus.

The Prime Minister's assessment of Hitler's military strategy, April 4th 1940. France fell to Germany at the end of June.

Franklin D. Roosevelt

I have said this before, but I say it again and again and again: your boys are not going to be sent into any foreign wars.

The US President campaigns for re-election on October 30th 1940. He changed his mind after Japan bombed Pearl Harbor in December 1941.

Defeat of Germany means defeat of Japan, probably without firing a shot or losing a life.

Presidential memo, July 16th 1942.

He doesn't want anything but security for his country, and I think that if I give him everything I possibly can and ask nothing from him in return, noblesse oblige, he won't try to annex anything and will work with me for a world democracy and peace.
Assessment of Stalin's war aims, 1944.

The Crimea Conference . . . spells the end of the system of unilateral action, the exclusive alliances, the spheres of influence, the balances of power, and all the other expedients that have been tried for centuries – and have always failed.
Addressing Congress after meeting Churchill and Stalin at Yalta, March 1st 1945.

Adolf Hitler

By this revolution the German form of life is definitely settled for the next thousand years.
On his accession to power, 1934.

We are winning international respect.
On his National Socialist government, 1934. What's regrettable about this claim is that it was true: Britain and France pursued a policy of appeasement until the end of 1938.

It is the last territorial claim that I have to make in Europe.
On the annexation of the Sudetenland, 1938.

The United States will not be a threat to us for decades – not in 1945 but at the earliest in 1970 or 1980.
November 12th 1940. He ought to have known better than to believe the campaign speeches of US politicians.

Thank God, I've always avoided persecuting my enemies.
Echoes of the Parable of the Pharisee in the Temple: 1941.

The Russians are finished. They have nothing left to throw against us.
The Führer reassures General Franz Halder in July 1941.

Reichsmarschall Hermann Goering

No enemy bomber can reach the Ruhr. If one reaches the Ruhr, my name is not Goering. You can call me Meyer.
Addressing the Luftwaffe, 1939. He never got round to changing his name.

Sir Kingsley Wood

Are you aware that it is private property? Why, you will be asking me to bomb Essen next!
The Secretary of State for Air is horrified by an RAF plan to fire-bomb the Black Forest in 1939.

Dame Irene Ward

How long is the Minister prepared to hold up the skirts of the Wrens for the convenience of His Majesty's sailors?
The Conservative MP complains about delays in supplying uniforms for the Women's Royal Naval Service: House of Commons, 1940.

John Foster Dulles

Only hysteria entertains the idea that Japan contemplates war against us.
The former presidential adviser and future Secretary of State in 1941. Hysteria was vindicated a few months later.

William P. Lambertson

My stand has constantly been that this hysteria about national defence is hooey, and I am ready to stake my political future on that proposition.
The Representative from Kansas goes on the US Congressional Record, September 26th 1940.

Wendell Wilkie

We won't be at war with Japan within forty-eight hours, within forty-eight days, within forty-eight years.
The US Presidential candidate tries out his statesmanship at a dinner on December 7th 1941. Bad news from Pearl Harbor ruined the dessert.

Winston S. Churchill

I could not help being charmed, like so many other people have been, by Signor Mussolini's gentle and simple bearing and by his calm detached poise in spite of so many burdens and dangers.
Writing in The Times, *January 21st 1927.*

The story of Hitler's struggle cannot be read without admiration for the courage, the perseverance, and the vital force which enabled him to challenge, defy, conciliate, and overcome all the authorities and resistance in his path.
Reviewing Hitler's Mein Kampf *in his book* Great Contemporaries.

The service rendered by Finland to mankind is magnificent. They have exposed for all the world to see the military incapacity of the Red Army and of the Red Air Force. Many illusions about Soviet Russia have been dispelled by these fierce weeks of fighting in the Arctic Circle. Everyone can see how Communism rots the soul of a nation; how it makes it abject and hungry in peace, and proves it base and abominable in war.
BBC broadcast celebrating a setback for Britain's future ally on January 20th 1940.

Josef Goebbels

We rule by love and not by the bayonet.
1936

My Führer, I congratulate you! Roosevelt is dead. It is written in the stars that the second half of April will be the turning point for us.
Memo to Hitler, April 13th 1945. It certainly was a turning point; both had committed suicide by the end of the month.

1945 – PRESENT

Dean Acheson

Never in the past has there been any place on the globe where the vital interests of American and Russian people have clashed or even been antagonistic, and there is no reason to suppose there should be now or in the future ever such a place.
The US Under-Secretary of State looks forward to doing business with the USSR after 1945.

Arthur Caldwell

Two Wongs don't make a white.
Australia's Minister for Immigration extends a big 'G'day!' to the right sort of settler in 1947.

Warren Austin

They should settle this problem in a true Christian spirit.
The US delegate to the UN offers a solution to the Arab–Israeli War of 1948.

Mr Dobi

This great man of the Soviet peoples struck me as a wise, kindly old man. His eyes reflect peace and kindness, that is why the peoples he is leading are so attached to him.
The President of the Yugoslav Smallholders' Party has a good meeting with Comrade Stalin in 1948.

Dwight David Eisenhower

My decision to remove myself completely from the political scene is definite and positive.
1948. Eisenhower was President of the US from 1953 to 1961.

Harry S Truman

We are not at war.
The US President explains the situation vis-à-vis Korea in 1950. While it is true

that the US did not declare war with North Korea, it is also true that the US did not declare war on Iraq in 1990. In both cases it was providing 'military assistance' to the United Nations.

Senator Joseph McCarthy

I have here in my hand a list of 205 that were known to the Secretary of State as being members of the Communist Party and who, nevertheless, are still working and shaping policy in the State Department.
February 9th 1950: counting Reds under the beds . . .

Last night I discussed Communists in the State Department. I stated that I had the names of 57 card-carrying members of the Communist Party.
February 10th 1950: still counting . . .

I frankly feel, in the view of the number of cases – there are 81 cases – that it would be a mistake to disclose these names on the floor.
February 20th 1950: count complete.

How can we account for our present situation unless we believe that men high in this government are concerting to deliver us to disaster? This must be the product of a great conspiracy, a conspiracy on a scale so immense as to dwarf any previous venture in the history of man. A conspiracy of infamy so black that, when it is finally exposed, its principals shall be forever deserving of the maledictions of all honest men.
Senate speech, June 14th 1951.

I think it is a shoddy, unusual thing to do to use the floor of the Senate to attack your opponent without any proof whatever.
1956. How true . . . Senator McCarthy's campaign, as Chairman of the Un-American Activities Committee, of using the Senate for just this purpose had finally come unstuck two years earlier when he accused the US Army of 'coddling communists'. By then he had ruined the careers of hundreds of innocent government employees and film industry workers.

The Mayor of Châteauneuf-du-Pape

The flights, landings and take-offs of airships called 'flying saucers' and 'flying cigars' of any nationality are forbidden on the territory of the community of Châteauneuf-du-Pape.
Mayoral decree, 1954.

Sir Anthony Eden

We are not at war with Egypt. We are in a state of armed conflict.
The British Prime Minister takes a leaf out of President Truman's Korea notebook in 1956. As events in Suez unfolded, his government turned out to be in a state of crisis; he resigned shortly afterwards.

Guy Mollet

France will remain in Algeria. The bonds linking metropolitan France and Algeria are indissoluble.

The French Prime Minister ends all discussion on the subject of Algerian independence, February 9th 1956. Algeria gained independence in 1962.

Fulgenico Batista

I give Castro a year. No longer.

The deposed dictator speaks from exile, 1959. Ah, but a year is a long time in Cuba . . .

Edward Koch

I'll never run again. Politics is a filthy business.

. . . Except in New York, obviously. The future Mayor of the Big Apple signs off after failing to become an Assemblyman in 1962.

John F. Kennedy

Should I become President I will not risk American lives by permitting any other nation to drag us into the wrong war at the wrong place at the wrong time through an unwise commitment that is unwise militarily, unnecessary to our security, and unsupported by our allies.

No entanglement in Vietnam: the presidential candidate issues a pledge to the Democratic National Committee on October 12th 1960.

Lyndon Baines Johnson

I didn't just screw Ho Chi Minh. I cut his pecker off.

The President reports on the effect of US bombing, July 13th 1964.

We are not about to send American boys nine or ten thousand miles away from home to do what Asian boys ought to be doing for themselves.

Seeking re-election, LBJ campaigns in Akron, Ohio, on October 21st 1964. Between 1964 and 1968 the number of US troops in Vietnam increased from 20,000 to 500,000.

Richard Milhous Nixon

Mother, I want to be an old-fashioned lawyer, an honest lawyer who can't be bought by crooks.

Words spoken to his mother in 1925 by the young Tricky Dicky, aged 12.

We must defend our Constitution against a great wave of indifference to authority, disrespect of its law, and opposition to its basic principles which threatens its basic existence. Shall we of the present generation allow this instrument to be cast into disrepute? Shall we be responsible for its downfall?

Contribution to High School debating competition, 1928. He won $50 for it.

Wanted: Congressman candidate with no previous political experience to defeat a man who has represented this district in the House for ten years. Any young man, resident of the district, preferably a veteran, fair education, may apply for the job.
Republican Party newspaper ad., Whittier, Calif., 1946. Nixon applied, got the job, and defeated Representative Jerry Voorhis by smearing him as a Communist.

I'm not a quitter and incidentally Pat's not a quitter. After all, her name was Patricia Ryan and she was born on Saint Patrick's Day.
Nixon's 'Checkers' speech, 1952. Mrs Pat Nixon was in fact born on March 16th, the day before St Patrick's Day.

You'll remember the 'Checkers' speech, I suppose. Well, I want you to be the first to know – I staged it.
Boasting at a lunch of the Radio and Television Executives Society, September 14th 1955.

Let's get one thing straight: where our opponents misrepresent and distort the record . . . I shall consider it a duty and a privilege to set the record straight.
Election speech as Vice-Presidential candidate, September 18th 1958.

Wherever any mother or father talks to his child, I hope he can look at the man in the White House and, whatever he may think of his politics, he will say: 'Well, there is a man who maintains the kind of standards personally that I would want my child to follow.'
The Presidential candidate: TV debate with John F. Kennedy, 1960.

Just think about how much you're going to be missing, you won't have Nixon to kick around anymore because, gentlemen, this is my last press conference.
Richard 'Not A Quitter' Nixon signs off after losing to Pat Brown for the Governorship of California on November 7th 1962.

The press are good guys . . . I like the press . . . The press are very helpful with their questions.
Nixon begins to feel the urge to be kicked around again in 1965.

Let us begin by committing ourselves to the truth, to see it like it is and tell it like it is; to find the truth, to speak the truth and to live with the truth. That is what we will do.
Speech accepting the Republican Party nomination as Presidential candidate, August 8th 1968.

I won without having to pay the price or make any deals.
Speech acknowledging victory over Hubert Humphrey, November 1968.

They're just scum.
Comment on the killing of four students at Kent State University by the National Guard during an anti-Vietnam War protest, May 13th 1970.

See also **The Fog of War** *(p. 48) and* **Telling It Like It Isn't** *(p. 119).*

WATERGATE

On June 17th 1972 the offices of the Democratic Party National Committee in the Watergate complex in Washington, DC, were broken into by a team of burglars working for a White House 'dirty tricks' team known as the 'The Plumbers' and operating within an umbrella organization called the Campaign to Re-elect the President (CREEP). Nixon moved quickly to squash the story, but the investigations of the Washington Post duo of Bob Woodward and Carl Bernstein uncovered a trail that led all the way back to Nixon and unearthed the existence of taped Oval Office conversations secretly recorded by the President himself. Their reporting led eventually to the President's resignation under threat of impeachment, and to criminal convictions for some of his senior aides. Nixon himself was pardoned by **Gerald Ford** (*see p. 31*).

Within our own staff, under my direction, Counsel to the President Mr Dean has conducted a complete investigation of all leads which might involve any present members of the White House or anybody in Government. I can say categorically that no-one in the White House staff, no-one in this administration, presently employed, was involved in this bizarre incident.
President Richard M. Nixon, public statement, August 29th 1972. Counsel to the White House Mr James Dean was himself one of the Watergate conspirators.

I expect the first four years of my sixties to be very interesting.
Nixon: 60th birthday interview, January 9th 1973.

I would have made a good pope.
Nixon discovers his true vocation at last: 1980.

Spiro T. Agnew

Aha. Haha. Hahahaha. Heeheeheehee. Aha, aha, ha – wheeeeeaaa hahahaha, ooh, hoo, hoohoohoheeheehahaha . . . [etc].
Response to the statement: 'Spiro T. Agnew for Vice-President of the United States!!??!!', Democratic Party broadcast, 1968. He was, however, elected.

I can give a show we can sell them, just like we were selling Wheaties.
James Dean to Richard Nixon, March 21st 1973: caught on tape.

Two of the finest public servants it has been my privilege to know.
Nixon, April 30th 1973, announcing the sacking of conspirators Bob Haldeman and John Erlichman.

I reject the cynical view that politics is inevitably, or even usually, a dirty business.
Nixon, April 30th 1973.

There can be no whitewash at the White House.
Nixon, April 30th 1973.

Watergate is water under the bridge.
Nixon, September 1973.

I urge the Congress to join me in mounting a major new effort to replace the discredited president . . .
Nixon: State of the Union Address, January 1974. He meant to say 'precedent'.

I have no intention of resigning. The President is not going to leave the White House until January 20th 1977.
July 1974. The President resigned on August 8th.

This country needs good farmers, good businessmen, good plumbers . . .
Ex-President Richard M. Nixon: farewell address to White House staff, August 9th 1974.

When the President does it, that means it is not illegal.
Nixon makes jurisprudence sound so simple in an interview with David Frost on May 19th 1977.

A Nixon–Agnew administration will abolish the credibility gap and re-establish the truth, the whole truth, as its policy.
Campaign speech, August 1968.

After all, what does a politician have but his credibility?
What indeed? Inauguration statement, January 1969.

Someone set up these people to have them caught . . . to embarrass the Republican Party.
The Veep draws a line under Watergate, September 22nd 1972.

The charges against me are, if you'll pardon the expression, damned lies. I am innocent of these charges. If indicted I shall not resign.
August 1973, on charges of financial corruption in his home state of Maryland. The man who abolished the credibility gap resigned on October 10th and was replaced by **Gerald Ford** *(see p. 31).*

Chou En Lai

We are firmly convinced that no force whatsoever can disrupt the great unity between the Chinese and the Soviet peoples.
The Chinese Premier sets the seal on proletarian fraternity, 1965. The Chinese and Soviet armies spent much of the following decade in a stand-off in Outer Mongolia.

Richard Daley

Get this thing straight once for all. The policeman isn't there to create disorder. The policeman is there to preserve disorder.
The Mayor of Chicago speaks up for the Boys in Blue after a police riot during the Democratic National Convention, 1968.

Viscount Montgomery

This sort of thing may be tolerated by the French – but we are British, thank God.
The hero of El Alamein, now a member of the House of Lords, on a Parliamentary Bill to legalize homosexual acts between consenting adults, 1965.

Harold Wilson

I myself have always deprecated – perhaps rightly, perhaps wrongly – in crisis after crisis, appeals to the Dunkirk Spirit as an answer to our problems.
The Leader of the Opposition derides 'muddling through' as an instrument of policy, July 22nd 1961.

I believe that the Spirit of Dunkirk will once again carry us through to success.
The Prime Minister commends 'muddling through' as an instrument of policy, December 12th 1964.

Over my dead body. There will be no devaluation.
Television interview, October 1967. The Cabinet decision to devalue the Pound was taken on November 16th. Prime Ministerial hara-kiri did not ensue.

From now the pound abroad is worth 14 per cent or so less in terms of other currencies. It does not mean, of course, that the pound here in Britain, in your pocket or purse or in your bank, has been devalued.
. . . Except, of course, when it comes to paying for imported goods and raw materials. Prime Ministerial broadcast, November 19th 1967.

This is not a lightly given pledge. It is a promise. We shall achieve the 500,000 target, and we shall not allow any developments, any circumstances, however adverse, to deflect us from our aim.
Election meeting, Bradford, March 1966, on Labour's target for the annual rate of council house building. 400,000 were completed in 1967, but in January 1968 the Housing Minister, Anthony Greenwood, announced that the target had been abandoned because 'there are too many uncertainties for it to be possible for anyone to say exactly how many will be built in 1970'.

The cumulative effects of the economic and financial sanctions might well bring the rebellion to an end within a matter of weeks rather than months.
The Prime Minister explains how he will bring the rebel Rhodesian government of Ian Smith to its knees, January 1966. It was still there when Wilson left office a decade later.

Ian Smith

We now have a Rhodesian constitution and if anybody thinks it can be improved, I would like to know where.
1971.

We have the happiest Africans in the world.
1971.

I am determined to give the Africans a fair crack of the whip.
1972.

There are going to be no dramatic changes in Rhodesia.
1975. Apart, of course, from its change of name to Zimbabwe in 1980, and one or two other things.

John Stokes MP

Why should white Rhodesians give up everything for some half-baked untried theory of one man, one vote?

1965: The Conservative Member for Oldbury & Halesowen on the constitutional frippery responsible for the election of British MPs since 1886.

The Rt Hon Anthony Wedgwood Benn, MP

We thought we could put the economy right in five years. We were wrong. It will probably take ten.

The President of the Board of Trade revises a forecast in 1968.

Franz Josef Strauss

I would prefer trying to grow pineapples in Alaska to being Chancellor.

The heavyweight Bavarian right-winger rules himself out in 1968 . . .

I hope the German people are never so desperate as to believe they have to elect me as Chancellor.

. . . and in 1971 . . .

I am not a candidate for Chancellor under present political circumstances.

. . . and again in 1979. In 1980 he ran for Chancellor, and lost.

Alexandr Dubček

I was asked at the airport whether our sovereignty was jeopardized and I am saying frankly that it is not.

The leader of the 'Prague Spring' speaks to the press in August 1968. A few days later the Soviet army invaded Czechoslovakia and Dubček was flown to Moscow for 'consultations'. He arrived handcuffed and in chains.

Leonid Brezhnev

The Soviet army was invited to protect the sovereignty of the People's Republic of Czechoslovakia.

August 1968. Hence the joke that did the rounds of Prague after the invasion: Q: 'What are 60,000 Soviet troops doing in Czechoslovakia?' A: 'Looking for the people who invited them.'

Henry Kissinger

Of all the men running, Richard Nixon is the most dangerous to have as President. I would never work for that man. That man is a disaster.

Speaking in 1968, shortly before his decision to . . . work for that man.

I have no question that the President will insist on the full disclosure of the facts.

'Nixon has nothing to hide on Watergate,' the Chief Foreign Policy Adviser tells the American Newspaper Publishers' Association on April 23rd 1973.

The CIA had nothing to do with the coup.
The US Secretary of State (Designate) reassures his confirmational Congressional hearing that the CIA was not involved in its own plan to overthrow the elected Government of Chile; September 17th 1973.

The Reverend 'Doctor' Ian Paisley MP, MEP

I've never made an inflammatory statement in my life.
The man who once described his Roman Catholic fellow-citizens as 'damnable acolytes of the Antichrist' deplores his reputation in 1969.

We are not going to stand idly by and be murdered in our beds.
An intriguing insight into Free Presbyterian sleeping habits, early 1970s.

The Rt Hon Joan Lester MP

Members exercising their integrity threaten to destroy the whole credibility of the Labour Party.
Putting her National Executive comrades back on the right lines in 1971 and confirming what many of us always thought about 'political principle'.

Evelyn King

Softly spoken but direct, General Amin is typical of independent Africa's newer and more independent approach to world affairs.
A Tory MP's encomium to Uganda's new dictator in the Daily Telegraph, *1971.*
See also: **Telling It Like It Isn't** *(p. 131).*

'Big Daddy' Field Marshal President Idi Amin Dada

In view of the success of my economic revolution in Uganda, I offer myself to be appointed Head of the Commonwealth.
The Great Dictator offers to give HM The Queen a rest in 1975.

Uganda has among the best prisons in the world and people from many countries are eager to visit them.
Interview in The Guardian, *January 1976. In an enlightened attempt to save labour, prisoners in Amin's gaols were required to execute each other with sledgehammers.*

Your experience will be a lesson to all of us men to be careful not to marry ladies in very high positions.
A comradely message to Lord Snowdon after his divorce from Princess Margaret in 1978.

As Conqueror of the British Empire I am prepared to die in defence of the motherland, Uganda.
April 1979, shortly before fleeing to Libya after Tanzanian troops invaded his country.
See also: **Telling It Like It Isn't** *(p. 131).*

David Bleakley

I have never been prouder to be a citizen of Belfast than at this time. Protestant and Catholic, rich and poor, are maintaining a standard of community stability that compares with anything that has ever been recorded in the annals of Europe.

The Northern Ireland Minister for Community Relations addresses the Ulster Institute for the Deaf in 1972. Three bombs cut short his remarks.

Werner Maihofer

Baader had the perfidy to shoot himself in the back of the head to try to make us look like murderers.

A typical terrorist trick deplored by the West German Minister of the Interior, 1977.

President Mobutu of Zaire

The people of Zaire are not thieves. It merely happens that they take more things, or borrow them.

. . . Which only goes to show that Irish logic travels well. 1978.

George McGovern

I am one thousand per cent for Tom Eagleton and have no intention of dropping him from the ticket.

The 1972 US Presidential candidate supports his running mate after it is revealed that he had electro-convulsive treatment for mental illness. McGovern swapped him for Sargent Shriver a few days later.

Billie Snedden

Wherever I go in this country, people know there is a problem.

The leader of Australia's Liberal Party scores an own goal in the 1974 General Election, which was won by Gough Whitlam's Labor Party.

Park Chung Hee

We have no political prisoners – only Communists and others involved in conspiracies against the country.

The President of South Korea makes democracy safe, 1974.

Edward Heath

This would, at a stroke, reduce the rise in prices, increase productivity and reduce unemployment.

These words, although not directly spoken by Mr Heath, were contained in a Conservative Central Office policy briefing during the June 1970 General Election, which he won. In the next four years inflation broke the 25% barrier, productivity fell and unemployment rose.

Our only problem at the moment is the problem of success.

The Prime Minister, November 1973. Among the problems that were to vex his administration were strikes by miners and power workers, fuel and food shortages, electricity rationing and a national three-day working week.

I intend to see to it that you have a Government that is capable of leading the country through the difficult times ahead.
So saying – in February 1974 – the Prime Minister called a snap election, using the slogan 'Who Governs Britain?' He lost.

John Stonehouse

To ask the Home Secretary whether he will review the arrangements for preventing drowning accidents.
Parliamentary question tabled on May 7th 1974 by the MP for Walsall North, who may have found the answer useful when faking his own death by drowning.

Lord Kagan

If you ask me if I enjoy being taxed, the answer, of course, is no. But ... I hope that the tax will change the pattern so that merit and hard work are rewarded at the expense of merely having.
The Prime Minister's Special Adviser on the merits of a progressive tax policy, August 1974. In 1980 he was gaoled for defrauding the Inland Revenue of money due to them on wealth he 'merely had'.

Gerald Ford

Mr Nixon was the thirty-seventh President of the United States. He had been preceded by thirty-six others.
President Ford explains his decision to pardon his predecessor, 1974.

To the great people of the Government of Israel – Egypt, excuse me.
Ford proposes a toast to Egyptian President Anwar el-Sadat, October 28th 1975.

Whenever I can I watch the Detroit Tigers on radio.
Ford endears himself to John Doe, 1976.

I say that if Lincoln were alive today he would turn over in his grave.
Ford gives new life to an old joke during the 1976 Presidential campaign.

There is no Soviet domination in Eastern Europe, and there never will be under a Ford administration.
Ford discusses Poland with his Democrat Presidential rival Jimmy Carter, October 6th 1976.

When a man is asked to make a speech, the first thing he has to decide is what to say.
Ex-President Ford shares his insights, 1977.

Hubert Horatio Humphrey

There are too many guns in the hands of people who don't know how to use them!
The Democrat elder statesman's comment on Sarah Jane Moore's bungled attempt to assassinate President Gerald Ford.

I say some things and, gosh, I wish I hadn't said them!
HHH proves himself a jewel among politicians; date unknown.

Jimmy Carter

I have looked on a lot of women with lust. I've committed adultery in my heart many times. God recognizes I will do this and forgives me.
An interview with Playboy, *November 1976.*

Because of the greatness of the Shah, Iran is an island of stability in the Middle East. This is a great tribute to you, Your Majesty, and to your leadership, and to the respect, admiration and love which your people give to you.
The US President salutes an ally, December 31st 1977.

The great president who might have been – Hubert Horatio Hornblower!
At least it proved he'd read a book: attempting to invoke the glory of the old Democrat warhorse at the New York Convention of 1980.

Andrew Young

Ayatollah Khomeini will one day be viewed as some kind of saint.
But by whom? The US Ambassador to the UN shoots from the lip in 1976.

Mohammed Reza Pahlavi

Nobody can overthrow me. I have the support of 700,000 troops, all the workers, and most of the people. I have the power.
The Shah of Iran believes what US Presidents tell him; March 6th 1978.

I should like very much to take a vacation.
January 1979. He got his wish in August, when Islamic fundamentalists drove him into exile and installed Ayatollah Khomeini as President of Iran.

Grand Ayatollah Ruhollah Khomeini

There is no laughter in Islam.
Certainly not in his sort: a 1980 interview.

Earl Butz

Coloureds want only three things: first, a tight pussy; second, loose shoes; third, a warm place to shit.
In Rolling Stone, the last recorded public utterance of the US Secretary for Agriculture before his resignation in 1976.

Ian Gow MP

If paternity leave were granted it would result in a direct incitement to a population explosion.
1979. It wasn't granted; there hasn't been a UK population explosion. QED.

Lord Whitelaw

I do not intend to prejudge the past.
Wille Whitelaw MP becomes Secretary of State for Northern Ireland, 1972.

He is going round the country stirring up apathy.
Harsh words for Harold Wilson, 1970.

We are examining alternative anomalies.
Explaining Government thinking in the Commons, 1981.

Baroness Thatcher, formerly the Rt Hon Margaret Hilda Thatcher, PC, MP

Every Prime Minister should have a Willie.
A (spoken) tribute to Lord Whitelaw after his elevation to the Lords.

I would not wish to be Prime Minister, dear. I have not had enough experience for that job. The only full Ministerial position I've held is Minister for Education and Science. Before you could even think of being Prime Minister you'd need to have done a good deal more jobs than that.
Interviewed on children's TV, 1973. In 1975, with no further Ministerial experience, she changed her mind.

Where there is discord, may we bring harmony . . .
Britain's new Prime Minister quotes St Francis of Assisi on the steps of Number Ten after her election victory, April 1979. There followed a severe recession, record unemployment, riots in Brixton and Toxteth, the miners' strike and the Poll Tax, among other harmonies.

It is exciting to have a real crisis on your hands, when you have spent half your political life dealing with humdrum issues like the environment.
14th May 1982, on the Falklands conflict.

There is no such thing as Society. There are individual men and women, and there are families.
Interviewed in Woman's Own, *October 31st 1987.*

The National Health Service is safe in our hands.
Press conference during 1987 General Election campaign.

But, Michael, there is no such thing as raw, untreated sewage.
Discussing the humdrum environment in a BBC TV interview with Michael Buerk, 1989.

We have become a grandmother.
Speaking to reporters on March 4th 1989, the Prime Minister appears to confirm those who suspected her of suffering delusions of royalty.

The Chancellor's position is unassailable.
Endorsement for Nigel Lawson in 1990, shortly before she made his position untenable.
See also: **Telling It Like It Isn't** *(p. 139) and* **The Scott Inquiry** *(p. 42).*

Ronald Reagan

It's silly talking about how many years we will have to spend in the jungles of Vietnam when we could pave the whole country and put parking stripes on it and still be home by Christmas.
The military strategist runs for the Governorship of California and is interviewed by the Fresno Bee, *October 10th 1965.*

A tree's a tree. How many more do you need to look at?
Quoted in the Sacramento Bee, *March 12th 1966.*

I don't believe a tree is a tree and if you've seen one you've seen them all.
Quoted in the Sacramento Bee, *September 14th 1966.*

I favour the Civil Rights Act of 1964 and it must be enforced at gunpoint if necessary.
October 20th 1965.

I would have voted against the Civil Rights Act of 1964.
1968. Even at gunpoint, presumably.

The thought of being President frightens me. I do not think I want the job.
Still content to be Governor of California in 1973.

We were told four years ago that 17 million people went to bed hungry every night. Well, that was probably true. They were all on a diet.
TV campaign speech, October 27th 1964.

Who?
Response to the mention of French President Giscard d'Estaing on The Today Show, *November 14th 1979.*

All the waste in a year from a nuclear power plant can be stored under a desk.
Quoted in the Burlington Free Press, *February 15th 1980. It would have to be a very large and highly toxic desk.*

Alaska has a greater oil reserve than Saudi Arabia.
The Presidential candidate derides energy conservation campaigners in The Washington Post, *February 20th 1980. Saudi oil reserves exceed those of Alaska by a ratio of approximately 40 to 1.*

Trains are not any more energy efficient than the average automobile. Both get about 48 passenger miles to the gallon.
The candidate gets it straight about fuel conservation in The Chicago Tribune, *May 10th 1980. (The facts: the average US train gets about 400mpg; the average US car gets about 43.)*

Approximately 80% of our air pollution stems from hydrocarbons released by vegetation, so let's not go overboard setting and enforcing tough emission standards for man-made sources.
Launching National Hate A Tree Week during the Presidential election campaign, 10th September 1980.

I know Teddy Kennedy had fun at the Democratic convention when he said that I said that trees and vegetation cause 80% of the air pollution in this country. Well, he was a little wrong about what I said. First of all, I didn't say 80%, I said 92%, 93%, pardon me. And I didn't say air pollution, I said oxides of nitrogen.
Clarifying the statement on October 9th 1980.

My administration will work very closely with you to bring about a spirit of co-operation between the President and the air traffic controllers.
Letter to Air Traffic Controllers' Union president Robert Poli, October 20th 1980. When air traffic controllers went on strike in 1981 Reagan sacked them all and hired non-union replacements.

A drastic reduction in the deficit will take place in the fiscal year '82.
Speaking at a news conference, March 5th 1981. In the fiscal year 1982 the US Treasury deficit rose to $110.7 bn, breaking the 1976 record of $70 bn.

We've laid a firm foundation for economic recovery in 1982.
October 18th 1981. By the end of 1982 US unemployment had risen to 10.4%.

My fellow Americans, I have signed legislation to outlaw Russia for ever. We begin bombing in five minutes.
The President tests a radio mike before an interview and does not realize he is on the air, 1981.

I don't honestly know. I think, again, until someplace – all over the world this is being, research going on, to try and find the defensive weapon. There has never been a weapon that someone hasn't, come up with a defence. But it could – and the only defence is, well, you shoot yours and we'll shoot ours.
The realities of Mutually Assured Destruction inform the thinking behind the Strategic Defense Initiative, aka Star Wars. The President reported verbatim by the International Herald Tribune and quoted by Miles Kington in Moreover . . . *(Robson Books 1982). Mr Kington went on to demonstrate that this would make a passable e e cummings poem.*

Now would you join me in a toast to President Figueredo, to the people of Bolivia. . . no, that's where I'm going . . . to the people of Brazil.
1982. In fact he was in Bogotá, Colombia.

THE IRAN-CONTRA AFFAIR

We did not – repeat, did not – trade weapons or anything else for hostages, nor will we.
The President denies: November 13th 1986.

It sort of settled down to trading arms for hostages.
The President contra-denies: March 26th 1987.

I didn't know how that money [to support the Contras in Nicaragua] **was to be used and I have no knowledge that there was ever any solicitation by our people with these people.**
He doesn't know: May 5th 1987.

As a matter of fact, I was very definitely involved in the decisions about support to the freedom fighters. It was my idea to begin with.
But on the other hand, he's sure: May 15th 1987.

My answer therefore and the simple truth is, I don't remember – period.
The President puts it all behind him on February 2nd 1987.

HRH Prince Philip

A few years ago everybody was saying we must have much more leisure, everybody is working too much. Now that everybody has got so much leisure – it may be involuntary, but they have got it – they are now complaining they are unemployed. People do not seem to be able to make up their minds, do they?
Some straight-from-the-shoulder common sense from the Queen's Consort in a 60th birthday interview, 1981.

You'll all end up with slitty eyes if you stay too long.
A group of British students finds itself on the receiving end of some light-hearted banter during a Royal Visit to China in 1986.

I don't think a prostitute is more moral than a wife, but they are doing the same thing.
A consort's view of marriage: December 6th 1988.

Walter Mondale

Knowing of your congregation's deep involvement in the major social and constitutional issues of our country is a great inspiration to me.
1978: The Vice President of the USA writes a reference for Rev Jim Jones, who used it to persuade the Guyanan government to let him set up a large religious commune there. When Jones came under Congressional investigation he persuaded all its members to destroy themselves and their children with cyanide-spiked Kool Aid.

Alexander Haig

As of now, I am in charge of the White House.
But he wasn't. A trembling and perspiring Secretary of State hails the attempted assassination of President Reagan in 1981.

The Rt Hon David Steel PC, MP

Go back to your constituencies – and prepare for government!
Peroration to his closing speech at the 1981 Liberal Party Conference. They're still preparing . . .

Dame Shirley Williams

I am not interested in a 'Third Party'. I do not believe it has any future.
Shirley Williams MP in 1983, shortly before helping to form a Third Party, the SDP. She was right: it had no future.

James Watt

Every kind of mix you can have. I have a black, I have a woman, two Jews and a cripple.
The US Interior Secretary chooses a Committee in 1983, before being sacked.

Winnie Mandela

Together, hand in hand, with our matches and our necklaces, we shall liberate this country.
April 1986: the self-styled 'Mother of the Nation' encourages 'necklace killing': a form of 'ideological' murder in which the victim is garlanded with a petrol-filled tyre which is then set alight.

George Bush

Read my lips: no new taxes.
A Presidential candidate is afterwards presumed to have been speaking through an alternative orifice on August 19th 1988.

Dan Quayle

Space is almost infinite. As a matter of fact, we think it is infinite.
Speech to the Space Council, reported in the Guardian *of March 8th 1989.*

It was an obscene period in our nation's history . . . no, not in our nation's but in World War II. We all lived in this century; I didn't live in this century but in this century's history.
Just a heartbeat away from the Presidency: a statesman's comment on the Nazi Holocaust, quoted in the Guardian *of March 8th 1989.*

What a waste it is to lose one's mind, or not to have a mind is very wasteful. How true that is.

We're going to have the best educated American people in the world.

Republicans understand the importance of bondage between parent and child.

If we don't succeed, we run the risk of failure.

The question is, whether we are going forward to tomorrow or we're going to go past to the back.

I will work towards the elimination of human rights in El Salvador.

Hawaii's always been a very pivotal role in the Pacific. It is in the Pacific. It's a part of the United States that is an island that is right here.
'Danger: High Doltage' was the comment of Education Digest *when it recorded these Vice-Presidential gems for posterity in 1992.*

Lord Tebbit, formerly The Rt Hon Norman Tebbit, MP

The Cricket test – which side do they cheer for?
The former Chairman of the Conservative Party outlines the entry criteria he would apply to immigrants from Commonwealth countries where tinted folk play England's Summer Game: interview in The Los Angeles Times, *April 19th 1990.*

The Rt Hon Norman Lamont PC, MP

I expect the recovery to begin, albeit relatively slowly at first, in the second half of this year.
The Chancellor settles nerves in the House of Commons, 23rd April 1991.

What we are seeing is the return of that vital ingredient, confidence, and green shoots of economic spring are appearing once again.
Speaking in the House of Commons as Britain sank deeper into economic winter, 9th October 1991.

Maastricht is truly dead. Historians will probably see the Treaty as a bit of a fossil.
Interviewed the day before his leader signed the Maastricht Treaty.

Membership of the ERM remains at the heart of the Government's economic policy.
Britain's very own financial Stormin' Norman settles the money markets hours before they force Britain's withdrawal from the Exchange Rate Mechanism in September 1992.
See also: **Telling It Like It Isn't** *(p. 142).*

The Rt Hon David Hunt MP

John Major will, I predict, turn out to be one of the great political figures of our time.
A Conservative politician emits a TV soundbite and, at some cost to his credibility, secures himself a Cabinet post in November 1990.

Edith Cresson

In Anglo-Saxon countries men prefer the company of other men . . . In England 25 per cent of the men are homosexual.
The then French Prime Minister does her bit for the entente cordial in 1991 . . .

Ants . . . little yellow men who sit up all night thinking how to screw us.
. . . and makes an impact on Franco-Japanese relations, too.

The Rt Hon John Major PC, MP

I am not forecasting a recession over the next twelve months.
But it happened anyway. The Chancellor speaks in the House of Commons, December 4th 1989.

I am confident the period of low growth will be short-lived.
It depends on what one means by 'short'. House of Commons, March 20th 1990.

My aim is to create a nation at ease with itself.
The Prime Minister celebrates his accession, November 1990.

Westminster is an example to other authorities. I hope they follow that example.
Setting the standard, July 1991. Westminster Council was at that time taking a rest from selling off cemeteries for 5p each before plunging itself into the 'Homes-for-Votes' scandal.

We have no plans to widen the scope of VAT.
Press conference during the 1992 General Election campaign. VAT was subsequently extended to domestic gas, electricity and coal.

Neil Hamilton has my full confidence and support.
Downing St statement, November 1994, shortly before Mr Hamilton's dismissal for his part in the 'cash for Parliamentary Questions' scandal.
See also: **The Scott Inquiry** *(p. 42).*

Councillor Alex Segal

The problem can be simply stated: if it is accepted that owner-occupiers are more likely to vote Conservative, then we approach the 1990 election with an enormous handicap . . . The short-term objective must be to target the marginal wards and as a matter of utmost urgency redress the balance by encouraging a pattern of tenure which is more likely to translate into Conservative votes.
A briefing to his fellow Conservative Westminter City Councillors advocates a policy usually known as 'gerrymandering': January 1987.

Dame Shirley Porter

When you have read the documents and after we've had our discussion, it would be helpful if you'd swallow them in good spy fashion otherwise they might self-destruct!
September 1986: at a Conservative Councillors' seminar, the leader of Westminster City Council seems aware that the policy isn't quite kosher.

The Rt Hon Kenneth Clarke PC, MP

Their only concern is for their wallets.
The Secretary of State for Health says all there is to say about doctors opposed to his NHS reforms, 1990.

At Consett you have got one of the best steelworks in Europe. It doesn't employ as many people as it used to because it is so modern.
The Chancellor enthuses on BBC Radio Newcastle, March 3rd 1995. Consett steelworks closed in 1975; the town is now famous for 'Phileas Fogg' snacks.

Consett . . . is also one of the major centres in Western Europe for disposable baby nappies.
On March 16th 1995 the Chancellor, hoping to make up for his earlier gaffe, praises a factory that closed in 1991.

Pat Robertson

Indeed, it may well be that men of goodwill like Woodrow Wilson, Jimmy Carter and George Bush . . . are in reality unknowingly and unwittingly carrying out the mission and mouthing the phrases of a tightly-knit cabal whose goal is nothing less than a new order for the human race under the domination of Lucifer and his followers . . .

Rest assured, there is a behind-the-scenes Establishment in this nation, as in every other. It has enormous power. It has controlled the economic and foreign policy objectives of the United States for the past seventy years.
Definitely a Man To Watch: the prominent US Republican, former presidential contender and leader of the million-strong 'Christian Coalition' airs a familiar conspiracy theory in his book The New World Order, *1991.*

The Rt Hon Douglas Hurd MP

The investigation has revealed no evidence to support suggestions of involvement by other countries. This matter does not, therefore, affect our relations with other countries in the region.
1990: the British Foreign Secretary pins responsibility for the Lockerbie bombing of 1988, in which 270 people were murdered, firmly on Colonel Qaddafi and Libyan intelligence agents. By 1991 the governments of Britain, Germany and the USA were fully aware of strong evidence to suggest that the bombing was financed by Iran and organized by Syria. Iran and Syria co-operated with Britain and the USA during the Gulf War of 1990–91.

Nicholas Fairbairn MP

If we had spent £167 million on condoms we wouldn't have had these problems in the first place.
A robust attitude to food aid for Africa, May 12th 1991.

The Rt Hon Neil Kinnock PC

Yeah! Oh yeah!
Triumphant greetings to a Labour Party election 'victory' rally in Sheffield, April 1992. A majority of the electorate said 'no'.

The sideways shuffles of those who . . . call themselves Social Democrats offer no means of progress . . . And when the shufflers finally take themselves off to stale centrist pastures in boardrooms, the House of Lords or European Commissions in a sort of moveable *Any Questions?*

panel, only the faction watchers in the Lobby and coalition mongers in the City mourn.
The left-wing firebrand writes in the Political Quarterly *of Oct–Dec 1980. He is now European Commissioner for Transport.*

THE SCOTT INQUIRY

A public inquiry under Lord Justice Scott was announced in Parliament at the end of 1992, following the collapse of the 'Matrix Churchill Case' in November. Three directors of the engineering firm of Matrix Churchill Ltd had been charged with breaking Government rules concerning arms exports by shipping large quantities of arms-making equipment to Iraq. They faced long prison sentences.

Things went wrong for the prosecution when the judge refused to recognize the Public Interest Immunity Certificates (PIICs) which had been signed by five Government Ministers under instruction from the Attorney General, Sir Nicholas Lyall. Their effect would have been to gag the defence by denying it access to Government papers proving their case – that the defendants had, in fact, been acting all along with Government approval and encouragement. One of them had even been recruited by MI6 after expressing his concerns about the uses to which his products might be put. The trial collapsed when the former Defence Procurement Minister, Alan Clark, readily agreed under cross-examination that he'd been aware of the matter all along, and that the rules had been re-worded to allow just this sort of trade to take place.

Evidence was taken from several Ministers and officials, past and present. The following is a selection of their more memorably Regrettable utterances.

We should not in future approve orders for any defence equipment which in our view would significantly enhance the capability of either side to prolong or exacerbate the conflict.
1984: Government guidelines on exports to Iraq and Iran.

We should not approve orders in future for any defence equipment which in our view would be of direct and significant assistance to either country in the conduct of offensive operations.
1988: Government guidelines on exports to Iraq and Iran.

Of course I was economical with the actualité.
In evidence at the Matrix Churchill trial, former Defence and Trade Minister Alan Clark cheerfully owns up to misleading the public about guidelines and guns, November 1992; the trial collapsed immediately.

I have no knowledge of this at all.
Margaret Thatcher says she knew nothing about her own Government's altered guidelines on Day 48 of the Scott Inquiry.

Of course I couldn't read everything that crossed my desk.
Margaret Thatcher denies knowledge of a 1988 memo from Defence official Alan Barrett recording her knowledge and approval of Matrix Churchill's trade with Iraq.

I quite simply misled myself on what I thought the situation was.
Eric Beston, Head of Export Control at the Department of Trade, explains to Lord Scott why he gave misleading evidence to the judge at the Matrix Churchill trial. He had earlier been shown his own memo of January 1991 in which he'd written: 'Cross-examination could prove tricky.' It did, eventually.

I get a bit confused when morality is invoked.
Sir Stephen Egerton, Assistant Under Secretary (Middle East) at the Foreign Office, in evidence on Day 11.

Cabinet Ministers explain why they signed PIICs:
I was concerned with people being exterminated, being done away with.
The Rt Hon Kenneth Baker, Home Secretary 1990–92.

I thought it was my duty.
The Rt Hon Peter Lilley, Secretary of State for Trade and Industry 1990–92.

No-one has ever claimed that Mr Henderson has been remotely prejudiced by the certificates.
The Rt Hon Kenneth Clarke, Home Secretary 1992–93, now Chancellor. Defendant Paul Henderson would have been extremely prejudiced by them. He would have gone to prison for something he didn't do.

I was obliged to sign.
The Rt Hon Malcolm Rifkind, Secretary of State for Defence since 1992.

Damage to the intelligence services from disclosure would be unquantifiable . . . I specifically take 'unquantifiable' to mean 'unquantifiably large' or 'unquantifiably small'.
A spot of Jesuitical casuistry from Tristan Garel-Jones, Minister of State at the Foreign Office, 1990–93.

You see, the thing about the Iraqis is, there is no point in asking something just as a kind of 'look here old chap', because they are not that kind of people.
David Mellor, Minister of State at the Foreign Office 1987–88, explains why he never raised military procurement with Saddam Hussein on his visit to Baghdad in 1988.

Since the beginning of the conflict between Iran and Iraq the Government has pursued a policy of impartiality.
It didn't. The Rt Hon John Major: written reply to Alf Morris MP, July 1989.

One of the charges at the time of course was that in some way I must have known because I had been the Chancellor, because I had been the Foreign Secretary, because I had been the Prime Minister and therefore I must have known what was going on.
Apparently he didn't: John Major explains the Case Of The Amazingly Ignorant Minister on Day 55.

Something that I was not aware that happened suddenly turned out not to have happened.
Clarification at last: John Major concludes Day 55.

If the Scott Report is seriously critical of my actions I shall resign from the Cabinet.
The Rt Hon Kenneth Clarke PC MP issues a solemn pledge – on BBC1's Question Time *and elsewhere – in 1994.*

Lord Goodman

Sir, Over the years I have had quite a lot to do with the honours system. May I say that, having read the speech of Mr David Hunt, the Secretary of State for Employment, strongly denying any connection between donations to the Tories and the conferring of honours, I concur in it and confirm that it is a system that, from a scrutiny close up, is respectable and honourable.
Letter to The Times, *July 3rd 1993. Of course he must be right.*

Lord Macalpine

I misjudged. I didn't make a judgement. It was all done third hand.
Pick your own explanation from the Tory Party treasurer after £440,000 benefactor Asil Nadir skipped bail from a North Dorset airfield in 1993.

President Bill Clinton

I tried it but I didn't inhale.
1992: the presidential candidate explains how, in his student days at Oxford, he almost didn't really smoke pot at all, much.

I have nothing else to say. We, we did, if, the, I, I, the stories are just as they have been said. They're outrageous and they're not so.
US Presidents seem to have a propensity for e e cummings. A response to allegations of past extra-marital sexual shenanigans in December 1993.

Tim Yeo MP

I am absolutely confident that I won't have to resign.
The Environment Minister speaks on January 4th 1994 after it is revealed that he has fathered two illegitimate children. He resigned the next day.

Michael Portillo MP

If any of you have got an A-level, it is because you have worked to get it. Go to any other country and when you have got an A-level, you have bought it.
The Spanish-born Chief Secretary to the Treasury puts Southampton University students right about foreigners, February 4th 1994.

Patrick Nicholls MP

The French are a nation of collaborators . . . Germany's unique contribution to Europe has been to plunge it into two World Wars . . . French wine is mostly inferior to that of Australia but in their own rule-twisting way it's probably hard for the French to find that out for themselves . . . The purpose of the Government's European policy is to avoid being thrown into some bastardised, federalised, European destiny, actively and fawningly crawling to France and Germany as the lesser countries insult us to the tune of their begging bowls . . . I wish I was not in the Community.
The Vice-Chairman of the Conservative Party writes an article in the Western Morning News *of November 23rd 1994.*

I bitterly regret any embarrassment I have caused.
He resigns on the evening of November 23rd 1994.

Martin O'Neill MP

The Labour Party is committed to the reintroduction of public ownership of the coal industry.
Speech by the Opposition spokesman on Energy, House of Commons, March 1994.

While we envisage a national role for coal in our energy strategy, we do not intend to re-nationalise the industry.
Speech to the Coal Industry Society conference, November 1994.

There has been no change in Labour's policy.
Letter to The Guardian, *November 1994.*

Robert Jones MP

I am very glad to support the Energy Conservation Bill. It is long overdue. I shall urge the government to support it.
The backbench Tory MP speaks out in 1993.

I deplore the Bill . . . Frankly we have much more practical things to get on with.
The Minister for Energy Conservation gives his verdict in 1994.

The Rt Hon Tony Blair MP

DAVID FROST: Do you have your own views on Clause Four, I mean would you oppose it being dropped?
TONY BLAIR: Well, I don't think that anyone actually wants that to be a priority of the Labour Party at the moment . . . I don't think anyone is saying now, looking ahead to the next two years in the run-up to the next general election, that this is the sort of thing we should focus on.
Interviewed on Breakfast With Frost, *June 12th 1994. At his Party's conference in September Blair announced a review of Clause Four; in January 1995 he began a high-profile nationwide campaign to have it scrapped.*

Her Majesty Queen Elizabeth II

Manchester is not such a nice place.
An off-the-top-of-the-crown remark to a St Petersburg student, 1994. She had to visit Manchester to make up for it. It rained.

John Maples

The Conservative Party has let voters down, been in Government too long, is complacent and has lost its sense of direction. We fail to fulfil promises, are clumsy at implementing policies, and shoot ourselves in the foot.
The Tory Party Vice-Chairman airs some views not intended for publication, November 1994.

Rod Richards MP

They're all the same. They're short, they're fat, they're slimy and they're fundamentally corrupt.
In a December 1994 interview with Barn *magazine, the junior Welsh Office minister gives an opinion of Welsh Labour councillors.*

Dame Angela Rumbold MP

I cannot bring myself to ask people favours. I am not that sort of person.
So what did they pay her for? January 1995: the Tory Party's Deputy Chairman, in evidence to the Nolan Committee on Standards in Public Life, denies she used her position to gain favours for the commercial lobbying firm that employed her at £12,000 p.a. as a 'consultant'.

Stephen Norris MP

You have your own company, your own temperature control, your own music and you don't have to put up with dreadful human beings sitting alongside you.

The Transport Minister is refreshingly frank in his views on private and public transport, February 8th 1995.

John Prescott MP

The Tories have done many things much damage to here in London, a proud once great city. London beat the racists in Tower Hamlets and the rest of the party proud of you doing it were and we much talk about outside the rest of London.

Let me leave you with one thought in view of the time which is important to put over a good idea. Why not employ more teachers in social productivity to challenge the economic productivity only so we shall show to the Tories where they are. Let us say something to the unemployed, yes you are after full employment years and we can go back forward now back to full employment.

Another e e cummings fan: the Deputy Leader of the Labour Party addresses the London Party Conference, February 26th 1995.

Jonathan Aitken MP

If it falls to me to start the fight to cut out the cancer of bent and twisted journalism in our country with the simple sword of truth and the trusty shield of British fair play, so be it.

April 1995. Time – and the outcome of Mr Aitken's libel action against the Guardian *and ITV's* World in Action *for allegations of dirty dealing in the Middle Eastern arms trade – will tell whether this call to arms will prove Regrettable.*

The Rt Hon John Major PC MP

For the last three years I've been opposed by a small minority in the party . . . To remove this uncertainty I have this afternoon tendered my resignation. . . .

June 22nd 1995. Prime Minister John Major resigns as leader of the Conservative Party and later announces his candidacy in the resulting leadership election.

This result puts to rest any question or speculation about the leadership of the Conservative Party.

Really? On July 4th 1995, John Major hails a result – Major 218, Redwood 89, abstentions/spoiled papers 20 – that left him with the support of two-thirds of his Parliamentary colleagues, and reduced the 'small minority' to a mere 109 Conservative MPs.

The Fog of War

'Theirs not to make reply,
Theirs not to reason why,
Theirs but to do and die.'

Alfred, Lord Tennyson:
The Charge of the Light Brigade.

Very occasionally, battles and wars are won as a result of accurate intelligence, meticulous planning and brilliant generalship. More often, as the following selection demonstrates, they are lost because of ignorance, incompetence or sheer lunacy – or else won in spite of it.

AD 70 – AD 1914

Vi et armis . . . sed non plus ultra

I will ignore all ideas for new works and engines of war, the invention of which has reached its limits and for whose improvement I see no further hope.

c. AD 70: Julius Frontinus, the Emperor Vespasian's chief military engineer, shows a shrewdness and foresight worthy of Earl Haig himself.

Our Regrettable History of Armed Conflict now skips 1700 years to . . .

The War of American Independence

A small action will set everything to rights.

Major John Pitcairn advises General Thomas Gage that the revolutionaries lack stamina and discipline, 1775.

The Napoleonic Wars

A man such as I am is not much concerned over the lives of a million men.

Napoleon Bonaparte makes what turns out to be a conservative estimate of the number of deaths caused by his campaigns.

What, sir, you would make a ship sail against the wind and currents by lighting a bonfire under her decks? I pray you excuse me. I have no time to listen to such nonsense.

In 1803, Napoleon dismisses the American engineer Robert Fulton, who suggested steam power as a useful means of defeating the Royal Navy.

No doubt he is a little mad at times, but in his lucid intervals he is an uncommonly clever fellow; and I trust that he will have no fit during the campaign, though I must say he looked a little mad as he embarked.

The Military Secretary in London attempts to reassure Wellington as to the competence of Sir William Erskine as a senior commander. Erskine, who had twice been confined in a lunatic asylum, was also acutely short-sighted and had to have the general position of the enemy pointed out to him. At the battle of Sabugal in 1811 he sent all his forces in the wrong direction.

Why on earth did I do that?
Lisbon, 1813: last words of Sir William Erskine, after he had thrown himself out of an upper storey window.

I tell you Wellington is a bad general and the English are bad soldiers; we will settle the matter by lunch time.
Napoleon briefs his commanders over breakfast on the day of the battle of Waterloo, June 18th 1815.

Ah, but what if . . .

Although the needle gun permits rapid fire as long as there is no stoppage, this does not constitute any real advantage, because rapid fire will merely exhaust the ammunition supply.
. . . the other lot have more ammunition? Austrian Feldzeugmeister Augustin rejects the new-fangled quick-firing gun, 1851. The Prussians adopted it and used it to trounce Austrian forces at Könnigrätz in 1866.

Points of view

Follow the enemy and try to prevent the enemy carrying away the guns.
October 25th 1854: Lord Raglan, on a hilltop, means one lot of guns in one enemy position; Lord Lucan, down in the valley, can only see another lot of guns in a different position. The result is the Charge (and loss) of the Light Brigade.

The American Civil War

My plans are perfect. May God have mercy on Lee, for I will have none.
General Joseph Hooker looks forward to a crushing defeat at Chancellorsville in May 1863. He was afterwards replaced by Ulysses S. Grant.

VERY FAMOUS LAST WORDS:

Nonsense, man! They couldn't hit an elephant at this dist –
Union commander General Sedgewick goes straight into the anthologies at the battle of Spotsylvania, 1864.

The Franco-Prussian War

We are ready, the Prussians are not. We are not lacking so much as a gaiter button.
July 4th 1870: Marshal Edmond Laboeuf, French Minister of War, is supremely confident. Prussia secured total victory within two months.

Possibly the worst Lieutenant-Colonel ever

Hold your horses, boys. There's plenty down there for us all.
Almost the last words of the man the Cheyenne called 'Squaw-killer': 'General' George Armstrong Custer at the Battle of Little Big Horn, June 25th 1876, at which he perished along with his 700 men. One horse survived.

A little spot of bother in the colonies: the two Boer Wars

You need not worry your head about the Boers fighting. I undertake to lead my regiment through South Africa from one end to the other, armed only with pickhandles.
Typical of his time, Colonel Tucker of the 80th Foot gives advance warning of a succession of British defeats in the first Boer War.

It appears certain that, after one serious defeat, they would be too deficient in discipline and organization to make any further real stand.
The strategy that lost the American Colonies: Military Notes on the Dutch Republics, *War Office Intelligence Department, 1899.*

The Boers are not like the Sudanese, who stood up to a fair fight. They are always running away on their little ponies.
Ah, the dear old Fuzzy-Wuzzies; they knew how to stand still and get shot! General Kitchener bemoans unsporting fighting habits during the Second Boer War: 1900.

MILITARY INTELLIGENCE (1)

On brains . . .

We shall always win by reason of pluck . . . always the most essential factor.
Major (afterwards Field Marshal) Douglas Haig, 1896.

War is a contest between two human intelligences rather than between two bodies of armed men. Ligny and Waterloo were won by sheer power of brain.
Staff College Introductory Lecture, 1900.

Brains! I don't believe in brains. You haven't any, I know, sir.
The Duke of Cambridge, Commander-in-Chief of the British Army, 1854–1895, pays tribute to one of his favourite Generals. Under his leadership, Britain's contribution to military literature dwindled to 1% of total output by 1900. 50% was published in Germany.

And bullets . . .

It must be accepted as a principle that the rifle, effective as it is, cannot replace the effect produced by the speed of the horse, the magnetism of the charge and the terror of cold steel.
They don't like it up 'em! That is, if you can get near enough . . . British Cavalry Training Manual, 1907.

Bullets have little stopping power against the horse.
BEF Commander-in-Chief Earl Haig concurs in 1914.

Make no mistake: this weapon will change absolutely nothing.
The Director-General of the French Infantry briefs his country's Parliament on the machine gun in 1910 . . .

A HERD OF DONKEYS
The Regrettable History of World War One

Ludendorff: The English fight like lions!
Col Max Hoffman: True. But don't we know that they are lions led by donkeys?

Feet on the ground
Aeroplanes are interesting toys, but of no military value.
Maréchal Foch addresses students at the Ecole Supérieure de Guerre, 1911.

Submarines would be unsporting
Most improbable and more like one of Jules Verne's stories.
Admiral Sir Compton Dombile on Danger!, *a short story by Sir Arthur Conan Doyle warning of the dangers of a submarine blockade.*

I reject the notion that territorial waters will be violated, or neutral vessels sunk. Such will be absolutely prohibited and will only recoil on the heads of the perpetrators. No nation would permit it, and the officer who did it would be shot.
Admiral Sir William Hannan Henderson concurs.

On entering the war zone tomorrow, we shall be securely in the care of the Royal Navy.
Captain William Turner, commander of the Lusitania, *takes the Admiralty at its word. 1198 people perished after she was torpedoed.*

Strictly for losers
My friend, we shall not have time to make them. I shall tear up the Boches within two months.
General Joseph Joffre rejects the notion that French troops will need helmets, November 1914. French soldiers went to the Front without them.

A purely defensive weapon
The machine gun is a much overrated weapon; two per battalion is more than sufficient.
Unless you're German, of course: General Douglas Haig, 1915.

Mechanical treachery

The idea that cavalry will be replaced by these iron coaches is absurd. It is little short of treasonous.

His master's voice: Haig's aide-de-camp after watching a tank demonstration in 1916.

A pretty mechanical toy.

A softer but no less stupid line from Lord Kitchener in 1917.

Blood and glory

Casualties? What do I care for casualties?

Major-General A. G. Hunter-Weston, nicknamed 'The Butcher of Hellas' after he used up three British divisions in daylight frontal attacks during the Gallipoli campaign. He once told an officer whose men had sustained 1300 casualties, 'You'll be glad you've bloodied the pups.'

Just like the Boers, only darker

The Turk is an enemy who has never shown himself as good a fighter as the white man.

A Staff Officer's briefing to troops before the Gallipoli landings, 1915, no doubt intended to be 'good for morale'.

Cannon fodder

With the enthusiasm of ignorance they will tear their way through the German line.

In 1903 Haig wrote: 'We must never forget that we are dealing with men of flesh and blood and nerves.' Now he's changed his mind as he plans for the battle of Loos, September 1915

Haig's 'Big Push'

You will be able to go over the top with a walking stick, you will not need rifles. When you get to Thiepval you will find the Germans all dead, not even a rat will have survived.

An anonymous Brigadier-General addresses the Newcastle Commercials on the morning of the Somme Offensive, July 1st 1916.

The men are in splendid spirits. Several have said that they have never before been so instructed and informed of the nature of the operation before them. The wire has never been so well cut, nor the artillery preparations so thorough.

Dear Diary: Field Marshal Earl Haig, July 1st 1916.

They advanced in line after line, dressed as if on parade, and not a man shirked going through the extremely heavy barrage, or facing the

machine-gun fire that finally wiped them out . . . I have never seen . . . such a magnificent display of gallantry, discipline and determination. The reports I have had from the very few survivors of this marvellous advance bear out what I saw . . . that hardly a man of ours got to the German front line.
Brigadier-General Rees, GOC 94th Infantry Brigade of 31 Division, on the evening of July 1st 1916.

The massive artillery barrage had done little damage to the German forces – and in any case our old friend Hunter-Weston ordered the barrage to stop before the advance began, thus allowing them to emerge and open fire. The barbed wire in many places had not been cut, and British troops carried no wire-cutters; German machine gun fire was concentrated in the places where it had been cut. Many British officers did in fact stroll over with walking sticks and furled brollies; some dribbled footballs, so well were they 'instructed and informed'.

By the time the Offensive petered out in November there were 1,000,000 casualties. 21,000 British troops died in the first half hour of July 1st.

The attack on the Somme bore out the conclusions of the British Higher Command, and amply justified the tactical methods employed.
Jolly good! Haig's official biographer Colonel Boraston sums up.

Here we go again

The experiment has been conclusive. Our method has been tried out. I can assure you that victory is certain. The enemy will learn this to his cost.
French General Robert Nivelle launched the Chemin des Dames offensive in December 1916, one month after the 'Big Push'. The Germans, who knew about it in advance, inflicted 120,000 casualties in five days. Nivelle, unlike Haig, was sacked following outbreaks of mutiny.

Every position must be held to the last man: there must be no retirement.
Field Marshal Earl Haig – described by Prime Minister Lloyd George as 'brilliant to the top of his boots' – sticks to his one-way strategy; April 12th 1918.

MILITARY INTELLIGENCE (2)

It is highly unlikely that an airplane, or fleet of them, could ever sink a fleet of Navy vessels under battle conditions.
Franklin D. Roosevelt, 1922.

It is not possible . . . to concentrate enough military planes with military loads over a modern city to destroy that city.
US Colonel John W. Thomason Jr opines in November 1937. Er . . . Guernica?

There is no such thing as the aerial battle. There is only the battle on the ground.
General Maurice Gamelin, 1936.

The tank was a freak. The circumstances which called it into existence were exceptional and are not likely to recur. If they do, they can be dealt with by other means.
That settles that. Major-General Sir Louis Jackson, 1919.

As for tanks, which are supposed by some to bring a shortening of wars, their incapacity is striking.
Marshal Henri Philippe Pétain pens a foreword to Is an Invasion Still Possible? *by General Chauvineau. The book's conclusion was 'Non'.*

On leaving Montmédy, we come to the Ardennes forests. If certain preparations are made, these are impregnable. This sector is not dangerous.
Marshal Pétain again: March 1934. His advice, when followed, made a nonsense of the 'Maginot Line'. The Ardennes were left virtually undefended, and German forces under Field Marshal von Rundstedt smashed through them.

Their tanks will be destroyed in the open country behind our lines if they can penetrate that far, which is doubtful.
Wrong on both counts: French General A. L. Georges, 1939.

The chances of Germany making a quick job of overwhelming Poland are not good.
US Major George Fielding Eliot reassures readers of the Boston Evening Transcript *on May 13th 1939. Beginning on September 1st, it took Germany five weeks to crush all Polish resistance.*

THE SECOND WORLD WAR

Réassurez-vous!

Nothing will happen before 1941.
General Gaston Bilotte, commander on the French North-eastern front, reassures corps commanders concerned about weapons shortages in May 1940.

We are not Poles. It could not happen here.
General Gamelin responds to reports that Germany may use blitzkrieg tactics on France: May 1940.

There are no urgent measures to be taken for the reinforcement of the Sedan sector.
The forest will protect us: General Charles Huntziger, commander of the French Second Army, May 13th 1940. Three days later, German forces broke through to Sedan. Six weeks after that, France surrendered.

Désespérez-vous!

In three weeks England will have her neck wrung like a chicken.
General Maxime Weygand, Commander-in-Chief of French Military Forces, bows rather gleefully to the inevitable on June 16th 1940. After victory in Europe Churchill commented: 'Some chicken, some neck.'

Like Carthage, England will be destroyed.
Jean Herold-Paquis signs off news bulletins on Vichy Radio.

Small yellow people of no particular account

War between Japan and the United States is not within the realm of reasonable possibility . . . A Japanese attack on Pearl Harbor is a strategic impossibility.
Major George Fielding Eliot, The Impossible War With Japan, *September 1938.*

Japan will never join the Axis.
General Douglas MacArthur in Manila on September 27th 1940, while morning newspapers reporting that Japan had joined the Axis were being printed.

The Hawaiian Islands are over-protected; the entire Japanese fleet and air force could not seriously threaten Oahu.
Captain William T. Pulleston, former Chief of US Military Intelligence, August 1941.

Well, don't worry about it. It's nothing.
Lieutenant Kermit Tyler, Duty Officer at the Shafter Information Centre, Hawaii, recalls the Lord Mayor of London (see p. 14) as he receives radar reports of 50 warplanes approaching Oahu at 180mph on December 7th 1941.

I had a good close-up, across the barbed wire, of various sub-human specimens dressed in dirty grey uniforms, which I was informed were Japanese soldiers . . . I cannot believe they would form an intelligent fighting force.
Air Chief Marshal Brooke-Popham, who also saw no need to improve Singapore's air defences in December 1941. The British force of antiquated Brewster Buffalo fighters was wiped out.

I do hope we're not getting too strong in Malaya, because if so the Japanese may not attempt a landing.
British officer in Singapore, December 1941. The Japanese did not need to attempt a landing . . .

I believe that defences of the sort you want to throw up are bad for the morale of troops and civilians.
Complacency must not be disturbed: Lieutenant-General Arthur Percival refuses to countenance landward defences, December 1941. A few months later, Japanese forces surged down the Malay peninsula and entered Singapore by the back door.

Nice ball game, shame about the . . .

It is significant that despite the claims of air enthusiasts no battleship has yet been sunk by bombs.
Caption to a photograph of the USS Arizona *in the official programme for the Army v. Navy football game, November 29th 1941. Eight days later the* Arizona *was bombed at her moorings in Pearl Harbor. She sank with the loss of 1102 lives.*

Patton the movie – the bit we all remember

Shut up that Goddam' crying. I won't have brave men here who have been shot seeing a yellow bastard crying. You're going back to the front lines and you may get shot and killed, but you're going to fight. If you don't I'll stand you up against a wall and have a firing squad kill you on purpose. I ought to shoot you myself, you Goddam' whimpering coward.
Lieutenant-General George S. Patton Jr. tries out his bedside manner with a shell-shock victim at the 93rd Evacuation Hospital, Sicily, August 10th 1943.

Forget the atom

Atomic energy might be as good as our present day explosives, but it is unlikely to produce anything very much more dangerous.
Winston Churchill, 1939.

This is the biggest fool thing we have ever done. The bomb will never go off, and I speak as an expert in explosives.
Admiral William Leahy advises President Truman in 1945.

KOREA, VIETNAM AND THE PRESENT

KOREA – A QUICK CAMPAIGN

There is no question whatever about the outcome of this struggle. We shall win.

US General Walton Harris Walker of Far East Command's Eighth Army, July 31st 1950.

The Chinese have 300,000 men in Manchuria. Of these probably not more than 100–125,000 are distributed along the Yalu River. Only 50–60,000 could be gotten across the Yalu River. They have no air force. Now that we have bases for our Air Force in Korea, if the Chinese tried to get down to Pyongyang there would be the greatest slaughter.

What, he worry? General Douglas MacArthur briefs President Truman, October 14th 1950.

These cookies are beaten!

Major-General Hobart Gay, commander of the US First Cavalry Division, October 23rd 1950.

After several hundred thousand Chinese troops crossed the Yalu River on November 6th the US-led UN force was forced to retreat. An armistice brought the ensuing stalemate to an end on July 27th 1953 and Korea was partitioned.

VIETNAM PART ONE – THE FRENCH CONNECTION

We shall never retreat or give up.

Admiral G. Thierry d'Argenlieu, French High Commissioner for Indo-China, November 24th 1946.

We will have victory in fifteen months.

General Jean de Lattre de Tassigny, C-in-C French Forces in Indo-China, doesn't rate the Vietminh very highly in December 1950.

There is no question that the Communist menace in French Indo-China has been stopped.

Uncle Sam lends moral support: General J. Lawton Collins, Chief of Staff of the US Army, October 27th 1951.

Light at the end of the tunnel – first reported sighting

A year ago none of us could see victory. There wasn't a prayer. Now we can see it clearly – like light at the end of the tunnel.

Lieutenant-General Henri-Eugene Navarre, C-in-C French Union Forces, September 28th 1953. As Churchill might have said: Some tunnel, some light.

Dienbienphu

We've taken the place and we shall stay there. . . . I foresee final victory in the spring of 1956.

General René Cogny, commander of French Union Forces, November 20th 1953.

First, the Vietminh won't succeed in getting their artillery through to here. Secondly, if they do get here, we'll smash them. Thirdly, even if they manage to keep on shooting, they will be unable to supply their pieces with enough ammunition to do us any real harm.

Colonel Charles Piroth, deputy commander of French forces at Dienbienphu, December 1953.

Victory after six more months of hard fighting.

Lt-Gen Navarre sees the light getting nearer on January 1st 1954.

If the Communists continue to suffer the losses they have been taking I don't see how they can stay in the battle.

The French Chief of Staff General Paul Ely, March 20th 1954. Dienbienphu fell to Vietminh forces on May 7th 1954. A spokesman for Lt-Gen Navarre announced: 'Dienbienphu has fulfilled the mission that was assigned to it by the high command.' On May 8th 1954 the French Government called for an end to hostilities in Indo-China.

VIETNAM PART TWO – THE YANKS ARE COMING

The Vietnamese have ample manpower and even today outnumber the enemy by 100,000. This matter can be resolved without bringing in one single American soldier to fight.

General John W. O'Daniel, Head of the US Military Mission of Advisers to the Government of South Vietnam, July 7th 1954.

We have exactly 342 men, the number allowed by the Geneva Armistice Committee. It would be a breeze if we had more.

General Samuel T. Williams, Head of US Advisory Group, June 12th 1957.

The risks of backing into a major Asian war by way of South Viet Nam are present but are not impressive. North Viet Nam is extremely vulnerable to conventional bombing, a weakness which should be

exploited diplomatically in convincing Hanoi to lay off South Viet Nam.
General Maxwell Taylor completes his fact-finding tour of South Vietnam and sends a cable to President Kennedy, November 1st 1961.

The training, transportation and logistical support we are providing in Vietnam has succeeded in turning the tide against the Vietcong.
An upbeat message from General Barksdale Hamlett, US Army Vice Chief of Staff, October 10th 1962.

Victory is in sight.
General Paul D. Harkins, Commander of US Forces, South Vietnam, March 5th 1963. At the end of the tunnel, perhaps?

The North Vietnamese cannot take the punishment any more in the South. I think we can bring the war to a conclusion within the next year, possibly within the next six months.
Like General Ely in 1954, General S. L. A. Marshall cannot see how the Communists can possibly fight on: September 12th 1966.

The troops will be brought home in 18 months.
General Harold K. Johnson, US Army Chief of Staff, August 12th 1967.

General William C. Westmoreland: an appreciation

It is inconceivable that the Viet Cong could ever defeat the armed forces of South Vietnam.
The Commander of US Forces in South Vietnam celebrates his appointment with a news conference: April 25th 1964.

The enemy is literally on the verge of starvation.
November 7th 1967.

We have reached an important point where the end begins to come into view.
Like, er, light at the end of a tunnel, perhaps? November 21st 1967.

The enemy is about to run out of steam.
February 2nd 1968.

I do not believe that the enemy can hold up under a long war.
Neither did Ho Chi Minh. February 25th 1968.

The enemy's only victories in the last few years have been in the propaganda field . . . I am confident the enemy is receiving false reports from field commanders . . . Time is on our side.
On a visit to LBJ's Texas ranch, May 30th 1968. A fortnight later General Westmoreland was appointed Chief of Staff of the US Army.

We're on our way up . . . The pendulum is beginning to swing.
Yet another beginning: April 16th 1972.

RSVP

Come and see the light at the end of the tunnel.
. . . Which turned out to be the Tet Offensive. Official invitation to the New Year's Eve Party at the US Embassy in Saigon, December 1967. In January 1968 the Vietcong briefly captured a large portion of the building.

Cruel to be kind

To save the town it became necessary to destroy it.
US commander during the Tet Offensive, 1968.

And then . . .

We have the enemy licked now. He is beaten. We have the initiative in all areas. The enemy cannot achieve a military victory; he cannot even mount another offensive.
Admiral John S. McCain, C-in-C US Pacific Forces, February 1969 – the year the Vietcong mounted 159 simultaneous raids in South Vietnam.

If we just keep up the pressure, these little guys will crack.
General Earl Wheeler, June 1970.

The Vietnam War has been reduced to what we technicians call a police action.
Wise words from Down Under: Major Ted Sioong of the Australian Army, 1971.

Peace with honor

If you Americans think you're going to just walk away and leave us, you'll never make it to the airport.
Colonel Luan, Chief of the South Vietnamese Police Force, April 1975. But they did, and on April 29th the last Americans left by helicopter from the compound of the US Embassy in Saigon. On May 1st the victorious North Vietnamese renamed the former capital Ho Chi Minh City.

Advice unheeded

Anyone who gets himself involved in a ground war in Indo-China needs his head examined.
General Douglas MacArthur, 1950.

1991–THE PRESENT

Oh mother!

The Mother of Battles will be our battle of victory and martyrdom.
He got it half right: Saddam Hussein encourages his troops on the eve of Operation Desert Storm in 1991.

A Major writes

The only other comparable regiment is the Royal Marines but they are a bit slower. They like to think a bit – and then go and get killed. The Paras just go out and get killed.
Army historian Major Charles Hayman extols the virtues of the Parachute Regiment in the Daily Telegraph, *November 29th 1994.*

Oh really?

The military phase of the Chechen campaign is effectively over.
President Boris Yeltsin after Russian troops captured the remains of the Parliament building in Grozny, January 19th 1995: a remark that became Regrettable almost as it was being uttered.

HOW TO SURVIVE A NUCLEAR WAR – OFFICIAL

(1) Be an American

The dangers of atomic war are overrated. It would be hard on little, concentrated countries like England. In the United States we have lots of space.
Colonel Robert Rutherford McCormick, February 23rd 1950.

(2) Dig a hole

Dig a hole, cover it with a couple of doors and throw three feet of dirt on top. It's the dirt that does it. You know, dirt is just great stuff. If there are enough shovels to go around, everybody's going to make it.
Go bury yourself, says US Deputy Under-Secretary of Defence for Research and Engineering, Strategic and Theater Nuclear Forces T. K. Jones in 1981.

A cleansing holocaust

Nuclear war could alleviate some of the factors leading to today's ecological disturbances that are due to current high-population concentrations and heavy industrial production.
An official at the US Office of Civil Defense throws a sop to the Deep Green lobby: 1982.

PEACE DIVIDENDS

Everything announces an age in which that madness of nations, war, will come to an end.
In Réflexions politiques sur les circonstances présentes, *the philosopher Jean-Paul Rabaut Saint-Etienne hails the outcome of the French Revolution: 1792.*

No more hatreds, no more self-interests devouring one another, no more wars, a new life made up of harmony and light prevails.
Victor Hugo sees the potential of balloon flight in 1842 – the beginning of what historians call 'The Decade of Nationalism'.

My dynamite will sooner lead to peace
Than a thousand world conventions.
As soon as men will find that in one instant
Whole armies can be utterly destroyed,
They will surely abide by golden peace.
Alfred Bernhard Nobel (1833–1896) waxes poetical.

To kill a man will be considered as disgusting as we in this day consider it disgusting to eat one.
1900: Andrew Carnegie greets the dawn of the twentieth century.

The submarine may be the cause of bringing battle to a stoppage altogether, for fleets will become useless, and as other war matériel continues to improve, war will become impossible.
But humankind stays much the same . . . Jules Verne is optimistic in 1904.

As a peace machine, its value to the world will be beyond computation. Would a declaration of war between Russia and Japan be made, if within an hour thereafter a swiftly gliding aeroplane might take its flight from St Petersburg and drop half a ton of dynamite above the enemy's war offices? Could any nation afford to war upon any other with such hazards in view?
An early version of Mutually Assured Destruction: John Brisben Walker, owner and publisher of Cosmopolitan, *March 1904.*

It seems pretty clear that no civilized people will ever again permit its government to enter into a competitive arms race.
Nicholas Murray Butler, President of Columbia University, October 17th 1914.

Radio will serve to make the concept of Peace on Earth, Good Will Toward Man a reality.
General James J. Harbond, former World War One commander and Chairman of RCA: 1925.

People are becoming too intelligent ever to have another big war. I believe the last war was too much an educator for there ever to be another on a large scale.
Henry Ford, 1928.

Never in history has mankind been given more reason to look forward to the future with hope. For the blast which blew nineteenth-century nationalism to pieces at Hiroshima may also have cleared the way for a new Renaissance – a new era of co-operation leading up to the twentieth-century Empire of the World.
1946: as the Cold War begins, the American military historian Lynn Montross publishes War Through the Ages *and foresees the End of History.*

We now have an opportunity to build a New World Order, based on diplomacy and co-operation.
1990: as the Cold War ends and nineteenth-century nationalism prepares to rise from the grave, US President George Bush ushers in yet another Renaissance.

Culture Vultures

Like the Assyrian,
the critic comes down
as a wolf on the fold

The creative arts, a field of activity where humankind is at its most playful, finds it also at its most savage – that is, if we can regard critics as human. It is well known among writers, painters, composers, actors, singers and musicians that critics in general are, by definition, failed writers, painters, composers, etc. – except on the very rare occasions when they give good reviews. These, of course, are the exceptions that prove the rule.

Widening the definiton of the word 'critic' to include both the publisher and that peculiar sub-species, the talent-spotter, achieves two interesting and worthwhile results. It allows them to become sources of entertainment for the rest of us, and it also provides a rare and necessary opportunity for anyone who has ever tried to make a living out of talent to get his or her revenge. This is, surely, too rare an opportunity to be missed.

It does, though, have one unfortunate consequence: some of the most damning critiques of the creative turn out to have been written by fellow creators. Fortunately for us, they also turn out to be among the silliest.

ART

More than simply a matter of knowing what one likes

When the flush of a new-born sun fell first on Eden's green and gold,
Our father Adam sat under the Tree and scratched with a stick in the mould;
And the first rude sketch that the world had seen was joy to his mighty heart,
Till the Devil whispered behind the leaves, 'It's pretty, but is it Art?'
Wherefore he called to his wife, and fled to fashion his work anew –
The first of his race who cared a fig for the first most dread review.

Rudyard Kipling, *The Conundrum of the Workshops.*

THE RENAISSANCE – A MOST REGRETTABLE ERROR

Instant degradation followed in every direction – a flood of folly and hypocrisy. Mythologies, ill-understood at first, then perverted into feeble

sensualities, take the place of the representation of Christian subjects, which had become blasphemous under the treatment of men like the Caracci. Gods without power, satyrs without rusticity, nymphs without innocence, men without humanity, gather into idiot groups upon the polluted canvas, and scenic affectations encumber the streets with preposterous marble. Lower and lower declines the level of abused intellect; the base school of landscape gradually usurps the place of the historical painting, which had sunk into prurient pedantry, – the Alsatian sublimities of Salvator, the confectionery idealities of Claude, the dull manufacture of Gaspar and Canaletto, south of the Alps, and in the north the patient devotion of besotted lives to delineation of bricks and fogs, cattle and ditchwater.

First prize in the Sustained Curled Lip Contest: John Ruskin, the leading critic and cultural mentor of his day, puts his finger on what's to blame for the state of Art in the nineteenth century in Stones of Venice, *1851–53.*

Titian

Why should Titian and the Venetians be named in a discourse on art? Such idiots are not artists.

William Blake, no mean dauber himself, scribbles a note on a copy of Sir Joshua Reynolds' Discourses, *1807.*

There, against the wall, without obstructing rag or leaf, you may look your fill upon the foulest, the vilest, the most obscene picture the world possesses – Titian's Venus. . . . There are pictures of nude women which suggest no impure thought – I am well aware of that. I am not railing at such. What I am trying to emphasize is the fact that Titian's Venus is very far from being one of that sort. Without any question it was painted for a bagnio and it was probably refused because it was a trifle too strong.

Mark Twain, part-time writer of pornographic stories, finds offence in 'the attitude of one of her arms and hand' in Titian's masterpiece: A Tramp Abroad, *1880.*

Rembrandt

Rembrandt is not to be compared in the painting of character with our extraordinarily gifted English artist, Mr Rippingille.

John Hunt (1775–1848).

PRE-RAPHAELITES AND OTHERS

John Everett Millais

In the foreground of the carpenter's shop is a hideous, wry-necked, blubbering, red-haired boy in a nightgown, who appears to have received a poke playing in an adjacent gutter, and to be holding it up for the

contemplation of a kneeling woman, so horrible in her ugliness that (supposing it were possible for any human creature to exist for a moment with that dislocated throat) she would stand out from the rest of the company as a monster in the vilest cabaret in France or the lowest gin-shop in England.
Charles Dickens goes over the top for Christ in the House of his Parents *in* Household Words, *1850.*

Revolting . . . loathsome.
The Times, *1850, on the same painting.*

William Holman Hunt

The face of this wild fantasy, though earnest and religious, is not that of a Saviour. It expresses such a strange mingling of disgust, fear, and imbecility, that we turn from it to relieve the sight. The manipulation, though morbidly delicate and laboured, is not so massive as the mute passion displayed in the general feeling and detail demands. Altogether this picture is a failure.
The Athenæum *dismisses* The Light of the World *on May 6th 1854. Reproductions of it were sold by the hundred thousand; it became Britain's most popular religious painting and, in Frank Muir's words, 'perhaps the nearest thing the Church of England has had to an ikon'.*

Lawrence Alma-Tadema

The general effect was exactly like a microscopic view of a small detachment of black beetles, in search of a dead rat.
John Ruskin isn't overly impressed by The Pyrrhic Dance, *1869.*

THE IMPRESSIONISTS

This school has abolished two things: line, without which it is impossible to reproduce the form of a living being or an object; and colour, which gives form the appearance of reality . . . the practitioners fall into a senseless, mad, grotesque mess, fortunately without precedent in the history of art, for it is quite simply the negation of the most elementary rules of drawing and painting. A child's scrawls have a naïveté and a sincerity that make you smile, but the excesses of this school are nauseating or revolting.
Quite simply Not Art: Emile Cardon condemns the first Impressionist exhibition of 1874 in La Presse.

The new French School is simply putrescence and decomposition.
Phew! Dante Gabriel Rossetti doesn't like Impressionism.

They provoke laughter and yet they are lamentable. They display the profoundest ignorance of drawing, of composition and colour. When children amuse themselves with a box of colour and a piece of paper, they do better.
La Chronique des Arts, *April 14th 1877.*

Edouard Manet

Is this drawing? Is this painting? . . . I see garments without feeling the anatomical structure that supports them and explains their movements. I see boneless fingers and heads without skulls. I see side-whiskers made of two strips of black cloth that could have been glued to the cheeks. What else do I see? The artist's lack of conviction and sincerity.
On Déjeuner sur l'herbe*: Jules Castagnary in* Salons, *1863.*

This is a young man's practical joke, a shameful open sore not worth exhibiting this way.
On the same picture: Louis Etienne, Le Jury et les exposants.

The nude, when painted by vulgar men, is inevitably indecent.
That Picture again: Philip Gilbert Hamerton in Fine Art Quarterly Review, *October 1863.*

You scarcely knew if you were looking at a parcel of nude flesh or a bundle of laundry.
Jules Claretie reviews Venus et le Chat *in* Le Figaro, *June 23rd 1863.*

Pierre Auguste Renoir

He has no talent at all, that boy. Tell him please to give up painting.
Spoken with conviction and sincerity: Edouard Manet, 1864.

Just try to explain to Monsieur Renoir that the torso of a woman is not a mass of decomposing flesh, its green and violet spots indicating the state of complete putrefaction of a corpse.
Albert Wolff vents his spleen in Le Figaro, *c. 1865.*

Of the work of M. Auguste Renoir it is hard to speak with gravity. A glance at some of the canvases which bear his name will explain more fully than any words of mine the difficulty one might experience in taking such work seriously.
Fellow artist Philip Burne-Jones lets the side down in The Nineteenth Century *magazine, March 1905.*

James McNeill Whistler

I never saw anything so impudent on the walls of any exhibition, in any country . . . a daub . . . absolute rubbish . . . it had no pretence to be called painting.

John Ruskin again, this time underwhelmed by Symphony in Grey and Green, *1872.*

I have seen, and heard, much of cockney impudence before now; but never expected to hear a coxcomb ask two hundred guineas for flinging a pot of paint in the public's face.

Just as well he wasn't around to see Damien Hirst's pickled sheep! John Ruskin pens the most famous critique in Art history, on The Falling Rocket, *or,* A Nocturne in Black and Gold. *Whistler issued a writ for libel and was awarded a farthing damages; the costs bankrupted him but he did afterwards sell the painting for eight hundred guineas.*

Camille Pissarro

No intelligence can accept such aberrations.

Albert Wolff of Le Figaro *takes his refined aesthetic sensibilities to Durand-Ruel's gallery in Paris, 1876, views the work of the Impressionists' leader, and recoils in comfortable horror.*

Edgar Degas

Degas is nothing but a peeping Tom, behind the coulisses, and among the dressing-rooms of ballet dancers, noting only travesties of fallen debased womanhood, most disgusting and offensive.

The Churchman, *1886.*

Degas is repulsive.

The New York Times, *April 10th 1886.*

It is extraordinary that the pupil of Ingres should create such appalling creatures.

Artist and critic Wynford Dewhurst, Impressionist Painting, *1904.*

Henri Toulouse-Lautrec

Buy Maurins! Lautrec is merely a painter of a period.

1893: Edgar Degas advises art investor Henry Laurent, who duly 'invested' in several hundred canvases of a now largely forgotten painter.

POST-IMPRESSIONISM

Works of idleness and impotent stupidity, a pornographic show . . . The drawing is on the level of that of an untaught child of seven or eight years

old, the sense of colour that of a tea-tray painter, the method that of a schoolboy who wipes his fingers on a slate after spitting on them.
Eurgh! Wilfrid Scawen Blunt didn't have a good time at the first British exhibition of the Post-Impressionists at the Grafton Gallery, 1910.

If the movement is spreading it should be treated like the rat-plague in Suffolk. The source of the infection ought to be destroyed . . . Van Gogh is the typical matoid and degenerate of the modern sociologist. *Jeune Fille au Bleuet* and *Cornfield with Blackbirds* are the visualized ravings of an adult maniac. If that is art it must be ostracised, as the poets were banished from Plato's republic.
The voice of Middle England: Robert Ross in the Morning Post, *1910.*

Paul Cézanne

M. Cézanne gives the impression of being a sort of madman who paints in a fit of delerium tremens . . . why look for a dirty joke or a scandalous theme in the Olympia? In reality it is only one of the weird shapes generated by hashish.
'Marc de Montifaud', a female art critic, writes in L'Artiste *about* A Modern Olympia.

What use have we now for Monsieur Cézanne? So much for the dealers who believed that one day they would make a clean up with his works!
What price now for La Lanterne, *which wrote the painter off in 1905?*

Paul Gauguin

A decorator tainted with insanity.
No wonder he left for the South Seas. Kenyon Cox, Harper's Weekly, *March 15th 1913.*

FAUVISM

Certainly no man or woman of normal mental health would be attracted by the sadistic, obscene deformations of Cézanne, Modigliani, Matisse, Gauguin and the other Fauves.
John Hemming Fry, The Revolt Against Beauty, *1934.*

Henri Matisse

An unmitigated bore. Surely the vogue of these twisted and contorted human figures must be as short as it is artificial.
Harriet Monroe, Chicago Tribune, *February 23rd 1913.*

Raoul Dufy

Dufy is merely a childish scene-painter, a scribbler of all sorts of nursery nonsense.
Sir Lionel Lindsay (1874–1961), Addled Art.

CUBISM

The real meaning of this Cubist movement is nothing else than the total destruction of the art of painting.

Kenyon Cox, Harper's Weekly, *March 15th 1913.*

Pablo Picasso

It's the work of a madman.

French art dealer Ambroise Vollard on Desmoiselles d'Avignon, *Cubism's first realized statement, in 1907.*

His work presents an unhealthy apology for the aesthetics of capitalism, provoking the resentment of ordinary people.

An apparatchik *writes: V. Kemenev, USSR, c. 1935.*

ALL THESE GODDAM ISMS!

So-called modern or contemporary art in our modern beloved country contains all the isms of depravity, decadence and destruction. . . . Who has brought down this curse upon us; who has let into our homeland this horde of germ-carrying art vermin?

Ku Klux Kriticism: Representative George A. Dondero of Michigan addresses Congress on April 19th 1949.

THE ROYAL ACADEMY

Not what it was

The pride and self-respect which are the natural concomitants of genius will be more likely to keep a man out of the Academy than bring him into it.

The Times, *July 20th 1830.*

Plus ça change . . .

The reputation of the Academy has got to a point where election would be positively distressing to a serious painter.

Evening Standard, *February 22nd 1961.*

ALL THERE IS TO BE SAID, REALLY, ABOUT ART

It's a rummy business.

Towards the end of his life, J. M. W. Turner (1775–1851) was invited to make a speech about art to a Royal Academy dinner. This, in its entirety, is what he said.

BOOKS, ETC.

**Publish and be Damned . . .
but first Get Published**

Behold, my desire is, that the Almighty would answer me, and that mine adversary had written a book.

The Book of Job, *Chapter 31, Verse 35.*

---

(1) THE PUBLISHED

Honoré de Balzac

Little imagination is shown in invention, in the creating of character and plot, or in the delineation of passion . . . M. de Balzac's place in French literature will be neither considerable nor high.
Eugène Poitou, Revue des Deux Mondes, *December 1856.*

Charles Baudelaire

In a hundred years the histories of French literature will only mention it as a curio.
Emile Zola considers Les Fleurs du Mal *on the occasion of its author's death in 1867.*

Samuel Beckett

The suggestion that something larger is being said about the human predicament won't hold water, any more than Beckett's incontinent heroes can.
The Spectator *reviews the trilogy* Molloy, Malone Dies *and* The Unnameable *in 1959. Ten years later, the Nobel Prize Committee disagreed.*

Emily Brontë

All the faults of *Jane Eyre* are magnified a thousandfold, and the only consolation which we have in reflecting upon it is that it will never be generally read.
James Lorimer reviews Wuthering Heights *in the* North British Review, *1849.*

Truman Capote

A failure of the imagination.
Norman Mailer reviews In Cold Blood *in 1965 and derides a piece of 'faction'. Mailer's own 'failure of the imagination',* The Executioner's Song, *was published in 1979.*

Lewis Carroll

We fancy that any real child might be more puzzled than enchanted by this stiff, overwrought story.
Alice's Adventures in Wonderland *is reviewed in* Children's Books, *1865.*

Samuel Taylor Coleridge

What great poem has he written? We put this question to his disciples; for we cannot name one considerable poem of his that is likely to remain upon the thresh-floor of fame . . . We fear we shall seem, to our children, to have been pygmies, indeed, in intellect, since such a man as Coleridge would appear great to us!
London Weekly Review, *June 1828.*

Joseph Conrad

It would be useless to pretend that these works can be very widely read.
The Manchester Guardian *considers* Youth *and* Heart of Darkness, *December 10th 1902.*

Charles Dickens

He has never played any part in any movement more significant than that of a fly on the wheel.
The Saturday Review *swats the novelist, January 1857.*

We do not believe in the permanence of his reputation. Fifty years hence, most of his allusions will be harder to understand than the allusions in *The Dunciad*, and our children will wonder what their ancestors could have meant by putting Mr Dickens at the head of the novelists of the day.
The Saturday Review *takes a second swat: May 1858.*

Emily Dickinson

An eccentric, dreamy, half-educated recluse in an out-of-the-way New England village (or anywhere else) cannot with impunity set at defiance the laws of gravitation and grammar. Oblivion lingers in the immediate neighbourhood.
Thomas Bailey Aldrich, The Atlantic Monthly, *January 1892.*

John Donne

Dr Donne's verses are like the Peace of God; they pass all understanding.
King James I, c. 1610.

T. S. Eliot

If Mr Eliot had been pleased to write in demotic English, *The Waste Land* might not have been, as it is to all but anthropologists and literati, so much waste-paper.
The Manchester Guardian, *1917.*

William Faulkner

The final blowup of what was once a remarkable, if minor, talent.
Clifton Fulman reviews Absalom, Absalom *in* The New Yorker, *October 31st 1936. William Faulker won the Nobel Prize for Literature in 1949.*

Gustave Flaubert

Monsieur Flaubert is not a writer.
Review of Madame Bovary *in* Le Figaro, *1857.*

Edward Gibbon

Another damned, thick, square book! Always scribble, scribble, scribble! Eh, Mr Gibbon?
HRH The Duke of Gloucester, to whom the author had just presented a copy of Volume II of The Decline and Fall of the Roman Empire, *1778.*

Goethe

Sheer nonsense.
Francis Jeffrey, The Edinburgh Review, *on Goethe's novel* Wilhelm Meister.

Kenneth Grahame

As a contribution to natural history the work is negligible.
Well, quite. The Times Literary Supplement *reviews* The Wind in the Willows, *1908.*

Radclyffe Hall

I would rather put a phial of prussic acid into the hands of a healthy boy or girl than the book in question.
James Douglas finds reading The Well of Loneliness *(pub. 1928) a fate worse than death.*

Saskia Hope

Saskia Hope has learned her (or more probably his) writing style from bad translations of de Sade and movies by Spielberg.
Erotobibliophile Fiona Pitt-Kethley, The Mail on Sunday, *July 25th 1993. 'Saskia Hope' was a pseudonym of Janet M. Holt (1949–1993).*

Henry James

It is becoming painfully evident that Mr James has written himself out as far as the international novel is concerned, and probably as far as any kind of novel-writing is concerned.
William Morton Payne, The Dial, *December 1884. Despite this expert diagnosis, Mr James managed to squeeze out* The Bostonians, The Turn of the Screw, The Wings of the Dove, The Ambassadors *and* The Golden Bowl *in the years that followed.*

James Joyce

I finished *Ulysses* and think it a mis-fire. The book is diffuse. It is brackish. It is pretentious. It is underbred, not only in the obvious sense, but in the literary sense. A first-rate writer, I mean, respects writing too much to be tricky.
Hark who's talking! Virginia Woolf confides to her diary, September 6th 1922.

The telephone directory is, because of its rigorous selection and repression, a work of art compared to the wastepaper basket. And *Ulysses* is a wastepaper basket.
Gerald Gould, The English Novel of Today, *1924.*

My God, what a clumsy *olla putrida* James Joyce is! Nothing but old fags and cabbage-stumps of quotations from the Bible and the rest, stewed in the juice of deliberate, journalistic dirty-mindedness.
A Puritan speaks out: D. H. Lawrence, 1928.

John Keats

Here are Johnny Keats' p-ss a bed poetry, and three novels by God knows whom. No more Keats, I entreat: flay him alive; if some of you don't, I must skin him myself: there is no bearing the drivelling idiotism of the Mankin.
Lord Byron writes to John Murray, October 12th 1820.

Fricassée of dead dog.
Thomas Carlyle considers Keats' Collected Works.

The Phrenzy of the 'Poems' was bad enough in its way; but it did not alarm us half so seriously as the calm, settled, imperturbable drivelling idiocy of 'Endymion' . . . Mr Hunt is a small poet, but he is a clever man. Mr Keats is a still-smaller poet, and he is only a boy of pretty abilities, which he has done everything in his power to spoil . . . We venture to make one small prophecy, that his bookseller will not a second time venture £50 upon anything that he can write. It is a better and a wiser thing to be a starved apothecary than a starved poet; so back to the shop, Mr John, back to 'plaisters, pills, and ointment-boxes,' etc. But for Heaven's sake, young Sangrando, be a little more sparing of extenuatives and soporifics in your practice than you have been with your poetry.
Attributed to John Lockhart and John Wilson, Blackwood's Magazine, *August 1818.*

A Mr John Keats, a young man who had left a decent calling for the melancholy trade of Cockney-poetry, has lately died of a consumption, after having written two or three little books of verses, much neglected by the public. . . . The New School, however, will have it that he was

slaughtered by a criticism of the Quarterly Review – 'O flesh, how art thou fishified!' – We are not now to defend a publication so well able to defend itself. But the fact is that the Quarterly Review finding before it a work at once silly and presumptuous, full of the servile slang that Cockaigne dictates to its servitors, and the vulgar indecorums which that Grub Street Empire rejoiceth to applaud, told the truth of the volume, and recommended a change of manners and masters to the scribbler. Keats wrote on; but he wrote indecently, probably in the indulgence of his social propensities.

As Tennyson said of another critic: 'A louse in the locks of literature.' Blackwood's Magazine *has another go in 1821.*

Richard Freiherr von Krafft-Ebing

This book should convey solace by being put to the most ignominious use to which paper can be applied.

The British Medical Journal *reviews* Psychopathia Sexualis, *1876.*

D. H. Lawrence

Mr Lawrence has a diseased mind. He is obsessed by sex . . . we have no doubt that he will be ostracized by all except the most degenerate coteries in the literary world.

John Bull *reviews* Lady Chatterley's Lover, *October 20th 1928.*

Unfortunately, one is obliged to wade through many pages of extraneous material in order to discover and savour sidelights on the management of a Midland estate, and in this reviewer's opinion the book cannot take the place of J. R. Miller's *Practical Gamekeeper*.

How true; how very, very true! Field & Stream *in the 1940s reviews* Lady Chatterley's Lover *(1928).*

Would you approve of your young sons, young daughters – because girls can read as well as boys – reading this book? Is it a book that you would leave lying around your own house? Is it a book that you would wish your wives or your servants to read?

A muffled titter ran around the Court as Mr Griffith-Jones, senior Treasury Counsel, opened the case for the Prosecution in the trial of Penguin Books Ltd., under the Obscene Publications Act of 1959, for publishing the paperback edition of Lady Chatterley's Lover*: October 20th 1960.*

Thomas Mann

The novel *Buddenbrooks* is nothing but two thick tomes in which the author describes the worthless story of worthless people in worthless chatter.

Eduard Engel, 1901.

Herman Melville

. . . sad stuff, dull and dreary, or ridiculous. Mr Melville's Quakers are the wretchedest dolts and drivellers, and his Mad Captain is a monstrous bore.
The Southern Quarterly Review *considers* Moby Dick *in 1851.*

John Milton

If length be not considered a merit, *Paradise Lost* has no other.
Edmund Waller, 1680.

His fame is gone out like a candle in a snuff and his memory will always stink.
A stinker from William Winstanley, in his Lives of the Most Famous English Poets, *1687.*

Our language sank under him.
Joseph Addison, quoted by Samuel Johnson in his Lives of the Poets, *1779–81.*

George Orwell

***Nineteen Eighty Four* is a failure.**
Laurence Brander in George Orwell, *1954.*

Alexander Pope

Who is this Pope that I hear so much about? I cannot discover what is his merit. Why will not my subjects write in prose?
King George II.

George Sand

In the world there are few sadder, sicklier phenomena for me than George Sand and the response she meets with.
Thomas Carlyle (1795–1881).

Sir Walter Scott

Sir Walter Scott (when all's said and done) is an inspired butler.
William Hazlitt (1778–1830).

Then comes Sir Walter Scott with his enchantments . . . sets the world in love with dreams and phantoms; with decayed and swinish forms of religion; with decayed and degraded systems of government; with the silliness and emptiness, sham grandeurs, sham gauds, and sham chivalries of a brainless and worthless long-vanished society. He did measureless harm; more real and lasting harm, perhaps, than any other individual that ever wrote.
Mark Twain must have been made to study him at school.

William Shakespeare

I remember, the players have often mentioned it as an honour to Shakespeare, that in his writing, whatsoever he penned, he never blotted out a line. My answer hath been: would he had blotted out a thousand!

Ben Jonson is professionally jealous, and rather more concerned to tell a story against himself: c. 1630.

'Was there ever,' cried he, 'such stuff as great part of Shakespeare? Only one must not say so! But what think you – What? – Is there not sad stuff? What? – What?'

King George III, recorded in The Diary of Fanny Burney, *December 16th 1785.*

With the single exception of Homer, there is no eminent writer, not even Sir Walter Scott, whom I can despise so entirely as I despise Shakespeare when I measure my mind against his. It would positively be a relief to dig him up and throw stones at him.

Professionally jealous and a blithering idiot: George Bernard Shaw.

I think Shakespeare is shit. Absolute shit! He may have been a genius for his time, but I just can't relate to that stuff. 'Thee' and 'thou' – the guy sounds like a faggot. Captain America is classic because he's more entertaining.

A triumph for US public education: Gene Simmons of the rock group Kiss.

Percy Bysshe Shelley

The school to which he belonged, or rather which he established, can never become popular.

Philadelphia Monthly Magazine, *July 15th 1828.*

Laurence Sterne

Nothing odd will do long. *Tristram Shandy* did not last.

Samuel Johnson faithfully quoted in Boswell's Life. The Life and Opinions of Tristram Shandy, *first published between 1759 and 1767, is still in print.*

James Tiptree Jr.

It has been suggested that Tiptree is female, a theory I find absurd, for there is to me something ineluctably masculine about Tiptree's writing. I don't think the novels of Jane Austen could have been written by a man nor the stories of Ernest Hemingway by a woman, and in the same way I believe the author of the James Tiptree stories is male.

Robert Silverburg introduces James Tiptree Jr's Warm Worlds and Otherwise, *1975. Two years later 'James Tiptree' was revealed as Alice Sheldon, a 61-year-old spinster.*

Mark Twain

A hundred years from now it is very likely that 'The Jumping Frog' alone will be remembered.
Harry Thurston Peck, editor of The Bookman, *gets it wrong twice over in January 1901 (or will have done in a few years' time . . . probably).*

Walt Whitman

Walt Whitman is as unacquainted with art as a hog is with mathematics.
Cue the Middle White Calculator . . . The London Critic, *1855.*

William Wordsworth

Dank, limber verses, stuft with lakeside sedges,
And propt with rotten stakes from rotten hedges.
Walter Savage Landor (1775–1864).

This will never do. The case of Mr Wordsworth is manifestly hopeless; and we give him up as altogether incurable and beyond the power of criticism.
*At least Francis Jeffrey (*Edinburgh Review, *November 1814) never had to do him for A-Level. . . .*

Emile Zola

His instinctive inclination to depict demented persons, criminals, prostitutes, and semi-maniacs . . . his symbolism, his pessimism, his coprolalia, and his predilection for slang, sufficiently characterize M. Zola as a high-class degenerate. That he is a sexual psychopath is betrayed on every page of his novels.
Max Nordau (1849–1923), Degeneration.

(2) THE UNPUBLISHABLE

A selection of memorably regrettable rejection letters, many of which are, alas, unattributed due (perhaps) to a certain inexplicable coyness on the part of publishers. Where the year only is supplied, this refers to the year of eventual publication.

Jane Austen: NORTHANGER ABBEY

We are willing to return the manuscript for the same sum as we paid for it.
1803.

Richard Bach: JONATHAN LIVINGSTON SEAGULL

***Jonathan Livingstone Seagull* will never make it as a paperback.**
James Galton of the Popular Library. Paperback sales of the book, published by Avon Books, are in the region of 10 million.

J. G. Ballard: CRASH

The author of this book is beyond psychiatric help.
1973.

Len Deighton: THE IPCRESS FILE

Not only does it tend to bog down in the middle, but the author tends to stay too long with non-essentials. He seems to have little idea of pace, and is enchanted with his words, his tough style, and that puts me off.
1963. De gustibus non est disputandum, *as they say at launch parties.*

Charles Dickens: SORROWS OF CHILDHOOD

I am sorry, but Brutus sacrifices unborn children of his own as well as of other people – the 'Sorrows of Childhood', long in type and long a mere mysterious name, must come out. The paper really is, like the celebrated ambassadorial appointment, 'too bad.'
The editor of Household Words, *Charles Dickens, writes himself a rejection note in 1852.*

Arthur Conan Doyle: A STUDY IN SCARLET

Neither long enough for a serial nor short enough for a single story.
1887. So?

William Faulkner: THE SOUND AND THE FURY

You're the only damn fool in New York who would publish it.
1929: Alfred Harcourt of Harcourt, Brace, to editor Harrison Smith.

Gustave Flaubert: MADAME BOVARY

You have buried your novel underneath a heap of details which are well done but utterly superfluous.
1856. Superfluous to what?

Frederick Forsyth: THE DAY OF THE JACKAL

No reader interest.
W. H. Allen & Co., April 1970, reject the book Margaret Thatcher read twice.

Anne Frank: THE DIARY OF ANNE FRANK

The girl doesn't, it seems to me, have a special perception or feeling which would lift that book above the 'curiosity' level.
1952. Where do they find these people?

William Golding: THE LORD OF THE FLIES

It does not seem to us that you have been wholly successful in working out an admittedly promising idea.
1954. They obviously preferred The Coral Island *– but then R. M. Ballantyne*

never won the Nobel Prize, as Golding did in 1983. Lord of the Flies *became one of the best-selling 'literary novels' of all time.*

Gunter Grass: THE TIN DRUM

It can never be translated.

1962. It would be interesting to discover the basis for this sweeping – and massively incorrect – assertion.

Thomas Hardy: DESPERATE REMEDIES

The story is ruined by the disgusting and absurd outrage which is the key to its mystery. The violation of a young lady at an evening party, and the subsequent birth of a child, is too abominable to be tolerated.

1871. Why should it be so particularly abominable at an evening party?

Joseph Heller: CATCH-22

I haven't really the foggiest idea about what the man is trying to say. . . . Apparently the author intends it to be funny – possibly even satire – but it is really not funny on any intellectual level. He has two devices, both bad, which he works constantly . . . This, as you may imagine, constitutes a continual and unmitigated bore.

1961. Read all about it! Publisher admits to terminal stupidity!

Thor Heyerdahl: THE KON-TIKI EXPEDITION

This is a long, solemn, tedious Pacific voyage best suited, I would think, to some kind of drastic abridgement in a journal like the *National Geographic*. It's definitely not for us.

William Styron, editor at MacGraw-Hill, 1947. Rand McNally eventually published the book in 1952. It stayed at number one on the bestseller list for over a year.

John Irving: THE WORLD ACCORDING TO GARP

The story is only mildly interesting, and it does nothing new with language or with form. Thanks for showing it to us, though.

1979. This rejection – from The Paris Review *– was of a short story,* The Pension Grillparzer, *which is contained within the novel and (as the work of the fictional Garp) is rejected by a magazine. Irving submitted it on its own to several magazines, just to see what would happen. When this real-life rejection arrived he changed the manuscript to incorporate it in the published novel. 'It was so much better than the rejection I had written,' he confessed. A rare and encouraging case of The Biter Bit.*

Rudyard Kipling: PASSIM

I'm sorry, Mr Kipling, but you just don't know how to use the English language.

The editor of the San Francisco Examiner, *having published a short story by Kipling, writes to tell him not to submit any more: 1889.*

Judith Krantz: SCRUPLES

Scruples is a ridiculous title. Nobody will know what it means. We've got to get Crown to change it.
June 25th 1981. Howard Kaminsky, president of Warner Books, after Warner bought the paperback rights to the novel. Quite a lot of people now know what 'scruples' are . . .

John Le Carré: THE SPY WHO CAME IN FROM THE COLD

You're welcome to Le Carré – he hasn't got any future.
1963. Not with this publisher, anyway . . .

Anita Loos: GENTLEMEN PREFER BLONDES

Do you realize, young woman, that you're the first American writer ever to poke fun at sex?
1925. Rather a good selling point, as it turned out.

Norman Mailer: THE NAKED AND THE DEAD

In my opinion it is barely publishable.
1948. A nice double entendre.

Herman Melville: MOBY DICK

We regret to say that our united opinion is entirely against the book as we do not think it would be at all suitable for the Juvenile Market in this country. It is very long, rather old-fashioned, and in our opinion not deserving of the reputation which it seems to enjoy.
No whales please, we're British Juveniles. 1851.

Vladimir Nabokov: LOLITA

It should be, and probably has been, told to a psychoanalyst . . . it is overwhelmingly nauseating, even to an enlightened Freudian . . . It is a totally perverse performance all round . . . I am most disturbed at the thought that the writer has asked that this be published. I can see no possible cause that could be served by its publication now. I recommend that it be buried under a stone for a thousand years.
1955. The really enlightened Freudians would probably say this was evidence of a repressed desire for pubescent girls on the part of the publisher.

George Orwell: ANIMAL FARM

I am highly critical of many aspects of internal and external Soviet policy; but I could not possibly publish a general attack of this kind.
Too politically sensitive for Victor Gollancz in 1944.

It would be less offensive if the predominant caste in the fable were not pigs.
All a matter of good taste for Jonathan Cape.

It is impossible to sell animal stories in the USA.
There's no answer to the Dial Press of New York.
Animal Farm *was published by Secker & Warburg in 1945. It also did quite well in the USA.*

Marcel Proust: REMEMBRANCE OF THINGS PAST

My dear fellow, I may be dead from the neck up, but rack my brains as I may I can't see why a chap should need thirty pages to describe how he turns over in bed before going to sleep.
Marc Humblot of the publishers Ollendorf rejects Swann's Way *on February 12th 1912. Proust published it at his own expense the following year.*

Shel Silverstein: THE GIVING TREE

It falls between two stools – it ain't a kid's book and it ain't an adult one. I'm sorry but I don't think you're going to find a publisher for it.
William Cole of Simon and Schuster, 1963. By 1982, The Giving Tree *(published by Harper & Row in 1964) had sold over 2 million copies and its author had become America's best-selling children's writer.*

H. G. Wells: THE TIME MACHINE

It is not interesting enough for the general reader and not thorough enough for the scientific reader.
1895. General Reader: the search goes on . . .

THE WAR OF THE WORLDS

I think the verdict would be: 'Oh don't read that horrid book.'
1898. Or then again, perhaps not.

Oscar Wilde: LADY WINDERMERE'S FAN

My dear Sir,
I have read your manuscript. Oh, my dear Sir.
1892.

(3) ROBERT MAXWELL

No survey of the Regrettable World of Publishing would be complete without a passing glance at the great Publisher, Author, and Champion of the Oppressed. So here, in all his awful majesty, he is:

I was only giving these men their say. I should not be taken as agreeing with them.
Robert Maxwell, interviewed in the Guardian *in March 1990, refutes malicious and libellous rumours to the effect that he pandered to the monstrous egomania of the East European dictators by giving them 'the oxygen of publicity' in books published by his company, Pergamon Press.*

That these rumours were absolutely without foundation is amply borne out by the following quotations . . .

I wish you good health and power to continue your constant, tireless activity for the good of your country.
The author-publisher interviews President Ceausescu of Romania in Ceausescu: Builder of Modern Romania and International Statesman, *Pergamon, 1983.*

Hungary had no alternative but to call for the military help of the Soviet Union to prevent a civil war.
A history lesson from Mr Maxwell would appear to owe something to a certain Daily Worker *editorial:* Janos Kadar: Selected Speeches and Interviews, *Pergamon, 1985.*

Dear Mr President, how do you explain the fact that you have been holding the highest political state post in your country for such a long time?
A typically hard-hitting question for Todor Zhivkov in Todor Zhivkov: Statesman and Builder of New Bulgaria, *Pergamon, 1982. Surprisingly, the Dear President's reply omitted to mention poisoned umbrellas.*

CLASSICAL MUSIC
The Tin Ear of Appreciation

If a literary man puts together two words about music, one of them will be wrong.

Aaron Copland

Johann Sebastian Bach

Deprived of beauty, of harmony, and of clarity of melody.
The German composer and musicologist Johann Scheibe writes in Der critische Musikus, *May 14th 1737.*

Bela Bartok

Unmeaning bunches of notes, apparently representing the composer promenading the keyboard in his boots. Some can be played better with the elbows, others with the flat of the hand. None requires fingers to perform nor ears to listen to.
Musical Quarterly, *July 1915.*

Ludwig van Beethoven

Beethoven's Second Symphony is a crude monstrosity, a serpent which continues to writhe about, refusing to expire, and even when bleeding to death still threshes around angrily and vainly with its tail.
First night review in Zeitung für die elegante Welt, *1828.*

Seems to lose its way in complete disorder . . . too much that is harsh and bizarre in it.
The Allgemeine musikalische Zeitung *doesn't like the Eroica symphony, 1805.*

An orgy of vulgar noise.
Louis Spohr – violinist and composer of difficult things for Associated Board Grade examinations – is offended by the Fifth Symphony in 1808.

Much too long.
. . . for The Harmonicon *of London: all there was to be said about the Sixth Symphony in 1823 . . .*

If Beethoven's Seventh Symphony is not by some means abridged, it will soon fall into disuse.
. . . A lesson unlearned by Herr B.: Boston critic Philip Hale recommends surgery in 1837.

Eccentric without being amusing, and laborious without effect.
The Harmonicon *again, on the Eighth Symphony in 1827.*

So ugly, in such bad taste, and in the conception of Schiller's Ode so cheap that I cannot even now understand how such a genius as Beethoven could write it down.
In his Selbsbiographie *(1861), Louis Spohr finds the Ninth Symphony a bit like our own dear Duchess of York: vulgar, vulgar, vulgar!*

Beethoven always sounds to me like the upsetting of a bag of nails, with here and there an also dropped hammer.
John Ruskin's ear is pained: letter, February 6th 1881.

Hector Berlioz

What a good thing this isn't music.
Rossini, on Symphonie Fantastique, *c. 1830.*

One ought to wash one's hands after handling one of his scores.
A fastidious Felix Mendelssohn in 1834.

Berlioz, musically speaking, is a lunatic; a classical composer only in Paris, the great city of quacks. His music is simply and undisguisedly nonsense.
The Dramatic and Musical Review, *1843.*

He does not know how to write.
The French critic Pierre Scudo restores the reputation of Paris: 1852.

It needs no gift of prophecy to predict that Berlioz will be utterly unknown a hundred years hence to everybody but the encyclopaedists and the antiquarians.
The Boston Daily Advertiser, *1874.*

Johannes Brahms

I played over the music of that scoundrel Brahms. What a giftless bastard! It annoys me that this self-inflated mediocrity is hailed as a genius . . . Brahms is chaotic and absolutely dried-up stuff.
Peter Ilyich Tchaikovsky fills his pen with sour grape juice and confides to his Diary *on October 9th 1886.*

The real Brahms is nothing more than a sentimental voluptuary, rather tiresomely dressing himself up as Handel or Beethoven and making a prolonged and intolerable noise.
. . . But not comparing his mind with Shakespeare's. George Bernard Shaw, date untraced.

Anton Bruckner

The anti-music ravings of a half-wit.
Hans von Bulow gives his opinion of all Bruckner's symphonies, 1888. . .

Symphonic boa-constrictors.
. . . and Frederic Chopin agrees.

Frederic Chopin

Had he submitted his music to a teacher, the latter, it is to be hoped, would have torn it up and thrown it at his feet – and this is symbolically what we wish to do.
Ludwig Rellstab, Iris im Gebiete der Tonkunst, *1833.*

The entire works of Chopin present a motley surface of ranting hyperbole and excruciating cacophony . . . There is an excuse at present for Chopin's delinquencies; he is entramelled in the enthralling bonds of that arch-enchantress, George Sand, celebrated equally for the number and excellence of her romances and her lovers.
Take a cold shower, Mr Chopin! A touch of twentieth-century tabloid journalism in Musical World, *October 28th 1841.*

Claude Debussy

The audience . . . expected the ocean, something big, something colossal, but they were served instead some agitated water in a saucer.
Louis Schneider reports on La Mer in Gil Blas, *1905.*

Edward Elgar

Elgar is one of the Seven Humbugs of Christendom.
Hark who's talking: George Bernard Shaw (again).

Edvard Grieg

Two or three catch-penny phrases served up with plenty of orchestral sugar.
. . . and again: G.B.S. on Peer Gynt, *1892.*

Franz Liszt

Liszt is a mere commonplace person, with his hair on end – a snob out of Bedlam. He writes the ugliest music extant.
A 'snob' being in those days 'a vulgar and ostentatious person' . . . the Dramatic and Musical Review, *January 7th 1843.*

Turn your eyes to any one composition that bears the name of Liszt, if you are unlucky enough to have such a thing on your pianoforte, and answer frankly, if it contains one bar of genuine music. Composition indeed! – decomposition is the proper word for such hateful fungi, which choke up and poison the fertile plains of harmony, threatening the world with drought.
. . . Not to mention plague, earthquake, and showers of giant Venusian frogs! Musical World, *June 30th 1855.*

Gustav Mahler

If that was music, I no longer understand anything about the subject.
Maybe not, then: Hans von Bulow on the Second Symphony, c. 1890.

Felix Mendelssohn

Are you overrun in London with 'Champagne Charlie is my Name'? A brutal Thing; nearly worthless – the Tune, I mean – but yet not quite – else it would not become so great a Bore. No: I can see, to my Sorrow, that it has some Go – which Mendelssohn had not.
The poor chap simply couldn't lay down a decent tune . . . Edward FitzGerald writes to W. F. Pollock, November 11th 1867.

Wolfgang Amadeus Mozart

You ask my opinion about taking the young Salzburg musician into your service. I do not know where you can place him, since I feel that you do not require a composer, or other useless people. . . . It gives one's service

a bad name when such types run about like beggars; besides, he has a large family.
A Mother's Advice: the Empress Maria Theresa to the Archduke Ferdinand, 1771.

Far too noisy, my dear Mozart. Far too many notes.
Perhaps he should have taken it: the Archduke's response to The Marriage of Figaro, *May 1st 1786.*

Mozart died too late rather than too soon.
The important judgement of pianist Glenn Gould, 1984.

Jacques Offenbach

He has written nothing that will live, nothing that will make the world better. His name as well as his music will soon be forgotten.
How soon? The Chicago Tribune*'s unkind obituary of October 7th 1880.*

Sergei Prokoviev

Mr Prokoviev might well have loaded up a shotgun with several thousand notes of various lengths and discharged them against the side of a blank wall.
The Love of Three Oranges *is not tuneful enough for Edward Moore of the* Chicago Tribune, *December 31st 1921.*

Giacomo Puccini

Puccini represents an evil art – Italian music, to wit – and his success would have meant the proliferating influence in England of that evil art. Wherefore, it has been my duty to throw back the score of *Tosca* at him. Puccini: may you prosper, but in other climes! Continue, my friend, to sketch in scrappy incidental music to well-known plays. But spare England: this country has done neither you nor your nation nearly so much harm as she has done other nations. Disturb not the existing peaceful relations.
But England was not spared despite the efforts of J. F. Runciman of The Saturday Review, *July 21st 1900.*

Nikolai Rimsky-Korsakov

What a name! It suggests fierce whiskers stained with vodka!
Er, what about the music . . .? Funnily enough, the Musical Courier, *in chauvinistic mood, didn't like that either: October 27th 1897.*

Gioacchino Rossini

Rossini would have been a great composer if his teacher had spanked him enough on the backside.
A flogging from Ludwig van Beethoven, date unknown.

Camille Saint-Saëns

It is one's duty to hate with all possible fervour the empty and ugly in art; and I hate Saint-Saëns the composer with a hate that is perfect.
Cor! J. F. Runciman warms up for Puccini in The Saturday Review *of December 12th 1896.*

Richard Strauss

An hour of original music in a lunatic asylum.
Claude Debussy considers Till Eulenspiegel, *1895.*

Better to hang oneself than write music like that.
Paul Hindemith doesn't like the Alpensymphonie *in 1917.*

Igor Stravinsky

The music of *Le Sacre du Printemps* baffles verbal description. Practically it has no relation to music at all as most of us understand the word.
The Musical Times, *1913.*

Peter Ilyich Tchaikovsky

Tchaikovsky's First Piano Concerto, like the first pancake, is a flop.
Professor Nicolai Feopemptovich Soloviev of St Petersburg writes in Novoye Vremya, *November 13th 1875.*

The violin is no longer played; it is pulled, torn, drubbed . . . Tchaikovsky's Violin Concerto gives us for the first time the hideous notion that there can be music that stinks to the ear.
. . . and criticism that stinks to posterity. Edouard Hanslick of the Neue Freie Press *of Vienna, December 5th 1881.*

The finale of the Fourth Symphony of Tchaikovsky pained me by its vulgarity. Nothing can redeem the lack of nobleness, the barbarous side, by which, according to ethnographs and diplomats, even the most polished Russian at times betrays himself.
The V-word again! The Musical Review *detects a bit of Old Ivan on February 26th 1880.*

. . . in the last movement, the composer's Calmuck blood got the better of him, and slaughter, dire and bloody, swept across the storm-driven score.
. . . while the Musical Courier *hears a touch of the tarbrush in the Fifth Symphony, March 13th 1889.*

Giuseppe Verdi

***Rigoletto* lacks melody. This opera has hardly any chance of being kept in the repertoire.**
Gazette Musicale de Paris, *May 22nd 1853.*

Richard Wagner

Wagner is a man devoid of all talent.
The well-known composer Cesar Cui writes to Rimsky-Korsakov in 1863.

Is Wagner a human being at all? Is he not rather a disease? He contaminates everything he touches – he has made music sick.
Friedrich Nietzsche, Der Fall Wagner.

With Wagner amorous excitement assumes the form of mad delirium. . . . It is a form of Sadism. It is the love of those degenerates who, in sexual transport, become like wild beasts. Wagner suffered from 'erotic madness', which leads coarse nature to murder and lust, and inspires higher degenerates with works like *Die Walküre*, *Siegfried*, and *Tristan und Isolde*.
Max Nordau, Degeneration.

There is no law against composing music when one has no ideas whatsoever. The music of Wagner, therefore, is perfectly legal.
Paris National, *1850.*

This revelling in the destruction of all tonal essence, raging satanic fury in the orchestra, this demoniacal, lewd caterwauling, scandal-mongering, gun-toting music, with an orchestral accompaniment slapping you in the face . . . the diabolical din of this pig-headed man, stuffed with brass and sawdust, inflated, in an insanely self-destructive aggrandizement . . .
. . . and so on. J. L. Klein, in Geschichte des Dramas, *does not care for Herr Wagner's music.*

The latest bore – but it is colossal – is *Tannhäuser*. I think I could compose something like it tomorrow, inspired by my cat scampering over the keys of the piano.
Prosper Mérimée, Lettres à une inconnue, *March 21st 1861.*

Wagner is a madman, a madman from pride. His music of the future is a monstrosity. Sterile by nature like all monsters, Wagner is impotent to reproduce himself.
Henri Prévost, Etude sur Richard Wagner.

Of all the *bête*, clumsy, blundering, boggling, baboon-blooded stuff I ever saw on a human stage, that thing last night beat – as far as the story and acting went – and of all the affected, sapless, soulless, beginningless, endless, topless, bottomless, topsiturviest, tuneless, scrannelpipiest – tongs and boniest – doggrel of sounds I ever endured the deadliness of, that eternity of nothing was the deadliest, as far as its sound went.
Words almost failed him: John Ruskin advises Mrs Burne-Jones not to bother with Die Meistersinger, *June 30th 1882.*

IT'S ONLY ROCK 'N' ROLL

That's the way it's been in town
Ever since they tore the juke box down.
The Grateful Dead, lyrics from Stella Blue

The big question in the music business today is: 'how long will it last?' It is our guess that it won't.
The music biz journal Cashbox *delivers its verdict on a passing fad, 1955.*

It will be gone by June.
1955 again: Variety *is a little more specific.*

There is no doubt that 'Rock and Roll' music is the most dangerous thing that has ever happened. It is a monstrous threat. We must oppose it to the end.
Defending Fair Albion's shores, the popular musicologist Steve Race considers the Elvis Phenomenon in Melody Maker, *c. 1956.*

Rock 'n' Roll is phoney and false and sung, written and played for the most part by cretinous goons.
It takes one to . . . Frank Sinatra opines, 1958.

The teenage vogue for beat music and rock'n'roll is over. Now the demand is for pop music shows of a broad family appeal.
The BBC axes Oh Boy! *and* Dig This *in 1960.*

Our big objection to rock music is not only the beat, which I think comes out of the jungle, but the words and what the words are spelling out. Look at the lives of these artists: the dress, the glasses they wear . . . I believe it is demonic, the dress, the glasses they wear . . . Look at Elton John with his glasses and freaky clothes . . . I believe Elvis Presley and the Beatles and the Rolling Stones are going to answer to God for all the pollution of youth around the world. All this rock culture is stirring people up to do evil instead of to do good, just as the people were doing in Noah's day. Just look at their dress and the glasses they wear. God is going to rain judgement upon the earth – and this could happen any moment now with all the rock music and illicit sex and wine, women and the glasses they wear.
The Rev. Jack Wyrtzen sees Satan in psychedelic specs, c. 1970.

The Beatles

I regretted my decision immediately, the noise was deafening.
Brian Epstein visits Liverpool's Cavern Club on November 9th 1961 and makes a note on his calendar . . .

I want to manage those four boys. It wouldn't take me more than two half days a week.
. . . but, on reflection, he was little bit impressed with one of the acts.

We don't like their sound. Groups of guitars are on the way out.
A Decca Records executive turns them down in 1962.

We don't think they'll do anything in this market.
Forget the USA, boys: Capitol Records' chief Alan Livingston is negative before their first tour in 1964.

The Beatles are not merely awful, I would consider it sacrilegious to say anything less than that they are godawful. They are so unbelievably horrible, so appallingly unmusical, so dogmatically insensitive to the magic of the art, that they qualify as crowned heads of anti-music, even as the impostor popes went down in history as 'anti-popes'.
William F. Buckley Jr breaks the outrage barrier: On the Right, *1964.*

The Beatles? They're a passing phase, symptoms of the uncertainty of the times and the confusion about us.
The Voice of God, aka Billy Graham, 1965.

Ian Dury and the Blockheads

I refused to write the music as I didn't really get off on the words. I thought any song that starts off, 'Arseholes, bastards, fucking cunts and pricks,' is not exactly going to be a Number One world hit.
Sometime Blockheads musician Chas Jankel exercises his skill and judgement in 1979. The song in question – Plaistow Patricia *– appeared on the album* New Boots and Panties, *which was in the Top Twenty for over a year.*

Bob Dylan

Message songs, as everybody knows, are a drag. It's only college newspaper editors and single girls under fourteen that could possibly have time for them.
Oh, right, Bob. Dylan puts it all behind him, c. 1970.

Buddy Holly

The biggest no-talent I ever worked with.
Why I Fired Him: Paul Cohen of Decca Records, 1956.

John Lennon

You'll never work again!
Revenge is . . . ultimately embarrassing. Manager Allan Williams decides he's had enough bolshiness, and quits: 1961.

Elvis Presley

Listen, son, you ain't goin' nowhere. You oughta go back to drivin' a truck.

September 25th 1954: Jim Denny, manager of Grand Ole Opry, fires the young crooner in 1954 after one performance.

This boy is a country rooster crowin' who shouldn't be allowed to sing after the sun comes up in the mornin'.

A black radio station man in Tennessee rejects That's Alright, Mama, *1954.*

If I play this they'll run me outa town. I gotta play pure an' simple white country music.

A white radio station man in Tennessee rejects That's Alright, Mama, *1954.*

This is a weapon of the American psychological war aimed at infecting part of the population with a new philosphical outlook of inhumanity. . . in order to prepare for war.

The East German magazine Young World *gives a bad review, 1956.*

I tell you flatly, he can't last.

Jackie Gleason, 1956.

Nothing in this great, free continent is going to make me put that boy on my programme.

Ed Sullivan says No in 1956 . . . a week later he paid the singer $17,000 for the privilege of changing his mind.

Singing in any form is foreign to Elvis.

Jack Payne tells Daily Mail *readers all about it, 1956.*

Mr Presley has no discernible singing ability . . . his phrasing, if it can be called that, consists of the stereotyped variations that go with a beginner's aria in a bath-tub. For the ear he is an unutterable bore.

Jack Gould in the New York Times, *1956.*

Who will sing 'Blue Suede Shoes' ten years from now?

D. W. Brogan puts it squarely to readers of the Manchester Guardian, *1956.*

Cliff Richard

Hardly the kind of performance any parent could wish their child to witness.

On the cutting edge of things, the Musical Express *dismisses Britain's answer to Elvis in 1958.*

The Rolling Stones

The singer'll have to go – the BBC won't like him.
New Manager Eric Easton doesn't rate Mick Jagger in 1963.

I give the Stones about another two years. I'm saving for the future. I bank all my song royalties for a start.
Mick Jagger takes a realistic view in 1964.

Tommy Steele

How long can this Tommy Steele last? Five months?
Mr Justice Harman tries a contractual lawsuit in 1957.

Led Zeppelin

Four shrieking monkeys are not going to use a privileged family name without permission.
A stern warning from Frau Eva von Zeppelin. It went unheeded.

PLAYS AND PLAYERS

Come, leave the loathèd stage,
And the more loathsome age;
Where pride and impudence, in faction knit,
Usurp the power of wit!

Ben Jonson (1573–1637): Ode To Himself

Samuel Beckett: WAITING FOR GODOT

It is pretentious gibberish, without any claim to importance whatsoever. It is nothing but phoney surrealism with occasional references to Christ and mankind. It has no form, no basic philosophy and absolutely no lucidity. It's too conscious to be written off as mad. It's just a waste of everybody's time and it made me ashamed to think that such balls could be taken seriously for a moment.
The Nobel Prizewinner's dramatic masterpiece is not well-made enough for Noël Coward in 1960.

Erskine Caldwell: TOBACCO ROAD

It isn't the sort of entertainment folks buy in the theatre, nor ever have bought within my memory.
Burns Mantle of the New York Daily News, *December 5th 1933.* Tobacco Road *opened on December 3rd 1933 and ran for 3182 performances – one of the five longest runs on Broadway.*

***Agatha Christie:* THE MOUSETRAP**

Compared to other current West End successes this new murder mystery is very weak.

Sunday Dispatch, *1952. Unlike its contemporary 'successes'* The Mousetrap *is, as everyone surely knows, still running. It is also a well-known fact that 'a theatre critic' named the murderer on the grounds that 'the play will soon close anyway' – but extensive research has so far failed to find the evidence.*

Henrik Ibsen – *definitely an enemy of the people. . .*

A DOLL'S HOUSE, 1889.

Unnatural, immoral.

The People.

Morbid and unwholesome.

The Observer.

ROMERSHOLM, February 1891.

These Ibsen creatures are neither men nor women, they are ghouls.

Gentlewoman.

GHOSTS, March 1891.

An open drain; a loathsome sore unbandaged.

Daily Telegraph.

Garbage and offal.

Truth.

Repulsive and degrading.

Queen.

Foul and filthy.

Era.

HEDDA GABLER, April 1891.

A bad escape of moral sewer-gas.

Pictorial World.

Photographic studies of vice and morbidity.

Saturday Review.

THE MASTER BUILDER, February 1893.

Hopeless and indefensible.

Globe.

Three acts of gibberish.

Stage.

Sensuality . . . irreverence . . . simply blasphemous.
Morning Post.

THE WILD DUCK, May 1894.

Commonplace and suburban . . . bald and unconvincing.
Daily Telegraph.

Arthur Miller: DEATH OF A SALESMAN

Who would want to see a play about an unhappy travelling salesman? Too depressing.
Cheryl Crawford turns down an invitation to stage Miller's most famous and successful work, 1948.

Eugene O'Neill: STRANGE INTERLUDE

***Strange Interlude* will probably interest a comparatively small public. It is solid grey in tone, slow-paced and repetitious in performance, and forbidding in length.**
January 31st 1928: once again, Burns Mantle of the New York Daily News *lays a critical egg.* Strange Interlude *was O'Neill's greatest popular success.*

John Osborne: LOOK BACK IN ANGER

Mr Osborne will have other plays in him, and perhaps he will settle down, now that he has got this off his mind.
Kenneth Tynan would not have loved J. C. Trewin of the Illustrated London News, *May 1956.*

Harold Pinter: THE BIRTHDAY PARTY

If the author can forget Beckett, Ionesco and Simpson he may do much better next time.
. . . but these playwrights never listen, do they? Not, at any rate, to the critic of the Manchester Evening News *in May 1958.*

William Shakespeare

There is an upstart crow beautified with our feathers. That with his tyger's heart wrapt in a player's hide, supposes he is as well able to bombast out a blank verse as the best of you, and being an absolute Johannes Factotum, is, in his own conceit, the only Shakescene in a country.
Miaow! Robert Greene (1558–1592), Groatsworth of Wit Bought with a Million of Repentance.

Whaur's yer Wully Shakespeare noo?
An anonymous Scottish theatregoer hails the première of the Rev. John Home's play, Douglas, *in 1756.*

Shakespeare's name, you may depend on it, stands absolutely too high and will go down.
Lord Byron writes to James Hogg, March 1814.

ROMEO AND JULIET

A play, of itself, the worst that ever I heard in my life.
Samuel Pepys, March 1662.

A MIDSUMMER NIGHT'S DREAM

The most insipid, ridiculous play that ever I saw in my life.
Samuel Pepys, September 1662.

TWELFTH NIGHT

Acted well, though it be but a silly play.
Samuel Pepys, January 1663.

KING LEAR

A strange, horrible business, but I suppose good enough for Shakespeare's day.
Quite so, ma'am: Queen Victoria finds it unedifying.

HAMLET

I saw Hamlet Prince of Denmark played; but now, the old plays begin to disgust this refined age, since his majesty has been so long abroad.
John Evelyn, Diary, *November 26th 1661.*

It is a vulgar and barbarous drama, which would not be tolerated by the vilest populace of France, or Italy . . . one would imagine this piece to be the work of a drunken savage.
Vive la différence! Voltaire, 1748.

OTHELLO

To anyone capable of reading the play with an open mind as to its merits, it is obvious that Shakespeare plunged through it so impetuously that he had finished it before he had made his mind up as to the character and motives of a single person in it.
Not everybody's mind is as open as George Bernard Shaw's in 1897.

George Bernard Shaw: MRS WARREN'S PROFESSION, 1905.

Superabundance of foulness . . . wholly immoral and degenerate.
New York Herald.

Offensive . . . contemptible . . . abominable.
New York Post.

Decaying and reeking.
New York Times.

A dramatized stench.
New York Sun.
The Lord Chamberlain refused Mrs Warren's Profession *a licence for production in Britain until the 1920s.*

THREE PLAYS FOR PURITANS

One might still be hopeful for Mr Shaw's future as a dramatist, despite his present incompetence, if there were any hint in his plays of creative power. But there is no such hint.
Arnold Bennett considers Caesar and Cleopatra, The Devil's Disciple, *and* Captain Brassbound's Conversion *for* The Academy, *February 9th 1901.*

The Irish actor and the Scottish Play

I think it's time there was an innovation to protect the author and the actors and the public from the vagaries of the director. Given a good play and a good team and a decent set, you could put a blue-arsed baboon in the stalls and get what is known as a production.
Peter O'Toole, interviewed by Playboy *in 1965. In 1980 he put himself in the stalls and directed* Macbeth. *The production was so gloriously awful it attracted full houses of people eager to see just how bad it was.*

Sarah Kane: BLASTED

***Blasted* is about the origins and effects of violence. The subject it treats is shocking but central to the world we live in. It addresses the subject with passion and wit and is a moral and compassionate piece of writing.**
James MacDonald, director of the play at the Royal Court Theatre, January 1995. The action takes place in a squalid hotel bedroom occupied by a tabloid reporter and his retarded girlfriend, whom he subjects to violent and graphic sexual assault. There are scenes of enforced masturbation and oral sex, culminating in intercourse while the girl is apparently unconscious. A soldier bursts in and proceeds to describe all the atrocities he has committed while putting down a civil insurrection outside. He then rapes the journalist, bites out his eyeballs, and eats them. A dying baby is brought in; when it is dead, the journalist starts eating its corpse. Ms Kane, 23, had one previously staged production, a trilogy of monologues entitled Sick.

The Ultimate Regrettable Theatrical Quote:
WRITE ME A MURDER

This one is going to run and run and run.
Fergus Cashin, Daily Sketch.
The play ran for less than a month. Mr Cashin's encomium subsequently entered British culture, courtesy of Private Eye *magazine, as a by-word for a sure-fire flop.*

MUSICAL TURKEYS

Annie Get Your Gun

Irving Berlin's score is musically not exciting – of the real songs, only one or two are tuneful.
Critic Lewis Kronenberger, PM, *May 17th 1946.*

Fiddler on the Roof

It seems clear to me this is no smash hit, no blockbuster.
Variety *squashes the Detroit tryout, July 28th 1964. The show ran for 3342 performances on Broadway.*

Grease

I don't think we can do anything with these reviews. It's a disaster. Close it.
February 14th 1972: Matthew Serino, whose advertising agency handled the show, advises against bringing it to Broadway, where it broke all records; it finally closed on April 16th 1980.

Oklahoma!

No legs, no jokes, no chance.
Broadway impresario Michael Todd nixes a show that ran for 2248 performances, 1943.

THE SILVER SCREEN

The cinema is little more than a fad. It's canned drama. What audiences really want to see is flesh and blood on the stage.

Charlie Chaplin, c. 1916.

Who the hell wants to hear actors talk?
Harry M. Warner, President of Warner Bros. Pictures, c. 1927.

(1) THE CASTING COUCH

Fred Astaire

Can't act. Can't sing. Slightly bald. Can dance a little.
An MGM executive casts an eye over his screen test in 1928.

Lucille Ball

Try another profession. Any other.
The head instructor at the John Murray Anderson Drama School gives his considered professional verdict in 1927.

Joan Bennett

Your daughter is sweet, but she'll never photograph.
Paramount's Walter Wanger breaks it gently to the young hopeful's mother in 1928. After starring for Sam Goldwyn, United Artists and Fox, Miss Bennett was signed by Wanger – who then married her.

Dirk Bogarde

Nice of you to come, but your head's too small for the camera, you are too thin, and . . . I don't know what it is exactly about your neck . . . but it's not right.
Earl St John of the Rank Organization auditions a misfit, 1939.

James Cagney

He's just a little runt.
Howard Hughes rejects the vertically challenged actor for a lead part in The Front Page, *1927.*

Maurice Chevalier

URGE CANCEL CHEVALIER DEAL STOP PUBLIC WILL NOT REPEAT WILL NOT ACCEPT ACCENTS STOP EVEN RUTH CHATTERTON TOO ENGLISH FOR AMERICA STOP FRENCH ACCENTS EVEN WORSE STOP
1928: a frantic telegram from Paramount fails to prevent the unacceptable Frenchman being signed up for his first American hit, Innocents of Paris.

Joan Collins

I'm sick of being a movie floozie!
1953: the star of The Decameron *and* The Cosh Boys *aspires to higher things. She went on to star in* The Bitch *and* The Stud.

Joan Crawford

Don't get carried away, dear. It says 'six months'.
Mother knows best as her daughter is offered a $75-a-week 'try-out' contract by MGM in 1924.

Bette Davis

Who did this to me?
Sam Goldwyn reacts to her screen test in 1930.

No-one faintly like an actress got off the train.
A studio gofer sent to greet one of the cast of Bad Sister *returns unaccompanied from the station, 1931.*

I think Joan Blondell will be a big star, Anne Dvorak has definite possibilities, but I don't think Bette Davis will make it.
Director Mervyn LeRoy considers the female unknowns in Three on a Match.

Clint Eastwood

You have a chip on your tooth, your Adam's apple sticks out too far, and you talk too slow.
Close the door on your way out: a Universal Pictures executive does what he has to do in 1959 (see also Burt Reynolds, *p. 103).*

Clark Gable

It's awful – take it away!
MGM's Irving Thalberg views a screen test, 1920s.

His ears make him look like a taxi-cab with both doors open.
Howard Hughes rejects another hopeful for The Front Page, *1927.*

What can you do with a guy with ears like that?
Jack Warner turns him down for Little Caesar *in 1930.*
Gable persisted, and made 12 film appearances the following year. He went on to be 'King of Hollywood' in 1937 and Rhett Butler in 1939.

Cary Grant

You're too bow-legged and your neck is far too thick.
A Paramount executive views his screen test in 1931.

Hugh Grant

If I do them early on in a film, I find it very sexy. The thing is, I have always found strangers sexy.
The Star of Four Weddings and a Funeral *talks candidly about cinema sex scenes, May 1995. On June 27th Los Angeles police charged Grant with 'lewd conduct in a public place' after arresting him in a car with a 'known prostitute'.*

Jean Harlow

My God, she's got a shape like a dustpan!
Screenwriter Joseph March judges a screen test by an unknown named Harlean Carpenter for Hell's Angels, *1930 . . .*

In my opinion, she's nix.
. . . and Howard Hughes agrees with him.

Marilyn Monroe

You'd better learn secretarial work, or else get married.
Emmeline Snively, director of the Blue Book Modelling Agency, counsels a wannabe in 1944.

Mary Pickford

I suppose we'll have to say goodbye to little Mary Pickford. She'll never be heard of again and I feel terribly sorry for her.
Cecil B.'s brother, playwright William C. DeMille, fails to prevent one of his ingénues leaving Broadway for Hollywood in 1911.

Ronald Reagan

Reagan doesn't have the presidential look.
Stick to cowboys, Ron, advises a United Artists casting executive for The Best Man, *1964.*

Robert Redford

He's just another California blond. Throw a stick at Malibu, you'll hit six of them.
A casting executive dismisses the star of Barefoot in the Park *as a contender for a lead in* Butch Cassidy and the Sundance Kid *in 1969.*

Burt Reynolds

You have no talent.
United Artists executive averts his gaze from Clint Eastwood's Adam's apple and kills two turkeys with one stone, 1959.

(2) MOVIE ACUMEN

Gone With The Wind

Forget it, Louis. No Civil War picture ever made a nickel.
MGM's Irving Thalberg advises Louis B. Mayer not to bid for the film rights to Margaret Mitchell's novel in 1936 . . .

Irving knows what's right.
. . . and Mayer takes his advice.

I wouldn't pay fifty thousand bucks for any damn book any damn time.
Jack Warner turns them down, too.

I bet it's a pip!
Bette Davis turns down the part of Scarlett O'Hara in 1938.

It's going to be the biggest flop in Hollywood history. I'm just glad it'll be Clark Gable who's falling flat on his face and not Gary Cooper.
Phew, that was close! Gary Cooper breathes again, 1938.

Do you think I'm a damn fool, David? This picture is going to be the biggest white elephant of all time.
Director Victor Fleming rejects Selznick's offer of 20% of the profits and insists on a flat fee, 1939.

Heaven's Gate

Why do they want to see the rushes?
Director Michael Cimino can't understand why United Artists executives should be panicking about a film already $25 million over budget and several hours too long. It turned out to be the biggest flop in movie history.

Jesus of Nazareth

Twelve? Who needs twelve? Couldn't we make do with six?
Playing God: producer Lew Grade sees a way of economizing on disciples.

One Million Years BC

The characters and incidents portrayed and the names used herein are fictitious and any similarity to the names, characters or history of any person is entirely accidental and unintentional.
A disclaimer in case of writs from people who kill dinosaurs and say 'Ug', 1966.

The Seashell and the Clergyman

This film is apparently meaningless, but if it has any meaning it is doubtless objectionable.
The British Board of Film Censors bans Cocteau's film in 1956.

Who Framed Roger Rabbit

A deplorable development in the possibilities of animation.
. . . Says the doyenne of film critics Dilys Powell in 1988.

The Wizard of Oz

The part's too small.
Actor Ed Wynn reckons he deserves better things than the role of The Wizard, 1938.

That rainbow song's no good, it slows the picture right down. Take it out.
1939: an MGM producer – alas anonymous – suggests an improvement after the studio screening.

Muck and Brass

On the rocks with the Captains of Industry and the Helmsmen of Finance.

'Getting and spending, we lay waste our powers.'

William Wordsworth,
Miscellaneous Sonnets, *Vol. I, No. 33*

But first, a message from our sponsor . . .

The trade of advertising is now so near to perfection that it is not easy to propose any improvement.

The Idler *in 1759 has not yet heard of the Gold Blend Couple.*

The intrinsic nature of the vastly extended advertising of the new age will be influenced by the new growth of public intelligence . . . advertising will in the future world become more and more intelligent in tone. It will seek to influence demand by argument instead of clamour . . . Cheap attention-calling tricks will be wholly replaced, as they are already being greatly replaced, by serious exposition . . .

T. Baron Russell, in A Hundred Years Hence, *1905, has never been Tangoed.*

Peasants and priests and all sorts of practical and sensible people are coming back into power . . . They will not be affected by advertisements, no more than the priests and peasants of the Middle Ages would have been affected by advertisements. Only a very soft-headed, sentimental and rather servile generation could possibly be affected by advertisements at all.

What I Saw In America*: G. K. Chesterton, 1922. What on earth* did *he see?*

The Thompson Anti-Bandit Gun is a powerful deterrent. It strikes terror into the heart of the most hardened and daring criminal. The moral effect of its known possession is an insurance of its own.

'Serious exposition': Extract from a full-page advertisement in the New York Herald, *January 31st 1922, for the Thompson Sub-Machine gun. Known as the 'Chicago Typewriter', it reached the zenith of its fame on February 14th 1929 . . . in the St Valentine's Day Massacre.*

The bomb's brilliant gleam reminds me of the brilliant shine GLEAM gives to floors. It's a science marvel!

'Intelligent in tone': Advertisement in the Pittsburgh Press *during the week of the first H-Bomb tests in February 1954.*

T.T.I.T.K.

TV advertising shorthand for the format that sells household cleaning products. It stands for 'Two Tarts In The Kitchen.'

Pepsi Brings Your Ancestors Back From The Grave.

The Chinese version of the adman's jingle, Come alive with Pepsi.

If you bought our course, 'How To Fly Solo in Six Easy Lessons', we apologize for any inconvenience caused by our failure to include the last chapter, 'How to Land Your Plane Safely'. Send us your name and

address and we will send you the last chapter post-haste. Requests by estates also honoured.
Only for the 'soft-headed'? Classified ad in World Magazine, *1973.*

If you want well-being and hygiene – Vote Pulvapies!
For Mayor – Honourable Pulvapies.
'Argument instead of clamour' . . . Picoaza, Ecuador (pop. 4100), 1975: the promoters of Pulvapies Foot Deodorant cash in on a municipal election with advertisements depicting a mock ballot paper. The write-in vote elected the product Mayor.

Enjoy the charm of Grenada – unspoilt, peaceful and uncrowded.
. . . Until the United States invaded a week after the appearance of this beguiling advert in The Tatler, *November 1983.*

BEAVER ESPAÑA
You get two weeks being drunk and disorderly
SUMMER OF 69
It's not all sex, sex, sex, sex, sex, sex, sex, sex, sex, sex, sex, sex, sex, sex, sex, sex, sex, sex, sex, sex, sex, sex, sex, sex, sex, sex, sex, sex, sex, sex, sex, sex, sex, sex, sex, sex, sex, sex, sex, sex, sex, sex, sex, sex, sex, sex. There's a bit of sun and sea as well.
No more 'cheap attention-calling tricks'. . . . 1995: advertisements encourage the punters to enjoy what Club 18–30 is famous for. They were withdrawn after 432 complaints were made to the Advertising Standards Authority.

COMMERCIAL JUDGEMENT, FINANCIAL ACUITY

Up in smoke

Your cigar-ettes will never become popular.
Cigar makers F. G. Alton turn down an offer from Mr John Player, c. 1870.

Sheer nonsense

The public will never accept artificial silks. Lister's will stay with the real thing.
The Directors of Lister's Bradford Mill decide against buying the right to manufacture Rayon, invented by Hilaire de Chardonnet in 1884.

A SHORT HISTORY OF THE CAR INDUSTRY
Putting money on the horse . . .

Nothing has come along that can beat the horse and buggy.
1903: US businessman Chauncey Depew advises his nephew not to invest $5000 in the Ford Motor Company . . .

The horse is here to stay, but the automobile is only a novelty – a fad.
. . . and the President of the Michigan Savings Bank gives the same advice to Horace Rackham, Henry Ford's lawyer. Rackham ignored it and sold out his $5000 investment years later for $12.5 million.

. . . but not on the Germans

A study of the engine indicated that the unit was, in certain details, most inefficient . . . it is very doubtful whether it was even capable of giving reliable service had it produced a performance commensurate with its size. Looking at the general picture, we do not consider that the design represents any special brilliance . . . and it is suggested that it is not to be regarded as an example of first-class modern design to be copied by British Industry.
1946: a report by the Humber Motor Company . . .

British designers have nothing to learn in this brand of design.
. . . and one from the Ford Motor Company of Great Britain, after a delegation from the British motor industry had toured the Wolfsburg factory that produced the 'People's Car' – the Volkswagen – later known as the Beetle. It had been offered to Britain on a 'first refusal' basis. Britain refused it.

The Beetle sold over 20 million units until production ceased in the 1980s; manufacture subsequently resumed under licence in Spain.

ICI displayed a similar attitude to Agfa's colour film technology in 1947, finding it 'commercially uninteresting'. Agfa's technicians went to work for the US firm of Kodak instead.

It is doubtful . . . if German production would be such as to challenge our strong position in most markets outside Europe.
The conclusion of a Board of Trade report in 1950.

Horseless turkeys: (1) The Ford Edsel

LOOKS RIGHT! BUILT RIGHT! PRICES RIGHT!

The keynote slogan for what Madison agency Foote, Cone & Belding described as 'the greatest advertising campaign ever conceived' – the push to sell the Ford Edsel, which began rolling off the production lines in 1957 with predicted sales of at least 200,000 a year.

It looked appalling, a herbivorous dinosaur on four wheels. Public disfavour centred on the design of the radiator grille, which was likened to a chrome-plated lavatory seat. It was built very badly indeed: fewer than half the 100,000 models sold proved fault-free. The price was wrong, being pitched higher than other, less ugly and more reliable models in its class.

The Edsel is here to stay.
Henry Ford II, December 7th 1957, announcing a relaunch with a new design,

better engineering, lower price and a $20 million advertising budget – but it, too, failed. The project was scrapped in November 1958.

All one thousand of the new Ford dealers signed up in 1957 – some of whom had paid $100,000 for their Edsel franchises – closed their businesses. Ford itself lost about $350 million.

Horseless turkeys: (2) The Bricklin

Sooner or later you are going to drive a Bricklin. It might prove to be the first great sexual experience of your lifetime.
Advertising copy for the Bricklin gull-winged sports car in 1974.

I have a gut feeling for this man.
Prime Minister Hatfield of New Brunswick, Canada, whose government advanced $20,000,000 to Malcolm Bricklin, the car's manufacturer.

Most sexual experiences are probably more satisfying than that of driving a Bricklin. The bodywork, made of a fibreglass-acrylic material previously used for lavatory seats, leaked. Owners were advised not to drive in heavy rain. The shock absorbers had a tendency to fall off at speeds of over 35mph. The gull-wing doors would not open, close or lock properly. A few prototype models were sold, but they did not show up as profit; the dealership price of $5400 was $900 less that the manufacturing cost per model. It never went into full production.

Bricklin moved on, leaving the people of New Brunswick each $30 worse off.

Meanwhile, in Northern Ireland, Mr John DeLorean obtained several million pounds from the British taxpayer to manufacture . . . a gull-winged, fibreglass-acrylic sports car called . . . the DeLorean. Strangely enough, it had exactly the same faults as the Bricklin. DeLorean, too, moved on. But Mr Bricklin, to our knowledge, has never been prosecuted for cocaine possession.

Rare honesty?

The world has changed. So has Mazda.
One of the few occasions when a manufacturer comes close to saying, 'Okay, we got it wrong.' Mazda finally abandoned the Wankel rotary engine in 1976.

See **The Blunt Edge of Technology** *(p. 195).*

Fortress America

Though import sales could hit 425,000 in 1959, they may never go that high again.
Business Week, *January 17th 1958.*

With over 50 foreign cars already on sale here, the Japanese auto industry isn't likely to carve out a big slice of the US market for itself.
Business Week, *August 2nd 1968.*

By the end of the 80s, imports accounted for 28.5% of US car sales.

Roaring to success

The company is not bust. We are merely in a cyclical decline.

Lord Stokes, Chairman of British Leyland, explains the situation in 1974 – shortly before the taxpayer moved in to keep BL in business.

In its eventual reincarnation as Rover Cars, Britain's last volume car maufacturer was acquired by the German firm of BMW in 1994.

TELEPHONES, COMPUTERS, ROBERT MAXWELL AND OTHERS . . .

What, me worry?

I do not look upon any system of wireless telegraphy as a serious competitor with our cables. Some years ago I said the same thing and nothing has since occurred to alter my views.

Resign! Sir John Wolfe-Barry, Chief Executive of Western Telegraph Co., addresses shareholders at the 1907 Annual General Meeting.

You could put in this room, DeForest, all the radiotelephone apparatus that the country will ever need.

W. W. Dean, President of Dean Telephone Co., pours cold water on American radio pioneer Lee DeForest's demonstration in Dean's office, 1907.

A specialized market

I think there is a world market for about five computers.

Thomas J. Watson, Chairman of IBM, 1947.

There is no reason for any individual to have a computer in their home.

Ken Olson, President of Digital Equipment Corporation, addresses the World Future Society in Boston, 1977.

Autres Temps . . .

I can tell you how to make money in newspapers – own them!

Newspaper magnate Lord Thomson of Fleet in 1961. In 1966 he bought The Times. *When his son sold the title to Rupert Murdoch in 1981 it was losing £2 million a month.*

Bloom of success

I sling my ideas out to my staff and I say, 'Make them work!' I look for things where the trading systems are fuddy-duddy, archaic, then I move in.

. . . and move out: John Bloom of Rolls Razor Ltd., purveyor of cut-price washing machines and (in theory) much, much else: Spring 1964. In August 1964 Rolls Razor went bust owing £4m.

Terminal exhilaration

Few exercises exhilarate the financial world more than speculating what the Pennsylvania-New York Central Transportation Company will be

doing in ten years if the great plans now being laid for the system come to fruition.

Fortune Magazine *hails the merger of the two great US railroad companies in 1965. Penn Central went bust five years later, owing $4,600,000,000.*

Lord floored

In the long term I feel confident that with the increasing acceptance of tufted carpets we must go from strength to strength.

Carpet King Cyril Lord, August 1966. In the long term – two years, in fact, during which he built a factory that didn't make vinyl flooring and one that didn't make artificial astrakhan, but did manage to manufacture a sort of artificial turf that turned blue and slimy on exposure to the weather – his company went bust.

Don't panic!

On the evidence available, there appears to be no immediate danger of insolvency.

Conclusion of a Board of Trade inquiry into the trading position of the Fire, Auto & Marine Insurance Co., January 1967. It went into liquidation a week later, leaving several hundred thousand people uninsured and uncompensated.

But of course, it was all fun.

Emile Savundra, presiding genius of the Fire, Auto & Marine Insurance Co., called to account on TV by David Frost, February 1967.

Savundra was convicted of fraud, fined £50,000 and gaoled for eight years.

Every day, in every way . . .

The 1970s, barring any major set-to between the major powers, show a steady increase in our national prosperity.

UK Multinational Chairman Leonard Macham looks forward in The Times *of December 30th 1969. The seventies came and went without superpower confrontation; in the UK there was an oil crisis, a prolonged miners' and power workers' strike, a three-day week, a banking scandal, rampant inflation, rising unemployment, an IMF loan, a Winter of Discontent . . .*

Here tooday . . .

There's no way of saying exactly how much money we've invested. Naturally it's a risk. But we wouldn't have put so much money into something we didn't think was going to be a success. . . . If they don't catch on as recording artists at first, they'll just go on making more records until it catches. If they haven't made a hit by the time the film comes out, I'll be disappointed. The substantial difference this group has over every other group is getting themselves involved with people who are established successes in showbiz like Kirschner and Saltzman.

1970: Derek Coyte, of Eon Films, invests $2,700,000 in a film starring Toomorrow (sic), the Supergroup of the Seventies that was backed and managed *by Don Kirschner (the man behind the Monkees) and Harry Saltzman (the man behind James Bond and Michael Caine). It didn't quite work out, and the group sank without trace – except for one member, a teenage Australian chanteuse called . . . Olivia Newton-John.*

. . . gone tomorrow

I want to become the world's greatest international financier in the next ten years.

Jim Slater, of Slater-Walker Securities, 1972. Slater-Walker collapsed in 1975. Jim Slater is now a share tipster for the Independent. *His 1994 'fantasy portfolio' showed a modest loss.*

British Coal will still be around 100 years from now.

Advertisement for National Coal Board Technical Services in Business Administration, *1973.*

Stranger than non-fiction

We are absolutely certain of the authenticity of this autobiography and we wouldn't put McGraw-Hill's and *Life* magazine's name behind it if we weren't.

Donald M. Wilson of publishers McGraw-Hill announces publication of the tape-recorded memoirs of eccentric billionaire recluse Howard Hughes, December 7th 1971, and commences payment of a $750,000 advance to the 'go-between' and 'amanuensis' Clifford Irving – who, it turned out when Hughes gave a telephone interview on March 13th 1972, had made it all up. Irving and his wife were gaoled for fraud.

Sex 'n' shopping

Have you tried Cod Pieces?

Bird's Eye woo the housewife in 1976.

Light fingers

I have the ability to think like a thief.

Allen Klein on the quality that will make him a successful manager of John, George and Ringo (but not Paul) in 1972. Klein was gaoled for income tax evasion in 1979.

Nice smile, shame about the career

I call it the Mark Spitz Game Plan. My objective is to make an institutional tie-up for Mark very soon with two of the big blue-chip companies. It might be a GM or a Bristol-Myers, or somebody of that calibre. Then I'm planning to work out two TV specials in which Mark will star during the 1972–73 season. After that we're going heavily into the merchandising area worldwide . . . We feel that Mark Spitz will have a major motion picture career.

Hollywood agent Norman Brokaw on his new signing, 1972. In real life Mark

Spitz was good at swimming; he won five gold medals at the Munich Olympics. Then he became a dentist.

Making Georgia famous

I could become the Colonel Sanders of beer.
1977: Billy Carter, good ole li'l brother of the President of the United States, launches Billy's Beer courtesy of the Falls City Brewing Co.

I tried it once, but it gave me diarrhoea.
Mizz Lillian, the First Mother, doesn't like Junior's brew. Nor did anyone else; the brewery went bust in 1978.

The Icarus effect

Another brilliant, strategic move that should put Braniff in splendid shape for the 80s.
Salomon Brothers airline analyst Julius Saldutis hails the acumen of Braniff Chairman Harding Lawrence in Business Week, *March 19th 1979. The 80s saw Braniff go bust.*

I'm flying high and couldn't be more confident about the future.
Sir Freddie Laker is characteristically ebullient three days before the collapse of Laker Airways in 1982.

Robert Maxwell – a colossus of our age

There was a time until recently when the employer changed his machines, his methods or his workforce without asking or consulting anybody. Periodic and quite capricious unemployment was the most dreadful aspect of this situation. Most large employers now consult their workers or their representatives whenever they wish to make major changes.
Thank goodness! Robert Maxwell – himself very large indeed, as employers go – writes in Man Alive, *Pergamon Press, 1968.*

This is obviously the end of Mr Maxwell's dream of being the proprietor of a national newspaper.
Hugh Cudlipp, Chairman of IPC, after Rupert Murdoch beat Maxwell to the Sun, *September 1969.*

He is a man of great energy, drive and imagination, but unfortunately an apparent fixation as to his own abilities causes him to ignore the views of others if these are not compatible. . . . The concept of a Board being responsible for policy was alien to him.

We are also convinced that Mr Maxwell regarded his stewardship duties fulfilled by showing the maximum profits which any transaction could be devised to show. Furthermore, in reporting to shareholders and investors he had a reckless and unjustified optimism which enabled him

on some occasions to disregard unpalatable facts and on others to state what he must have known to be untrue . . .

We regret having to conclude that, notwithstanding Mr Maxwell's acknowledged abilities and energy, he is not in our opinion a person who can be relied on to exercise proper stewardship of a publicly quoted company.

Maxwell was fond of reminding journalists that these remarks had been 'the subject of a High Court action' – but not that he lost it. The report of the Department of Trade and Industry into Maxwell's stewardship of Pergamon Publishing, July 13th 1971, was largely forgotten for two decades afterwards.

I guarantee unconditionally that the Games will go ahead. I hope you will agree there is nothing more important than that. There will be no deficit at all. . . . I hope that will put paid to any nonsense . . . that I or any of my family will be handing out medals.

June 19th 1986: Maxwell steps in to save the Edinburgh Commonwealth Games, £4m short of funds with only a few weeks to go. (In due course, decathlete Daley Thompson's gold medal was hung round his neck by Robert Maxwell.)

When it comes to elbow-twisting on a major scale I am particularly good at it . . . The Games are financially secure. The job is virtually done.

Rejoice! Maxwell gives a press conference on July 18th, with six days to go.

Soon after the Games ended, Maxwell announced a deficit of £4m. By refusing to pay various contractors' accounts, he reduced it to £3.2m in October. By 1988 it had grown, with interest charges, to £3.8m.

I say to those who are here today and who manage the pension and investment funds that they are unfit to be the managers of those funds if they do not recognise the achievements of Mr Maxwell and invest in the company.

June 17th 1987: Henry Poole, analyst at Alexanders, Laing & Cruicksank and a broker for the British Printing and Publishing Corporation, gives a vote of confidence to the Chairman.

Our guaranteed circulation will be half a million.

Maxwell launches the London Daily News, *February 24th 1987. Circulation on day one was 400,000. After that it plummeted, sticking at around 100,000. On July 24th Maxwell scrapped the paper.*

It's not an ego trip. I don't go in for ego trips. It's not my style.

September 25th 1987: Maxwell changes the name of the British Printing and Publishing Corporation to Maxwell Communications Corporation. In October 1987, MCC released an eight-page colour brochure containing nine photographs of the eponymous Chairman. One was captioned: 'Robert Maxwell discussing world affairs with Henry Kissinger in Tokyo.'

In the work and life of Bob Maxwell we identify not merely one great talent but many: a remarkable innovator in the field of science and technology, an outstanding publisher, an exceptional communicator, manager, and a prominent and broadminded public figure.
... Also makes trains run on time and cures cancer. Corneille Radonco-Thomas & Francoise Garcin: Progress in Neuro-Psychophormeology & Biological Psychiatry, *Pergamon, 1988. Pergamon (R. Maxwell, prop.) was a notorious late (and in some cases non-) payer of authors' royalties.*

We must not abandon Gorbachev ... Don't you realise that Gorbachev wouldn't do anything without ringing me first?
Advice for Mirror *editor Roy Greenslade after the Soviet leader's virtual invasion of Lithuania, February 1990. Greenslade had wanted to publish 'horrific pictures from Vilnius'. Maxwell demurred.*

My way of running the Labour Party is now very, very successful.
Good news for Neil Kinnock in a Guardian *interview, March 1990.*

Even a one-eyed Albanian can work out there is going to be a premium to the issue price.
May 1990: on the eve of the flotation of Mirror Group Newspapers Maxwell insists the issue will be oversubscribed. Dealing in MGN shares opened on May 17th and they quickly fell from their offer price of 125p; underwriters Salomon Brothers admitted losses of £5m. Throughout 1990 and 1991 Maxwell used the devaluing shares in MCC and MGN as collateral for his huge and mounting debts. The pension funds became his only 'asset'.

By the time of Maxwell's death in November 1991, the many companies in the late tycoon's control had amassed debts in excess of £3,000,000,000.

It was directly linked to fresh allegations which will be made in the next few weeks. Of course there is a link. A story is going to break which would have made his position untenable.
November 6th 1991: Matthew Evans, Chairman of publishers Faber & Faber, links Maxwell's death to 'evidence' supplied to author Seymour Hersh that Maxwell was an agent of the Israeli intelligence service, Mossad, involved in gun running and money-laundering. The 'evidence' was false: Evans and Hersh had been hoaxed. Maxwell, a sufferer from chronic pulmonary oedema, died of a heart attack, probably while urinating over the rail of his yacht.

Postscript: the legend lives on

Piss off, or I'll call the police.
Son Kevin Maxwell threatens a group of early morning visitors to his house in January 1992. The visitors' reply: 'We are *the police.'*

Kevin Maxwell and his brother Ian were subsequently charged with various counts of theft and false accounting, and deemed penniless after divesting themselves of personal assets. As they awaited trial in March 1995, their lawyers had received around £4m of public money from the Legal Aid Board.

A sporting bet

It could no more lose money than I could have a baby.
Mayor Jean Drapeau of Montreal looks forward to hosting the 1976 Olympic Games, January 29th 1973. It lost around $1 billion, but M. Drapeau failed to make medical history.

The Bank of Crookery and Cocaine International

I don't hold myself responsible because I have not had anything to do with the affairs of BCCI for the past three years.
Agha Hassan Abedi, founder of the Bank of Credit and Commerce International, attempts to draw a veil over the sixteen years prior to that; July 15th 1991, a few days after BCCI collapsed under its own weight of criminality.

It's easy to say with hindsight that we were wrong to put all our eggs in one basket.
And with foresight too, surely? Donald MacLeod, Director of Finance for Comhairle nan Eilean (the Western Isles Council) which lost £23m in the failed bank – including £1.3m deposited 15 minutes before the Bank of England closed it down in July 1991. Churches in the Western Isles responded by organizing 'a day of penance and humiliation'.

Not wet leaves

It was the wrong kind of snow.
Manager Terry Worrall explains the failure of British Rail's anti-snow measures in February 1991.

Unobservant

I don't believe the *Observer* will be sold in the foreseeable future.
How long could Tom Bower, Robert Maxwell's unauthorized biographer and Observer *owner Tiny Rowland's official one, foresee in 1994 – one month prior to the sale of the paper to the trustees of the* Guardian*?*

What a worker

I shouldn't mind being a junior hospital doctor. It might be quite relaxing to do their job.
BT Chairman Sir Iain Vallance reckons he's worth every penny of his £663,000 annual salary, plus perks: February 1995.

Easy money

Don't panic! Derivatives are here to help . . . Send for your RISK-FREE trial issue now!
February 1995: a month that saw over-enthusiastic trading in the 'derivatives

market' bring about the extinction of Baring's Bank, and this flier for Derivatives Quarterly *magazine.*

Down the tubes?

We are not going bust.
We shall see: Sir Alistair Morton on Eurotunnel's £387m trading loss, April 1995.

GREAT ECONOMIC FORECASTS OF THE TWENTIETH CENTURY

The older I get the more convinced I am that most of the theories on which economics is based are bunkum.

Denis Healey, former Chancellor of the Exchequer, 1992.

The Great Wall Street nothing-very-much-at-all

Stocks have reached what looks like a permanently high plateau.
. . . Until you fall off the edge. Irving Fisher, Professor of Economics at Yale University, October 17th 1929. One week later, $6,000,000,000 was wiped off stock values on Wall Street.

The worst has passed.
Statement signed by the 35 major Wall Street dealing houses on October 24th. Five days later, another $10,000,000,000 was wiped off stock values – more than twice the amount of currency then in US circulation.

The end of the decline of the Stock Market will probably not be long, only a few more days at most.
Professor Irving Fisher has a second opinion on November 14th . . .

For the immediate future at least, the outlook is bright.
. . . and again, in The Stock Market Crash – And After, *published in 1930.*

These really are good times, but only a few know it. If this period of convalescence through which we have been passing must be spoken of as a depression, it is far and away the finest depression that we have ever had.
Henry Ford, President of Ford Motor Co., 1931.

I don't know anything about any depression.
J. P. Morgan, banker, 1931.
Economic decline continued until the outbreak of World War II in 1939.

Gee, post-war is hell!

There will be no cars, radios, washing machines or refrigerators after the war . . . women will have to return to their grandmothers' spinning wheel and men will have to build their own cottages.

Dr Hans Elias of Middlesex University, Massachusetts, has a go at doing a Party Political Broadcast for the Greens on October 4th 1942.

During the next four years, unless drastic steps are taken by Congress, the US will have nearly 8 million unemployed and will stand on the brink of a deep depression.

US Secretary of Commerce Henry A. Wallace spells out doom in November 1945. During 1945–50 US unemployment reached a peak of 4 million, and Gross National Product grew by 50%.

Not wholly miraculous

During the past two years it has been asserted with increasing frequency and vehemence that if, somehow, the German economy could be freed from materials and manpower regulations, price controls and other bureaucratic paraphernalia, then recovery would be expedited . . . Yet there has never been the slightest possibility of getting German recovery by this wholesale repeal, and it is quite possible that its reiteration has delayed German recovery.

Professor J. K. Galbraith, The German Economy, *1948. The 'post-war German economic miracle' is now widely attributed to the deregulation and abolishing of 'bureaucratic paraphernalia' which was begun shortly afterwards by Chancellor Erhart.*

Fool's gold

When the US government stops wasting our resources by trying to maintain the price of gold, it will sink to $6 an ounce rather than the current $35 an ounce.

Henry Reuss, Chairman of the Joint Economic Committee of Congress, 1967.

The US government stopped buying gold in 1971; ten years later the price had risen to $840 an ounce. Early in 1995 it stood at $380.

Possibly the most regrettable economic forecast of all time

In all likelihood, world inflation is over.

The Managing Director of the International Monetary Fund, 1957.

TELLING IT LIKE IT ISN'T

THE MEDIA AND THE PUNDITS

'Political pundits can predict any old nonsense, and when it doesn't come true no-one seems to mind.'

Craig Brown, newspaper columnist, 1994.

No childhood is complete without the statutory parental warning: 'Don't believe everything you read in the newspapers.' It is every bit as important as the injunction not to take sweets from strangers.

No-one should embark on a reporting career without taking to heart the lesson of Sir Walter Raleigh, who, imprisoned in the Tower, sought information on a brawl that had taken place below his cell window and, receiving two mutually contradictory eyewitness accounts of it, tore up in despair the History of the World he was trying to write.

And any expert tempted to inform popular opinion by hawking his or her informed insight to the press would do well to remember two little words: 'Hitler' and 'Diaries'.

For the delight of all those of us who don't aspire to be in the know, there follows a selection of regrettable reports and commentaries, together with the odd low-flying turkey plucked from the airwaves of radio and TV.

Specialist blunders in the fields of Science and Technology and of Entertainment will be found under their respective headings elsewhere in this book.

1800–1900

Sheer lunacy: the Sun *and the Moon*

The specimen of lunar vegetation, however, which they had already seen, had decided a question of too exciting an interest . . .

Dr Herschel has classified not less than thirty-eight species of forest trees, and nearly twice this number of plants . . . Of animals, he classified nine species of mammalia, and five of oviparia . . .

We were thrilled with astonishment to perceive four successive flocks of large winged creatures, wholly unlike any kind of birds, descend with a slow even motion from the cliffs on the western side, and alight upon the plain . . .

We counted three parties of these creatures, of twelve, nine and fifteen in number, walking towards a small wood near the base of the eastern precipices. Certainly they *were* like human beings, for their wings had now disappeared, and their attitude in walking was both erect and dignified . . . They averaged four feet in height, were covered, except on the face, with short and glossy copper-coloured hair . . . these creatures were evidently engaged in conversation; their gesticulation, more particularly the varied action of their hands and arms, appeared impassioned and emphatic. We hence inferred that they were rational beings.

A selection of cuttings from the New York Sun *of August 1835. Published as reports of telescopic observations on the moon made by Sir John Herschel's expedition to the Cape of Good Hope, they were in fact composed after work each evening by* Sun *journalist Robert Locke. Sales of the* Sun *soared accordingly; no-one publicly questioned the veracity of the reports. The* New Yorker *opined that they opened up a new era in scientific discovery, while a leader in the* New York Times *described them as 'plausible and possible.' Worldwide, convocations of scientists were held to consider the implications of these important discoveries. Mr Locke subsequently earned a few more pennies by publishing a book about it all.*

150 years later in Britain the Sunday Sport *carried the front page headline:*

WORLD WAR 2 BOMBER FOUND ON MOON

The American Civil War

Tennessee in no contingency will join the Gulf Confederacy.
New York Times *editorial, April 17th 1861. Tennessee joined the Confederacy 20 days later.*

No man of sense can for a moment doubt that the war will end in a month. The rebels, a mere band of ragamuffins, will fly on our approach like chaff before the wind. The Northern people are simply invincible.
Philadelphia Press *editorial, 1861.*

Fort Sumter must not be surrendered, if there is force enough in the United States to hold it . . . It must be reinforced at every hazard.
New York Times *editorial, April 13th 1861.*

The fall of Sumter was a substantial and crowning advantage, anticipated and provided for.
New York Times *editorial, April 15th 1861.*

The end is that Richmond is safe while Washington is menaced, and that Lee is master of the field . . . The conclusion must be plain that the great object of the Federals – the capture of Richmond – is absolutely unattainable.
The Times *sees no threat to the Confederate capital, August 16th 1864. Within a year Richmond had fallen to the 'Federals' and the Confederate general Robert E. Lee had surrendered.*

The Gettysburg Address

The cheek of every American must tingle with shame as he reads the silly, flat and dishwatery utterances of the man who has to be pointed out to intelligent foreigners as the President of the United States.
The Chicago Times *reacts to Lincoln's speech. Lincoln himself commented: 'I failed; I failed: and that is about all that can be said of it.'*

Anything more dull and commonplace it would not be easy to reproduce.
The Times *tends, on the whole, to agree with Mr Lincoln.*

The race for the White House, 1864

Mr Lincoln is already beaten. He cannot be re-elected.
New York Tribune *editor Horace Greely puts his readers straight on August 14th 1864. Lincoln won the election by 212 Electoral College votes to 21.*

The Franco-Prussian War

Nothing shall ever persuade me except the event that the Prussians will withstand the French.
The Times *editor John Thadeus Delane, July 1870. The persuasive event – the routing of the French Army at Sedan and the capture of Napoleon III – took place six weeks later.*

Hoaxed

Dear Sir,
I am not surprised at your friend's anger but he and you should know that to denounce the murders was the only course open to us. To do that promptly was plainly our best policy.

But you can tell him and all others concerned that though I regret the accident of Lord F. Cavendish's death I cannot refuse to admit that Burke got no more than his deserts.

You are at liberty to show him this and others whom you can trust also, but let not my address be known. . . .

Yours very truly,
Charles S. Parnell.

The Irish Nationalist MP appears to condone the Phoenix Park murders – the stabbing to death of Burke and Lord Cavendish by Fenian assassins in Dublin. The Times *printed the first 'Parnell letter' on April 18th 1887. All were forgeries, traced eventually to Richard Pigott, an Irish newspaper owner and blackmailer, who subsequently committed suicide. The error of judgment cost the Thunderer £200,000 in legal fees.*

It was not the last time The Times *was to fall victim to forged documents* *(see p. 135).*

So, farewell then, Karl Marx . . .

Marx's audacious attempt to destroy the bases of contemporary society with the aid of what seemed to be the cardinal principles of political economy has utterly failed.
The St Petersburg journal Grazhdanin, *March 13th 1883.*

The Socialist ideas he had tried to propagate failed to make a lasting impression.
The Daily Alta California*'s reckless use of the word 'lasting' gains it an entry: March 18th 1883.*

1900–1950

The SS Titanic

ALL SAVED FROM TITANIC AFTER COLLISION RESCUE BY CARPATHIA AND PARISIAN; LINER IS BEING TOWED TO HALIFAX AFTER SMASHING INTO AN ICEBERG

The New York Evening Sun *scoops the world; April 15th 1912.*

NORTH MAN LOST AT SEA

No proof exists for this supposed headline in the Aberdeen Press & Journal *but that didn't seem a good enough reason for leaving it out.*

World War One

The bankers will not find the money for such a fight, the industries will not maintain it, the statesmen cannot . . . There will be no general war.

The Independent *(USA) gives a platform to Stanford University President David Starr Jordan on February 27th 1913.*

While it is only natural that one should be stricken with horror at the brutal and shocking assassination of Archduke Francis Ferdinand, it is impossible to deny that his disappearance from the scene is calculated to diminish the tenseness of the situation . . . the news of his death is almost calculated to create a feeling of universal relief.

F. Cunliffe-Owen, International Affairs expert of the New York Sun, *gets it exactly wrong on June 29th, 1914.*

A great world war would be such an absurdity, such a monstrous outcome from relatively trivial causes . . . that any reasonable calculation of probabilities would yield only a slight percentage in favour of such an eventuality.

Days before Austria's declaration of war on Serbia (July 28th 1914), Vienna's eminently reasonable and finely-calculating Neue Freie Presse *cannot bring itself to believe the worst. In fairness it should be said that* 'a monstrous outcome from relatively trivial causes' *is a pretty fair description of World War One – but the Balkans have always been good at that sort of thing . . .*

In three months from now the war fever will have spent itself.

The London Chronicle, *August 5th 1914. War fever finally spent itself over four years later, after the loss of nearly eight million dead and over twenty-four million wounded.*

A truth more strangely regrettable than media speculation . . .

A *Daily Herald* cartoon by Will Dyson portrays the signatories to the Treaty of Versailles as they leave Paris. Clemenceau is turning to the others and saying, 'Curious, I seem to hear a child weeping.' In the background a child is shown above the caption, 'Class of 1940'.
The cartoon was published in 1919.

The Russian Revolution

It can't work – for Lenin and Trotsky are both extremely unpopular. Lenin will never be able to dominate the Russian people.
Herman Bernstein, Russian correspondent of the New York Times, *November 9th 1917.*

What are the Bolsheviki? They are representatives of the most democratic government in Europe. Let us recognise the truest democracy in Europe, the truest democracy in the world today.
Citizen Kane – sorry, William Randolph Hearst – gives his papers a line to follow in 1918.

The Bolshevist Government won't last six months more.
Walter Duranty, foreign correspondent of the New York Times, *May 27th 1920.*

There is abundant evidence that the Bolshevik terror is drawing steadily to its downfall . . . Of course the attempt to reverse economic laws and to ignore the most deeply seated impulses of human nature was certain to fail. It was only a question of time. Apparently that time is not to be very long.
Former US Secretary of State Elihu Root anticipates the inevitable in the New York Tribune *of November 11th 1921. It took a little longer, however – roughly seventy years, in fact.*

The Wall Street Crash and the Great Depression

EXPERTS PREDICT RISING MARKET
Bulls Ready to Back Bankers; Bear Move Touches Bottom

PUBLIC CONFIDENCE IN STOCKS RESTORED
BY MOVE OF 'BIG 4'
The New York Journal, *October 25th 1929, the day after $6 billion was wiped off share values on Wall Street. On October 29th shares fell a further $10 billion.*

Hysteria has now disappeared from Wall Street.
The Times, *November 2nd 1929. Prices fell steadily for another three years until by December 1932 $50bn had been wiped out.*

Business has come home again, back to its job, providentially unscathed, sound in wind and limb, financially stronger than ever before.
Business Week, *November 2nd 1929.*

In most of the cities and towns of this country, this Wall Street panic will have no effect.
Paul Block: syndicated editorial in Block Group papers, November 15th 1929.
See also: **Muck and Brass** *(p. 117) and* **Misleadership** *(p. 16).*

The race for the White House, 1932

In 1932 the chimneys will be smoking, the farmers will be getting good crops that will bring good prices, and so Mr Hoover will be re-elected.
The New York Times, *editorial, November 5th 1930.*

The re-election of President Hoover with at least 270 votes in the electoral college, four in excess of a majority, is predicted in a statistical study of vote percentages in the several states, based on a poll taken by the Hearst publications.
The New York Times, *report, November 5th 1932. In the real ballot Mr Hoover received 59 college votes. A certain Mr F. D. Roosevelt got 472. This was not the last time opinion polls proved unreliable.*

The race for the White House, 1936

FDR will be a one-term president.
New York Herald Tribune *political commentator Mark Sullivan, 1935. Roosevelt served a record three terms and had been re-elected for a fourth at his death.*

The race will not be close at all. Landon will be overwhelmingly elected and I'll stake my reputation as a prophet on it.
A little touch of the Isaiahs from William Randolph Hearst, August 1936.

I have never felt more certain of anything in my life than the defeat of President Roosevelt. By mid-October people will wonder why they ever had any doubt about it.
Another syndicated editorial from Paul Block, September 1936.

Landon 1,293,669; Roosevelt 972,897

Final Returns in The Digest's Poll of Ten Million Voters . . . the most extensive straw ballot in the field – the most experienced in view of its twenty-five years of perfecting – the most unbiased in view of its prestige – a poll that has always previously been correct.
The Literary Digest *goes over the top in its eve-of-poll edition of October 31st 1936.*

The real result: Roosevelt 523 college votes, Landon 8. FDR beat his rival by a margin of 11 million popular votes – the biggest majority ever recorded.

The resistible rise of Adolf Hitler

The day when they [the Nazis] were a vital threat is gone.

It is not unlikely that Hitler will end his career as an old man in some Bavarian village who, in the biergarten in the evening, tells his intimates how he nearly overturned the German Reich . . . The old man, they will think, is entitled to his pipe dreams. It is comforting to live on the memory of an illusion.

But did Harold Laski find comfort in the memory of his? The Great Sage of the Left pontificates in the Daily Herald, *November 21st 1932.*

. . . Not forgetting Il Duce

There can be no doubt as to the verdict of future generations on his achievement. He is the greatest figure of our age. Mussolini will dominate the 20th century as Napoleon dominated the early nineteenth.

Lord Rothermere lectures his public in the Daily Mail, *March 28th 1928.*

Ignorant and prejudiced people talk of Italian affairs as if that nation were subject to some tyranny which it would willingly throw off. With that rather morbid commiseration for fanatical minorities which is the rule with certain imperfectly informed sections of British public opinion, this country long ago shut its eyes to the magnificent work that the Fascist régime was doing. I have several times heard Mussolini himself express his gratitude to the *Daily Mail* as having been the first British newspaper to put his aims fairly before the world.

Ward Price proudly reports an endorsement from the Italian dictator in 1932.

HURRAH FOR THE BLACKSHIRTS!

1934 Daily Mail *headline to a report of a rally of Sir Oswald Mosley's Union of British Fascists. In 1939 proprietor Lord Rothermere described Hitler as 'a perfect gentleman'.*

The appeasing Thunderer

It might be worthwhile for the Czechoslovak Government to consider whether they should exclude altogether the project, which has found favour in some quarters, of making Czechoslovakia a more homogeneous state . . . The advantages . . . might conceivably outweigh the obvious disadvantages of losing the Sudeten German districts of the borderland.

A Times *leader on Hitler's proposed annexation of the Sudetenland on September 7th 1938.*

Peace for our time . . .

Britain will not be involved in war. There will be no major war in Europe this year or next year. The Germans will not seize Czechoslovakia. So go about your own business with confidence in the future and fear not.

Daily Express, *May 23rd 1938.*

The *Daily Express* Declares That Britain Will Not Be Involved In A European War This Year Or Next Year Either.
Daily Express, seven-column headline on September 30th 1938.

Another war that never really happened produced two memorable newspaper headlines:

EIGHTH ARMY PUSH BOTTLES UP GERMANS

and:

MACARTHUR FLIES BACK TO FRONT

Hitler and Stalin: unravelling the party line

The whispered lies to the effect that the Soviet Union will enter into a treaty of understanding with Nazi Germany are nothing but poison spread by the enemies of peace and democracy, the appeasement mongers, the Munichmen of Fascism.
So now you know, Comrades: the Daily Worker *of May 26th 1939 told you so.*

By compelling Germany to sign a non-aggression pact, the Soviet Union has tremendously limited the direction of Nazi war aims.
Er, on the other hand . . . The Daily Worker *reports the Nazi-Soviet Pact of August 23rd 1939. Nazi war aims were afterwards tremendously limited to the invasion of Poland, France, Belgium, Holland, Norway, Denmark . . . and, in 1941, the USSR.*

The modern German theory of victory by *Blitzkrieg* (lightning war) is untried and, in the opinion of many experts, unsound.
. . . Except in Poland, France, Belgium, Norway . . . Time, *June 12th 1939.*

The French Army is still the strongest all-round fighting machine in Europe.
Time, *June 12th 1939. France surrendered to Germany on June 22nd 1940.*

The race for the White House, 1940

Although the answer to the question, Does Mr Roosevelt want a third term? is definitely Yes, to the other question, If he does, can he get it? the answer is emphatically No.
But he got it anyway by defeating Wendell Wilkie. Political expert and Democratic Party historian Frank R. Kent misleads readers of The American Mercury *in January 1938.*

The race for the White House, 1948

FIFTY POLITICAL EXPERTS UNANIMOUSLY PREDICT A DEWEY VICTORY
A Newsweek *headline of October 11th 1948 that should have prompted Mr Dewey to throw in the towel immediately.*

Dewey is going to be the next President, and you might as well get used to him.
Wishful thinking in the New Republic *of October 25th 1948.*

DEWEY DEFEATS TRUMAN
G O P Sweep Indicated in States
President Harry S Truman posed for photographers with this early edition of the Chicago Daily Tribune *of November 3rd 1948 after defeating Dewey by 303 college votes to 189.*

1950–1975

The Korean War 1950–53

One or two divisions with terrific air power and a blockade of the coast can do the job.
Joseph Fromm, Regional Far East Editor, US News & World Report, *July 14th 1950.*

The time has passed when the Chinese could change the course of the war.
Newsweek, *November 6th 1950.*

Communist Premier Chou En-Lai's threat that China 'will not stand aside should the imperialists wantonly invade North Korea' is only propaganda.
Time, *October 9th 1950. Chinese intervention prolonged the conflict for three years; it ended it stalemate.*

Hungary, 1956

Soviet troops are now leaving Budapest and apparently are also leaving Hungary.
John MacCormac files for The New York Times *hours before 200,000 Soviet troops and 2500 tanks surrounded the city prior to storming it.*

The Soviet troops are assisting the Hungarian people to retain their independence from Imperialism.
Once again, the Daily Worker *sets Comrades' minds at rest: November 1956.*

Fidel Castro exposed

Senor Castro has been accused of Communist sympathies, but this means very little since all opponents of the regime are automatically called Communists. In fact he is further to the right than General Batista.
The Economist, *April 26th 1958.*

South Africa – the end in sight

Revolution is obviously coming to this country – and will obviously be successful – within the next five years.
Kirkpatrick Sale files a report for the Chicago Tribune, *1961.*

Vietnam

A sample of the leisure time goodies set before the American public this week: Safaris in Vietnam, for the Tourist Who Really Wants to Get Away From It All.
Newsweek*: 'Leisure in the 1960s', December 14th 1959.*

US aid to South Vietnam may be stepped up. *But no* US combat troops are going into the jungle to engage in shooting war with Communist guerrillas.
US News & World Report, *November 13th 1961.*

For the first time since we spun into the Vietnam mess, there is hope for the United States . . . The credit justly belongs to President Lyndon B. Johnson. He has made the war 'unlosable.'
Life*'s Senior Editor Sam Castan, November 30th 1965.*

From being on the verge of losing its position in South Vietnam lock, stock and barrel, the US has driven the main enemy to the brink of defeat. Never in modern times has there been a smoother, surer, swifter reversal in the tide of a struggle.
Fortune *magazine: 'The War We've Won', April 1967.*

The enemy is reeling from successive disasters. We are, in fact, winning the war.
William Buckley: syndicated column filed from Hong Kong in December 1969. The USA was, in fact, four years away from losing it.

The enemy is beating himself to death.
Syndicated columnist Joseph Alsop excitedly quotes the Chief American Civilian Adviser in Vietnam: June 16th 1972.

News from nowhere

The climax, when it came, was in the best Drake tradition but by then too little momentum remained to carry it to the required height.
The Guardian*'s Harry Whewell reviews a live TV show by the comedian Charlie Drake in 1961. Drake was knocked unconscious during transmission and the programme was faded out – an event Whewhell, who was also the paper's News Editor, inexplicably failed to notice at the time.*

Dallas, Texas

The Man Who Is Gunning For Kennedy.
An uncanny lack of prescience on the part of the Daily Express *is shown in this caption to a photograph of Republican rival Barry Goldwater on the morning of November 22nd 1963.*

MacMillan's successor named

HAILSHAM PREMIER
The Daily Express *reports the choice of Quintin Hogg, Viscount Hailsham, as Prime Minister and Leader of the Conservative Party, November 1963. In fact the Tories chose Sir Alec Douglas-Home.*

Miracle in Printing House Square

NIZAM OF HYDERABAD IS DEAD
The Times, *February 23rd 1964.*

NIZAM OF HYDERABAD SLIGHTLY BETTER
The Times, *February 24th 1964.*

Empty Thunder

'University of the Air' . . . The very term is an illusion in that it holds out hopes it cannot possibly fulfil . . . to speak of a university of the air is to encourage hopes that the television viewer will be offered the range and depth of courses open to the university student. This would be misleading nonsense.
The Times, *April 3rd 1965. Britain's university of the air – the Open University – was launched in 1969 and currently offers a full range and depth of university courses to over 75,000 students – as well as offering a fascinating time-capsule insight into early 1970s fashions.*

Remembering the Surbiton Five

It is possible that the five girl typists of Surbiton will, when the history of these confused times is written, become as famous as the six martyrs of Tolpuddle.
At last, the Daily Mirror*'s prediction of 1968 comes true! The typists had volunteered to work 30 minutes extra per day without pay to aid the 'I'm Backing Britain' campaign, which had the informal approval of the Labour Government the* Mirror *supported. A reader's offer of 'I'm Backing Britain' T-shirts backfired when they turned out to be labelled 'Made in Portugal'.*

The race for the White House, 1968

It will be a Johnson-Humphrey ticket again in '68.
US News & World Report, *February 13th 1967.*

Lyndon Johnson's long legs are very firmly wrapped around the Donkey, and nothing short of an A-bomb – someone else's A-bomb – could knock him off.

National Review, *December 1967. Johnson withdrew his candidacy in March 1968 after narrowly defeating Eugene McCarthy in the New Hampshire primary.*

Victims of patriarchal oppression

Lesotho Women Make Beautiful Carpets

Bangkok World, *date unknown.*

Next to godliness

BELFAST CHOSEN AS MODEL CITY

The National Society of Christians has selected Belfast as 'The Model City of the World, 1970'.

The Society, which is based in the USA, says that Belfast 'possesses a zealous Christian attitude and participates with an active interest in religious functions.'

Reported without a trace of irony in The Belfast Newsletter, *1970.*

NOTE: In some of our copies the article *The Power of the Papacy* described the Pope as His Satanic Majesty. This should have read The Roman Antichrist.

A zealous Christian attitude in the Protestant Telegraph, *Belfast.*

Full frontal error

Certainly pubic hair will become a fashion emphasis, if not necessarily blatant.

Mary Quant hands out a fashion tip to Daily Mirror *readers at the beginning of 1970. Her own, she added, was 'trimmed into a dainty heart shape' in readiness for the exciting year ahead.*

Big Daddy Field Marshal President Idi Amin Dada: an apology

**GOOD LUCK TO PRESIDENT AMIN . . .
GOOD RIDDANCE TO OBOTE**

General Amin, a beefy, soft-spoken man of the Madi tribe, sets an example of self-restraint. First reports seem to suggest . . . a military government which, with any luck, may turn out to be of like nature and ambitions to those which have successfully brought law and order and relatively clean administration to Ghana and Nigeria.

Daily Telegraph *editorial, January 1971.*

THE CHAMP WHO ROSE FROM THE RANKS TO SEIZE POWER

Military men are trained to act. Not for them the posturing of the Obotes

or the Kaundas who prefer the glory of the international platform rather than the dull but necessary task of running a smooth administration. Amin looks capable of that task.
Daily Express *editorial, January 1971.*

A thoroughly nice man . . . as gentle as a lamb.
Daily Mirror, *January 1971.*

Without doubt, a benevolent, honest, dedicated and hardworking man.
Financial Times, *1972.*

One feels that Uganda cannot afford General Amin's warmhearted generosity.
The Times, *1972.*

President Amin has the support of the Ugandan people who still believe he is bringing them real independence. He is admired by all Africans . . . it is possible that this semi-literate peasant from the West Nile district can write a new chapter in East Africa's history.
Judith Listowel, The Times, *January 1973.*

Every Inch a Field Marshal!
Evening Standard *report of Amin's address to the UN, 1975.*

Amin was driven from Uganda by the Tanzanian army in 1979. He had ruined the economy, expelled thousands of Uganda's Asians, and murdered some 300,000 of his fellow-citizens.

The death of Life

You'd have to have a death wish to kill *Life* magazine.
James R. Shepley, President of Time Inc., January 1970. In December 1972 he suffered a bout of tedium vitae *and closed the magazine down.*

A gush too far

There are some marriages that are so ideal and easy looking that you wonder why the rest of us can't manage it too. It's something to do with being each other's match and equal, of keeping together so that half isn't left behind, and maintaining some secret balance and link between the two – hard to define but immediately recognizable when you meet it. Barbara and John Stonehouse have always seemed to me to be married in that way.
Ann Sharpley, Evening Standard, *January 1971. In November 1974 John Stonehouse MP faked his own drowning in order to disappear with his secretary, Sheila Buckley.*

The race for the White House, 1972.

McGovern has about as much chance as Pat Paulsen of getting the Democratic presidential nomination in Miami.
Arizona Republic *editorial, March 12th 1972. Uh, Pat* who?

If I had to put money on it, I'd say that on January 20th 1973 the man with his hand on the Bible will be John V. Lindsay.
Psephological gurus Jerry Bruno and Jeff Greenfield, The Advance Man, *1972. John V. Lindsay pulled out of the primaries and McGovern won the nomination.*

Senator Thomas Eagleton . . . a casting director's ideal for a running mate.
The New York Times, *July 14th 1972. MacGovern dumped Eagleton 12 days later and chose Sargent Shriver. They were heavily defeated by the incumbent, Nixon, in November.*

Oh no he wasn't

MARTIN BORMANN ALIVE
The Daily Express *is hoaxed on November 25th 1972.*

Water under the gate: Nixon and the media

Sincerity is the quality that comes through on television.
The Washington Star, *September 15th 1955.*

A political has-been at 49.
Newsweek, *November 19th 1962.*

Nixon is a very much better man today than he was ten years ago . . . I do not reject the notion that there is a new Nixon who has outlived and outgrown the ruthless politics of his early days.
Walter Lippmann, The Washington Post, *October 6th 1968.*

A predictable election-year Mickey Mouse, of course, but surely the Democrats are pushing our sense of humour too far.
A Richmond News *Leader editorial pours scorn on the suggestion that the Watergate burglary may have been organized by Republicans, June 22nd 1972.*

As shameful as Watergate is, the case has a hopeful or reassuring aspect: nothing is being swept under the rug.
Orlando Sentinel, *January 13th 1973.*

If the press continues its zealous overkill on this affair, it is not likely to destroy either President Nixon or the Nixon Administration but it will

gravely injure something more important – the faith of the people in the freedom of the press.
The Burlington Free Press *upholds the inalienable right of the media not to investigate or report things: April 25th 1973.*

A racing certainty

Jim Slater has now earned himself a position of paramount respectability in the City for his novel and wide-ranging techniques.
The Times *puffs Slater Walker Ltd in 1969 at a time when Mr Slater's 'novel and wide-ranging techniques' were earning him a great deal of money.*

Slater Walker is now safe from calamity
Patrick Hutber, writing in the Sunday Telegraph *shortly before the collapse of Slater Walker in 1975.*

1975–THE PRESENT

The race for the White House, 1976

Is Teddy Running? Are You Kidding . . . Do Birds Sing In The Morning?
Clay Felker pens a headline for the front page of New York *magazine, March 24th 1975. Teddy Kennedy did not run.*

Jimmy Carter's Running for WHAT?
Headline of editorial in the Atlanta Constitution, *July 10th 1974.*

Well, I can tell you who it won't be. Jimmy Carter . . . looks more like a kid in a bus station with his name pinned to his sweater on his way to summer camp than a President on his way to the White House.
Dick Tuck, 'Who'll Be Our Next President? Read It Here First', Playboy, *March 1976.*

Jimmy Carter swept the primaries, won the Convention with a landslide on the first ballot, and beat Gerald Ford comfortably.

Yes! it's Charles and . . . who?

Express Exclusive
Engagement next week
Sons will be Protestant, daughters Catholic
CHARLES TO MARRY ASTRID – official

John Warden of the Daily Express *scoops the known Universe on June 17th 1977. HRH Prince Charles married Lady Diana Spencer in 1981.*

Middle East peace hopes dashed

It is far more likely that the Vatican conclave will elect a black Pope than any serious agreement will emerge from it.
The Village Voice *calls time on the Camp David Summit on August 21st 1978. On March 26th 1979 the Summit concluded with the signing of a peace treaty by Presidents Carter and Sadat and Prime Minister Begin.*

The race for the White House, 1980

I would like to suggest that Ronald Reagan is politically dead.
NBC political correspondent Tom Pettit on The Today Show, *January 22nd 1980.*

Dear Diary . . . mein Gott!

I am 100% convinced that Hitler wrote every single word in those books – it's the journalistic scoop of the post-World War Two period.
Peter Koch, editor of the German magazine Stern, *April 22nd 1983, after a joint acquisition with the London* Times *of exclusive serialization rights to 62 handwritten volumes of Adolf Hitler's diary.*

[These diaries] all belong to the same archive, and whereas signatures, single documents, or even groups of documents can be skilfully forged, a whole coherent archive covering 35 years is far less easily manufactured. Such a disproportionate and indeed extravagant effort offers too large and vulnerable a flank to the critics who will undoubtedly assail it . . . The archive, in fact, is not only a collection of documents which can be individually tested: it coheres as a whole and the diaries are an integral part of it.

This is the internal evidence of authenticity . . .
In The Times *of April 24th 1983 the historian Hugh Trevor-Roper (Lord Dacre) gives his seal of approval.*

The following day the first serious public doubt was cast on the authenticity of the 'diaries' and by the end of May they had been conclusively exposed as a forgery. The 'skilful' methods used to fabricate the diaries included buying them from a stationers, dropping them on the floor and walking on them, and spilling instant coffee over them. They had never, in fact, been 'individually tested' by anybody.

It is one thing to forge a contemporary document, in which only the handwriting and the content must be made plausible, and another to manufacture an ancient document, avoiding the perils of anachronism not only in writing and content but in paper and ink.
How true! 1976: Hugh Trevor-Roper (as he then was) writes A Hidden Life: The Enigma of Sir Edmund Backhouse, *and reveals the revered Sinologist as . . . a diary-forger.*

Lèse-majesté

I don't know what all the fuss is about. It's just a second-rate Royal marrying an overweight Sloane.

BBC journalist David Dimbleby looks forward to commentating on the marriage of HRH Prince Andrew to Miss Sarah Ferguson in July 1986.

Better stick to tealeaves

TERRY WAITE: In the Year of the Cat we do not expect to see headlines screaming of hostages in plight. As a result, Terry Waite, the Archbishop of Canterbury's special envoy, will have a chance to put his feet up and live more of a normal life.

In the Cat Year I expect Terry to spend more time at home . . . But if there is trouble under the Cat's influence it will not last long.

Depending, of course, on what one means by such words as 'normal', 'home' and 'long'. Barry Fantoni's Chinese Horoscope for February 1987–February 1988, the year in which Terry Waite was kidnapped by Hizbollah and began his record-breaking stay in captivity in Beirut.

Gay Gordons

The most frightening fact about AIDS is that it can be spread by normal sex between men and women. This is still rare in Scotland.

Comforting news from a land where sheep outnumber people: the Sunday Mail, *March 1987.*

Conflicting reports

Prisoner Release Could Help Set Mandela Free

Financial Times, *September 7th 1987, Page 1.*

Prisoner Exchange Unlikely to Entail Release of Mandela

Financial Times, *September 7th 1987, continuation on Page 2.*

Junk journalism

Roll up, it's Liberace's junk stall . . . Fans will be falling over themselves to spend £6m on a heap of rubbish from the pianist's tatty treasure trove.

The Star, *April 1988. Much of the pianist's tatty treasure was bought by Express Newspapers proprietor Lord Stevens of Ludgate to be distributed as prizes in a competition run by . . . the* Star.

Persecution, or what?

We've already hunted the grey whale into extinction twice.

Ms Andrea Arnold airs her Green credentials in an ITV interview, May 1990.

Clear as mud

The impression was not so much to be entirely literal as to give the

groundsweep of what it was about and in that sense he is accurate, speaking from a strategic spreadangle.

A Foreign Office press officer clarifies a remark by Douglas Hurd: April 1990.

The race for Number Ten, 1992

Lawson helped bring about the second army of unemployed and the failed businesses whose condition now seems likely to drive the Tories disgraced out of power . . . Mr Kinnock was magnificent. The party he made, now poised for power tomorrow . . . Unless all polls are nonsense, which I don't believe, or my perceptions are worthless, something I humbly doubt . . .

Edward Pearce of the Guardian *forecasts the outcome of the General Election in April 1992. The Tories won with a majority of 20 seats.*

No cause for alarm

Iraqi leaders will not want to undermine the ruling regimes in the Gulf States.

Royal Institute of International Affairs *press release, 1991.*

No risk of war in the Gulf

Terrible and wrong as a war would be, there is something comforting in the fo-fummery of Mr Bush. A man truly disposed to war, and ready to commit all the attendant crimes, does not talk like that.

Edward Pearce rules out conflict: The Guardian, *January 2nd 1991. The bombing of Baghdad began a fortnight later.*

The Soviet Coup: resistance is useless

Please let us understand that we are talking about power – Faith, Hope and Power, and the greatest of these is Power. In the Soviet Union, the generals have it and the crowds on the Moscow streets have it not. Nothing else matters.

But the crowds on the Moscow streets won anyway: Edward Pearce writes in the Guardian, *August 21st 1991.*

Maxwell of the Mirror

(1) I have no intention of making anyone redundant.
(2) I will never interfere in editorial freedom.
(3) Union recognition will continue.

Cap'n Bob nails his colours to the mast on acquiring the Mirror, *July 1984.*

Under my management editors in the Group will be free to produce their newspapers without interference with their journalistic skills and judgement.

For all those who missed it the first time: a pledge renewed in July 1985.

One of Britain's most successful businessmen of the past decade . . . one of the most outstanding performers of the year.
Sunday Telegraph, *March 1991.*

Robert Maxwell says he'll only allow his sons Ian and Kevin to take over his vast empire if they are capable. 'Money you haven't earned isn't good for you,' he says.
A gush from Woman's Realm, *August 8th 1991.*

I am only concerned about needless anxieties which the programme may cause to pensioners in our group.
Maxwell tells Mirror *readers why he's issued a writ against a BBC* Panorama *programme, September 1991.*

The truth is our only currency.
Facing bankruptcy in more ways than one, Maxwell writes in the Daily Mirror *of October 29th 1991, a week before his mysterious death.*

THE MAN WHO SAVED THE DAILY MIRROR
Front Page headline, Daily Mirror, *November 6th 1991, reporting Maxwell's death by drowning the day before.*

Robert Maxwell's premature death is a great loss to the world of business and publishing. He was the one man you could rely on in times of trouble.
Fellow press baron Lord Stevens of Ludgate, Daily Express, *November 6th 1991.*

I think he had more physical and moral courage than anyone I have ever met.
Former UK ambassador to Washington and ex-Maxwell employee Peter Jay, Today, *November 6th 1991.*

The publisher's final resting place is high on the hillside . . . It was from the Mount of Olives, according to Christian belief, that Jesus ascended into heaven after His resurrection.
John Jackson and Harry Arnold, The People, *November 10th 1991.*

A man who worked and aspired and achieved dreams unthinkable to the ordinary mortal.
Mary Riddell, Daily Mirror, *November 11th 1991.*

Joe Haines writes . . . the man who, in 1984, told colleagues, 'He is a liar and a crook and I can prove it', shares his thoughts with Mirror *readers:*
Many of us who started off disliking him ended up captured by his kindness.
November 6th.

Many of us in the Mirror building despise those who are seeking, within hours of his death, to smear him further . . . They will get their comeuppance, one day.
November 7th.

From the moment Harold Wilson resigned, rumours, inventions and baseless gossip began, and those whom he hardly knew rushed to claim intimate insights into his life and secrets, with heavy hints of scandal behind both . . . As it was with Harold Wilson, so it was and will be with Robert Maxwell . . . tosh and falsehood.
Comparing past employers, November 11th.

MAXWELL:
£526 MILLION IS MISSING FROM HIS FIRMS
Front Page headline, Daily Mirror, *December 6th 1991 after it is revealed that Maxwell stole from the pension funds of his companies' employees.*

Joe Haines writes . . .
It's been an awful week, the worst I can remember, and I need someone to talk to . . . Now I think I'll go home and have a good bath.
Daily Mirror, *December 6th 1991.*

PS: AS YOU WERE . . .

(1) I have definitely got no plans for job cuts in editorial departments; nor has the board considered any.
(2) The editorial independence of our newspapers will be preserved and vested in our editors.
(3) Union recognition will continue.
More paper promises, destined to be broken: new supremo David Montgomery in the Daily Mirror *of October 23rd 1992.*
See also: **Muck and Brass** *(p. 113) and* **Books**, *etc. (p. 84)*

Green shoots . . . of mould?

ECONOMIC RECOVERY BEGINS TO BLOSSOM
Each week, we will note the economic news, and assign it Green Shoots points. A sighting of a blossom, such as a surge in gross national product, would merit five points, but a withering of the bud, such as a collapse in retail sales, would merit minus five.
Batting for Britain: The Sunday Times, *April 26th 1992.*

Recently there have been as many brown as green shoots, with few signs of sustained growth. We are therefore suspending the index until new signs of growth appear.
Small paragraph on the back page of The Sunday Times, *July 5th 1992.*
Not long afterwards the paper began its 'Lamont Must Go' campaign.

Chas 'n' Di . . . and Fleet Street's finest

From Fairytale Wedding to the Camillagate Tapes, the marriage of HRHs The Prince and Princess of Wales has been responsible for several thousand tons of newsprint. Whole forests perished after publication of Andrew Morton's *Diana: Her True Story* in 1992.

THE *SUN*

Senior Royal advisers say the book is almost certain to damage the couple's marriage beyond repair, when there had been a last chance to save it.
Front Page, 5th June.

It's the book the whole world is talking about . . . It's gripping, it's sad, it's history in the making. And it's all true. You can start reading it, chapter by chapter, only in the *Sun* next week. Order your copy today.
10th June.

The best thing for Prince Charles and Diana now will be to spend time together, quietly and away from the public gaze.
Editorial, 12th June.

The love that moved Diana to tears.
Page 1, 12th June.

You give pride and joy to us all, may you always remain just you.
Pages 2–3, 12th June.

Di's not like the Royals, she was never trained to hide her tears . . . Cry, Di, it's good for you . . . 10 tell-tale signs of a woman about to crack.
Page 9, 12th June.

At the end of the day, a smile . . .
Pages 22–23, 12th June.

THE *STAR*

Last night Britain sighed with sadness for Di – and sent her a massive wave of sympathy as she faced incredible strain. Friends and MPs lashed the 'shabby and intrusive' treatment she was receiving.
Front Page, 5th June.

Royal Marriage in Torment – Special Report: Pages 2, 3, 4 & 5.
Front Page, 5th June.

THE *DAILY EXPRESS*

Never, in 25 years at the journalistic cutting edge of this world, have I ever encountered such vitriolic indiscretion . . . It is exactly what the Royal

Family doesn't need at this time . . . Let the light in on the Royal Family, it has been observed, and it loses its mystery. I will therefore draw a veil over breakfast at Highgrove on Sunday morning and leave it to your imagination.
The responsible correspondent: Ross Benson's reaction to the publication of Diana: Her Story, *June 5th.*

Marriage in Crisis
Only doing his job: Ross Benson writes a series in the editions of June 8th, 9th and 10th.

THE *EVENING STANDARD*

The Royals: A Family at War
Page one headline, June 5th.

Suicidal Despair, Loveless Marriage.
Pages 2–3 headline, June 5th.

Is It Time to Leave the Royals Alone?
Leader page headline, June 5th.

THE *DAILY MIRROR*

***The Sunday Times* and the *Sun* which together have invested more than £500,000 in Andrew Morton's book suggest the Princess has somehow cooperated in the publication. Well, they would, wouldn't they? The *Mirror* today publishes the Princess's complete rebuttal of that claim in the most clear and precise terms.**
June 8th.

Diana last night warmly embraced the former flatmate who contributed to the controversial book about her marriage . . . Diana clearly told the world: 'I approve of everything she has done.'
June 11th

THE *DAILY MAIL*

It is painful to dwell on the melancholy state of the marriage of the heir to the throne.
Editorial, June 6th.

Diana: The Unhappiness Behind the Smile. Turn to Pages 17, 18 and 19.
Front page, June 6th.

Disaster? what disaster? oh, that disaster!

WHY DISASTER THEORISTS ARE WRONG

The spiralling stock market and property prices of the late Eighties were

going to end in tears . . . but even this has not happened, as the Bank of Japan and the Ministry of Finance have gently deflated the 'bubble economy' to bring people back to their senses . . .
'View From Tokyo': Terry McCarthy in The Independent, *February 15th 1992.*

TEARS FLOW OVER NIKKEI'S MISERY
The Tokyo stock exchange soap opera is going into a new weepie phase . . . By Friday morning, with the Nikkei at 18,286, well below the supposed psychological support level of 20,000, it was handkerchief time all round.
'View From Tokyo': Terry McCarthy in The Independent, *April 4th 1992.*

Everyone knew the peak was unnaturally and unhealthily high; that it was based on a grossly inflated property market and a dangerous upsurge in lending by freshly deregulated financial institutions; and that one day nemesis would strike. Now it has.
Editorial in The Independent, *April 10th 1992.*

Greyish Wednesday

Like his predecessor, John Major is not for turning. Once he has negotiated a deal or made a promise, he stands by it.

Last night . . . he said that even if other countries devalue or revalue their currency in the European exchange rate mechanism, Britain will not join in. Mr Major's speech should help steady the pound in the difficult days ahead.
Editorial, Daily Express, *Friday September 11th 1992.*

LAMONT POUND VICTORY
The Chancellor won a spectacular victory over the Germans last night – paving the way for a dramatic cut in interest rates.
Daily Mail, *Monday 14th September 1992.*

When the market opens this morning . . . it would not be surprising if the pound also strengthened its position against the mark. Shares should also leap as the prospect of interest rate rises finally recedes.
Daily Express *City Editor Tom McGhie, Monday September 14th 1992.*

For Britain, last night's package should ensure that sterling holds above its floor in the ERM for the five days remaining until the French vote.
Editorial, The Times, *Monday September 14th 1992.*

Currency gyrations and vague threats of financial crashes or interest rate rises have undermined confidence again over the past two months . . . Consumers and businessmen can now wake from that nightmare and start getting on with the job again, confident of eventual recovery.
Comment in the Business Section of The Times, *Tuesday September 15th 1992.*

Devaluation in Italy . . . may encourage the markets to celebrate their victory over the lira by taking a pot shot at the next weakest currency in the ERM, the pound. The evidence of yesterday is that this will not happen and that if the markets did they could be repelled.
The Independent*'s Hamish MacRae, Tuesday September 15th 1992.*

Sterling will be an altogether tougher nut to crack, with the reserves newly bolstered.
City Comment, Daily Telegraph, *Wednesday September 16th 1992.*

Mr Major . . . may well succeed, at least for a while. Until Sunday he is probably safe. The Bank of England can spend its reserves to protect sterling from the worst ravages of the market-place.
The Times, *Wednesday September 16th 1992.*

By lunchtime on Wednesday September 16th 1992 UK interest rates had risen to record levels. Britain then withdrew from the ERM and sterling was effectively devalued by around 30% against the mark.

It took until early yesterday evening for the government to bow before forces it should not have been fighting . . . a brief battle with the money markets in which victory would have been a miracle.
The Times, *Thursday September 17th 1992.*

Good news, bad news

REPOSSESSIONS FALL

The number of houses repossessed in the first half of this year is expected to show a further fall when figures are released on Wednesday.
The Sunday Telegraph, *July 25th 1993, page 2.*

Repossessions still rising
The Sunday Telegraph, *July 25th 1993, page 37.*

Gypsy Rose Lee writes . . .

Is the Prime Minister trying to tell us something? The new year's Honours List could almost be a resignation Honours List.
Andrew Rawnsley in the Observer, *January 1994.*

Major will leave of his own accord as soon as the European elections are over. Clarke should be in the saddle by mid-summer.
Paul Johnson in The Sunday Times, *January 1994.*

Tory grandees now believe it would be better to go down to honourable defeat under a new leader.
Ian Aitken in the Guardian, *January 1994.*

All eyes now look to Mister Clarke.
Alan Watkins, describing his past predictions as 'infallibly correct', in the Independent on Sunday, *January 1994.*

Not for sale

Last summer I suggested that British Aerospace would be in no particular hurry to sell Rover as it was released from its undertaking given to the government when it bought the car maker five years earlier. Today, after getting a glimpse of how well Rover performed in 1993, it still holds true.
Michael Smith, Business Editor, writes in the Observer *on January 30th 1994. British Aerospace sold Rover Cars to BMW the following day.*

Style gurus

It looks as if the dining room is on the way out. The kitchen, now that servants are a thing of the past, is the prime candidate for the dining area.
Daily Telegraph, February 19th 1994.

Kitchen dining is out . . . The dining room has re-emerged, complete with all the trappings.
The Times, *February 19th 1994.*

Autre temps, autre moeurs . . . but the same old news

IN THE HOSPITAL WHERE TOGETHERNESS IS A TONIC THE PATIENTS ARE FEELING BETTER ALREADY
Daily Mail *headline to a report and photograph of a mixed-sex ward, 1966.*

DEGRADATION THAT SHAMES THE NHS
It can come as something of a shock to patients, particularly women, to find themselves lying in a ward next to someone of the opposite sex.
The Daily Mail *finds a different use for the same photograph in 1994.*

Striking a balance

A World Cup without a home team is still managing to grip the country's armchair football fans, television viewing figures revealed today.
Evening Standard, *June 28th 1994.*

A World Cup without a home team is proving a turn-off for the country's armchair football fans, television viewing figures revealed today.
Evening Standard, *June 28th 1994.*

On a night that should have belonged to Elle MacPherson, Elizabeth Hurley managed to accrue more than her fair share of attention.
Evening Standard, *July 13th 1994.*

Miss Elle MacPherson monopolised the fickle paparazzis' attention at last night's West End première. Miss Elizabeth Hurley – she of That Dress – was largely ignored.
Evening Standard, *July 13th 1994.*

How terribly, terribly true

We all know that people with very meagre talents can become household names by appearing on television.
Noel Edmonds, interviewed in the Daily Telegraph, *July 1994.*

All quiet, no change

It is unlikely that interest rates will move before Eddie George and Kenneth Clarke meet again on 26th September.
George Sivell, The Times, *September 8th 1994.*

The absence of dramas between the Chancellor and the Bank of England has left the outlook for base rates unchanged.
Terry Byland, Financial Times, *September 12th 1994.*

Last Wednesday the Chancellor and the Governor of the Bank of England decided to leave base rates unchanged, almost certainly until November or later.
Gavyn Davies compares himself favourably with 'the average newshound' in The Independent, *September 12th 1994. That same day, base rates rose 0.5% to 5.75%.*

Playing both ends . . .

FURY AS IRISH PM GREETS GERRY ADAMS
PALS WITH MURDERERS

Two headlines from the Sun*'s Ulster edition report a peace-making meeting, September 1994. An editorial opined that the IRA are 'lucky they're not hanging from a rope'.*

HANDSHAKE OF HOPE

A slightly different perspective on the same event in the Sun*'s Eire edition included praise for this 'historic breakthrough'.*

It's a Knockout

Foreman is volunteering to be beaten up for large sums of money.
Paul Hayward looks forward to Foreman v Moorer: Daily Telegraph, *November 1st 1994.*

Foreman should not be allowed to fight for the title on humanitarian grounds.
Neil Allen, Evening Standard, *November 4th 1994.*

Foreman could end up badly hurt with his cherubic features turned into a grotesque and bloody mess. Fat's yer lot, Foreman!
The considered opinion of Colin Hart, the Sun, *November 5th 1994.*

Moorer will . . . punch Foreman to a shattered standstill by the eighth.
Pinpoint accuracy from Ian Gibb, Daily Mirror, *November 5th 1994.*

Foreman will lose. The only question is how badly he will be hurt.
James Lawton, Daily Express, *November 5th 1994.*
Result: Foreman regained the title by knocking out Moorer in Round Ten.

OUT OF THE AIR . . .

A selection of regrettable broadcast gems. Many of them are not strictly 'Regrettable' within the terms of this book, but proved too delicious to leave out.

At the present moment the whole Fleet is lit up. When I say 'lit up' I mean lit up by fairy lamps. It's fantastic. It isn't a Fleet at all . . . It's fairyland. The whole Fleet is in fairyland. Now if you'll follow me through . . . If you don't mind . . . the next few moments, you'll find the Fleet doing odd things. (*Prolonged silence.*) I'm sorry, I was telling some people to shut up talking . . . Oh, it's gone. It's gone. There's no Fleet. It's . . . it's disappeared. No magician who ever could have waved his wand could have waved it with more acumen than he has now at this present moment. The Fleet's gone. It's disappeared. I was talking to you in the middle of this damn (*cough*) in the middle of this Fleet and what's happened is the Fleet's gone and disappeared and gone.
A tired and emotional Lieutenant-Commander Tommy Woodroffe, whose BBC commentary on the 1937 Spithead Naval Review was faded out at this point.

If there's a goal now I'll eat my hat.
Tommy Woodroffe again, at the 1938 FA Cup final. There was. He did.

I guess that'll hold the little bastards.
Donald Carney – 'Uncle Don' – the Children's Programme presenter on Station WOR, speaking (as he thought) off-air: 1930s.

I belong to the fag-end of Victorian liberalism,
E. M. Forster 'outs' himself on the BBC Home Service, 1946.

Funny old game

Since the success of the long campaign to curtail hooliganism on English football grounds, the noisy dishonouring of opponents seems to be the lout's last liberty. . . . Human beings are not irreversibly programmed to display rancour towards their opponents at football matches. The European Cup finals of 1992, at Wembley, and 1994, in Athens, were the most enjoyable football nights I can remember, for the ambience created by the supporters. The stakes could hardly have been higher, yet the fans of Barcelona, Sampdoria and Milan found a way of supporting their

---

We are going to play a hiding and finding game. Now, are your balls high up or low down? Close your eyes a minute and dance around, and look for them. Are they high up? Or are they low down? If you have found your balls, toss them over your shoulder and play with them.
Music & Movement, *BBC Home Service for Schools, c. 1957.*

Summers will never be the same . . . The much loved and lamented Brian Johnston, BBC cricket commentator:
The bowler's Holding, the batsman's Willey.
There's Neil Harvey at leg slip, with his legs wide apart waiting for a tickle.
There has been a heavy fall of rain here at Trent Bridge but fortunately it didn't touch the ground.

Do you think the prisoners will regard you as just another screw?
Jack de Manio interviews Britain's first woman prison governor on the Today *programme, 1960s.*

Princess Margaret, wearing an off-the-hat face.
Max Robertson commentates on the wedding of Princess Anne and Captain Mark Phillips for BBC radio.

Juantorina opens wide his legs and shows his class.
Not David Coleman but Ron Pickering, at the 1976 Olympics.

The art of the quill has been practised since Caxton – and probably before.
Yes indeed! David Frost: TV interview, 1977.

You can rest assured there isn't going to be a hurricane.
In the event, few in the South of England found much rest. TV Weatherman Michael Fish achieves notoriety on October 16th 1987.

teams, of accepting defeat or victory, without needing to experience any emotion darker than disappointment.

In the wake of the 'Cantona Incident', Richard Williams contributes a long 'think piece' to the Independent on Sunday *on January 29th 1995 – the day a Genoa supporter was stabbed to death by a fan of AC Milan. Riot police used teargas to quell the vicious hand-to-hand fighting that ensued.*

Premature electrocution

Killer Nick Ingram fried to death at midnight in an American jail's electric chair . . . Crowds outside Jackson prison, near Atlanta, Georgia, cheered as the switch was pulled at 7 pm local time . . . Ingram was pronounced dead by doctors more than twenty minutes later.

Manchester (England)-based reporter John Burke-Davies gives readers of the Daily Sport *on the morning of April 7th 1995 an eye-witness account of the execution of murderer Nick Ingram, unaware that a judge had granted the killer a 24-hour reprieve. Ingram was electrocuted the following day.*

What a gas!

Because Sarin is slightly heavier than air, it hovers close to the ground to cause maximum fatalities.

Tuesday March 21st: page four of the Daily Express *reports the background to the gas attack on the Tokyo underground.*

Sarin is lighter than air, and would normally disperse quickly in the open air.

Tuesday March 21st: page five of the Daily Express *clarifies the facts.*

Getting it right?

As is inevitable in these occasions, instant theories were advanced on the basis of little or no evidence. One linked the bomb to the deadly raid by Federal agents on David Koresh's Davidian compound in Waco, Texas. Another, even more far-fetched, connected Wednesday morning's explosion with the scheduled execution in Arkansas of a White Supremacist. The more serious speculation was about the involvement of people connected to fundamentalist forces in the Middle East.

April 21st 1995. Two days after the Oklahoma City bombing the Economist *gets it seriously wrong. Three right-wing white extremists were later taken into custody in connection with the bombing. On April 20th* Today *had run the wildly speculative headline* IN THE NAME OF ISLAM . . .

And finally . . .

The following was spotted in 1976 on a billboard for the Carlisle Evening News. *Any reader who can shed light on its meaning is warmly invited to contact the author, who has been worrying about it – off and on – ever since . . .*

ERA POLO PUTS FEBRUARY MEDICINE GRAMMAR INTO OINTMENT HISTORY

THEY'RE NOT LIKE US

A BRIEF SURVEY OF REGRETTABLE PREJUDICE

RACE

They might make quite good servants

Races north of the Pyrenees never reach maturity; they are of great stature and of a white colour. But they lack all sharpness of wit and penetration of intellect.

c. 1100; the Moorish traveller Saïd of Toledo describes Europeans to his fellow-countrymen.

White on Black

I am apt to suspect . . . all the other species of man . . . to be naturally inferior to the whites. There never was a civilisation of any other complexion than white, nor even any individual eminent either in action or speculation.

What, not even Jesus Christ? The philosopher and polymath David Hume, 1766.

There is a physical difference between the White and the Black races which I believe will forever forbid the two races living together on terms of social and political equality.

Abraham Lincoln, 1858.

In the skull of the Negro the cranial capacity and the brain itself is much undersized. On the average it will hold thirty-five fluid ounces, as against forty-five for the Caucasian skull.

Wow, let's hear it for the elephant! Robert W. Shufeld: The Negro a Menace to American Civilisation, *1907.*

Most of the attacks on white women of the South are the direct result of a cocaine-crazed Negro brain.

Dr Christopher Koch, member of the Pennsylvania State Pharmacy Board, gives expert medical evidence to the US Congress in 1914.

Encyclopedia entries

The mental constitution of the negro is . . . normally good-natured and cheerful, but subject to sudden fits of emotion and passion during which he is capable of performing acts of singular atrocity, impressionable, vain, but often exhibiting in the capacity of servant a dog-like fidelity which has stood the supreme test . . . After puberty sexual matters take first place in the negro's life and thoughts.

Encyclopædia Britannica, *1911.*

The negro is greatly inferior mentally to the white and yellow races, and this has been attributed by some to the early closing of the cranial sutures, by which the normal development of the brain is arrested.
The Waverley Encyclopedia, *1930.*

They occupy rather a low level in the scale of humanity, and are lacking in those mental and moral qualities which have impressed the stamp of greatness on other races that have distinguished themselves in the history of the world.
The Nuttall Encyclopedia, *1930.*

Knowing their place . . .

Evidently you did not try to learn anything until you had reached maturity, because you know it is a biological fact that a Negro's skull, where the parts of it are connected by sutures, ossifies by the time a Negro reaches maturity and they become unable to take in information.
Whereas the skulls of US Congressmen. . . . Senator Theodore G. Bilbo of Mississippi writes in 1945 to a black schoolteacher in Chicago and advises her to be a charwoman.

. . . and looking alike

I have in front of me photographs of twelve Asian men, all of whom look exactly the same, which I'm sure you appreciate.
Judge Alexander Morrison addresses an all-white jury at Derby Crown Court, February 21st 1995. Afterwards he said his remarks had been misinterpreted.

Y'awl hear this!

I aint going to let no darkies and white folks segregate together in this town.
Eugene Connor, Police Commissioner for Birmingham, Alabama, 1950.

Shock, horror

15-YEAR-OLD PASADENA GIRL TELLS OF SCHOOL TERROR . . . I would never go into a swimming pool where there has been or are Niggers in it. I refused to take swimming for that reason. My mother phoned the Board of Education and stated as such. They could not understand such a thing as they said no one had ever refused to take swimming for that purpose. My mother told me she was proud that I was the first to refuse, but she prayed I wouldn't be the last . . . The next day I was told by the head physical education teacher that *'the Niggers are the same as whites, and the skin was the only difference'!* I told her maybe they were as good as her, but they sure were not as good as I am!
A 'Miss K. S.' writes to The Thunderbolt, *November 1970: quoted by Harland Ellison in* The Other Glass Teat.

Hey, what's the fuss?

This coloured thing, you don't really notice it at all; coloured servants out there don't really mind – they get their food and their board, so why should they mind? Gosh, you get coloured servants all over the world. They don't mind at all.

Gosh! Cliff Richard tells the Youth of Britain all they need to know about South Africa in 1963.

Er, quite

They shouldn't be killing the rhinos.

Kylie Minogue on the situation in South Africa: Clio *magazine, 1989.*

I'm not racialist, but . . .

One employer gave as his reason for not employing a coloured school-leaver: 'Your pigmentation would make you more allergic to frostbite in our frozen food.'

Daily Telegraph.

Most of the boarding-houses here are not large enough to take coloured and white guests at the same time.

Mrs Dorothy Brookes, Withernsea Landladies' Association, Yorkshire.

Oh yes, we Tory Councillors have done a lot for race relations. I do think it's very important. After all, but for the Grace of God, we'd be black ourselves, wouldn't we?

Anon Tory councillor. The foregoing were collected by the New Statesman *between 1968 and 1974.*

The abuses of science

Science shows us the infinite superiority of the Teutonic Aryan over all others, and it therefore becomes us to see that his ascendancy shall remain undisputed. Any racial mixture can but lower the result. The Teutonic race, whether in Scandinavia, other parts of the continent, England, or America, is the cream of humanity.

Science fiction writer H. P. Lovecraft, 1916.

The non-Nordic man takes up an intermediate position between the Nordic man and the ape.

Herman Gauch, New Elements of Scientific Investigation*, 1934.*

The blood particles of a Jew are completely different from those of a Nordic man. Hitherto one has prevented this fact from being proved by microscopic investigation.

Julius Streicher, 1935.

Christ cannot possibly have been a Jew. I don't have to prove that scientifically. It's a fact!
Joseph Goebbels, c. 1940.

There is no anti-Semitism in Russia. In fact, many of my best friends are Jews.
He really said it! Soviet President Alexei Kosygin, 1971.

What is a bloodsucker? When they land on your skin, they suck the life out of you to sustain their life. In the 20s and 30s and 40s, the Jews were the primary merchants in the black community . . . from our life they drew life and came to strength. They turned it over to the Arabs, the Koreans and others, who are now doing what? Sucking the lifeblood of our own community . . . You stand out there as if to say this is some of the same old garbage they said in Europe. I don't know about no garbage said in Europe.
Presumably Louis Farrakhan of the Nation of Islam has never heard of Kristallnacht *either: interviewed in* Time *magazine, February 20th 1994.*

GENDER

(1) ON WOMEN

The wisdom of the ancients

It is a great glory in a woman to show no more weakness than is natural to her sex, and not to be talked of, either for good or evil, by men.
Thucydides, 5th century BC.

Silence and modesty are the best ornaments of women.
Euripedes, 5th century BC.

A woman will bear any weight, if it's placed upon her by a man.
Only joking . . . ? Aristophanes, 5th–4th century BC.

Woman may be said to be an inferior man.
Aristotle, 4th century BC.

Women are all one and all a set of vultures.
Petronius, 1st century AD.

Religious insight

Unto the woman he said, I will greatly multiply thy sorrow and thy conception; in sorrow shalt thou bring forth children; and thy desire shall be to thy husband, and he shall rule over thee.
God lays down the law in Genesis, *3:16.*

Give not thy strength unto women, nor thy ways to that which destroyeth kings.
Proverbs, *31:3.*

Now concerning the things whereof ye wrote unto me: it is good for a man not to touch a woman.
The First Epistle of the Apostle Paul to the Corinthians, *7:1.*

Let the woman learn in silence with all subjection.
But I suffer not a woman to teach, nor to usurp authority over the man, but to be in silence.
For Adam was first formed, then Eve.
And Adam was not deceived, but the woman being deceived was in the transgression.
Notwithstanding she shall be saved in childbearing, if they continue in faith and charity and holiness with sobriety.
A lesson unlikely to be preached by women priests: The First Epistle of Paul the Apostle to Timothy, *2:9–15.*

As regards the individual nature, woman is defective and misbegotten.
St Thomas Aquinas, 1225–74.

To promote a Woman to bear rule, superiority, dominion or empire, above any Realm, Nation, or City, is repugnant to Nature; contumely to God, a thing most contrarious to his revealed will and approved ordinance, and finally it is the subversion of good Order, of all equity and justice.
A Presbyterian Speaks: John Knox, First Blast of the Trumpet against the Monstrous Regiment of Women, *1558.*

The ministrations of a male priesthood do not normally arouse that side of female human nature which should be quiescent during the times of the adoration of almighty God. . . . It would be impossible for the male members of the average Anglican congregation to be present at a service at which a woman ministered without becoming unduly conscious of her sex.
Beware the slumbering beast in Man! 1935: Unruly male members are cited by the Archbishop of Canterbury's Commission of Enquiry into the ordination of women. It decided against it.

The female sex is in some respects inferior to the male sex, both as regards body and soul.
Mid-century teaching . . . the 20th century. The Catholic Encyclopedia, *c. 1940.*

A Restoration view

A woman is a solitary, helpless creature without a man.
Dramatist Thomas Shadwell, c. 1642–92 – of whom Dryden wrote, 'Shadwell never deviates into sense.'

The Age of Enlightenment

Most women have no characters at all.
Alexander Pope, Moral Essays, *1732.*

Women are much more like each other than men; they have, in truth, but two passions, vanity and love; these are their universal characteristics.
That well-known leather settee, The Earl of Chesterfield: Letters to his Son, *December 19th 1749.*

A woman's preaching is like a dog's walking on his hinder legs. It is not done well; but you are surprised to find it done at all.
The fount of English Common Sense: Samuel Johnson, 1763, quoted in Boswell's Life of Johnson, *Volume 1.*

A small man's opinion . . .

Nature intended women to be our slaves . . . They are our property . . . They belong to us, just as a tree that bears fruit belongs to a gardener. What a mad idea to demand equality for women! . . . Women are nothing but machines for producing children.
Get back in your box, Josephine: Napoleon Bonaparte, 1769–1821.

Philosophy

The fundamental fault of the female character is that it has no sense of justice . . . Since every man needs many women, there could be nothing more just than that he should be free, indeed obliged, to support many women. This would also mean the restoration of woman to her rightful and natural position, the subordinate one.
Arthur Schopenhauer, 1788–1860.

When a woman becomes a scholar there is usually something wrong with her sexual organs.
Friedrich Wilhelm Nietzsche, 1888.

Science

Every well-sexed woman invariably throws her shoulders back and breasts forward as if she would render them conspicuous, and further signifies sensuality by way of a definite rolling motion of the posterior.
Our wise old friend Orson Squire Fowler: Sexual Science, *1870.*

There is a large number of women whose brains are closer in size to those of gorillas than to the most developed male brains. This inferiority is so obvious that no-one can contest it for a moment; only its degree is worth discussion . . . they are closer to children and savages than to an adult, civilized man. They excel in fickleness, inconstancy, absence of thought and logic, and incapacity to reason. Without doubt there exist some distinguished women . . . but they are as exceptional as the birth of any monstrosity as for example, a gorilla with two heads; consequently, we may neglect them entirely.
French anthropologist Gustave Le Bon, essay in Revue d'Anthropologie, *1879.*

It is the prime duty of a woman of this terrestrial world to look well.
Sir William Osler, Professor of Medicine at Johns Hopkins University and Physician-in-Chief at Johns Hopkins Hospital, in 1903.

Direct thought is not an attribute of femininity.
Thomas Alva Edison, The Woman of the Future, *article in* Good Housekeeping *of October 1912.*

Brain work will cause her to become bald, while increasing masculinity and contempt for beauty will induce the growth of hair on the face. In the future, therefore, women will be bald and will wear long moustaches and patriarchal beards.
Just like John Knox! Wisdom from the land of Nietzsche: Professor Hans Friedenthal of Berlin University, 1914.

The great question . . . which I have not been able to answer, despite my thirty years of research into the feminine soul, is, 'What does a woman want?'
The answer is almost certainly not 'a penis': Sigmund Freud, 1920.

Girls jumping rope

In this play the child rehearses the part he wishes or she wishes to assume in adult life. The girl jumping rope acts out the to-and-fro movement of the man during sex intercourse. Her own body takes the part of the active man, while the swinging rope imitates her own body adjusting to the movement of man's. In this game, girl acts both the role of man and of

the woman. Thus the girls go through unconscious preparation for their future sexual function as women.
Not many people would have thought of that. Psychologist Marion Sonnenberg, 1953, quoted in The Journal of Irreproducable Results.

Biologically and temperamentally, women were made to be concerned first and foremost with child care, husband care, and home care.
The wisdom of age: Dr. Benjamin Spock in 1979.

Politics

Extend now to women suffrage and eligibility; give them the political right to vote and be voted for, render it feasible for them to enter the arena of political strife, and what remains of family union will soon be dissolved.
The Catholic World, *1869.*

The Queen is most anxious to enlist every one who can speak or write to join us in checking this mad, wicked folly of 'Women's Rights', with all its attendant horrors, on which her poor feeble sex is bent, forgetting every sense of womanly feeling and propriety.
Queen Victoria writes to Sir Theodore Martin, May 28th 1870.

Women's participation in political life . . . would involve the domestic calamity of a deserted home and the loss of the womanly qualities for which refined men adore women and marry them . . . Doctors tell us, too, that thousands of children would be harmed or killed before birth by the injurious effect of untimely political excitement on their mothers.
The aptly-named American critic Henry T. Finck writes in The Independent, *January 30th 1901.*

I see some rats have got in; let them squeal, it doesn't matter.
Protesting Suffragettes interrupt a speech by David Lloyd-George, c. 1910.

The 'homo' is the legitimate child of the 'suffragette'.
Two phobias in one: novelist and painter Percy Wyndham Lewis, The Art of Being Ruled, *1920.*

The judicial view

The woman barrister looks and is ridiculous; and has been so since Portia. Neither should the sex sit on juries; no woman will believe that a witness wearing the wrong hat can be giving the right evidence.
James Agate, Ego 6, *1944.*

All Berkshire women are very silly. I don't know why women in Berkshire are more silly than anywhere else.
Judge Claude Duveen, Reading County Court, July 1972.

Some modern views

There are two kinds of women – goddesses and doormats.
And they all have eyes on the same side of their faces: Pablo Picasso, 1930.

Women do not find it difficult nowadays to behave like men; but they often find it extremely difficult to behave like gentlemen.
Well, dammit, they would, wouldn't they? Novelist Compton MacKenzie, 1940.

You treat a car like a woman. If you relate it to a woman – because it is a very highly strung and nervous piece of equipment – you can have this love affair with it. You have got to be able to understand it and comprehend its feelings and habits. You have to coax it sometimes to get the best out of it, you have to correct it and treat it gently, and at times, maybe on a different circuit, you have to give it a really good thrashing, because that is the only way it understands.
At least he didn't mention trading it in for a newer model. Racing driver Jackie Stewart, 1969.

Why should a married woman want a mortgage in her own name? We'll have husbands doing the housework next.
Eric Nash, branch manager of the Magnet & Planet Building Society, 1976.

A society in which women are taught anything at all but the management of a family, the care of men and the creation of the future generation is a society which is on the way out.
In fact the only hope for it is . . . Scientology??!! L. Ron Hubbard, Questions For Our Time, *1980.*

Every decision a woman makes is right.
Let's hear it for Lucrezia Borgia and Margaret Thatcher, says Germaine Greer in a Danish TV interview of the early 1980s.

Women have smaller brains than men.
They're a bit behind the times in Iran – and proud of it! Ali Akhbar Hashemi Rafsanjani, Iran's 'moderate' President, July 1986.

(2) ON MEN

One realizes with horror that the race of men is almost extinct in Europe. Only Christ-like heroes and woman-worshipping Don Juans, and rabid equality-mongrels.
. . . And the odd gamekeeper. D. H. Lawrence, Sea and Sardinia, *1921.*

The male is a biological accident; the y (male) gene is an incomplete x (female) gene, that is, has an incomplete set of chromosomes. In other

words, the male is an incomplete female, a walking abortion, aborted at the gene stage.
Valerie Solanas, Manifesto of the Society for Cutting Up Men, *1967.*

Every man is a rapist.
Andrea Dworkin, c. 1976 and often since.

The ethics of male sexuality are essentially rapist. The idea of the male sex is like the idea of an Aryan race . . . It is a political entity that flourishes only through acts of force and sexual terrorism.
John Stollenberg, Refusing to Be a Man.

Men are dangerous around small children, and should be kept as far away from them as possible.
Germaine Greer in The Independent, *1989.*

The things men do, one way or another . . .

It is the embodiment of the White-Male-With-Property Model.
A Task Force of the New York State Board of Education finds fault with the United States Constitution in 1989.

The nuclear family is the cornerstone of women's oppression. It enforces heterosexuality and imposes the prevailing masculine and feminine character structures on the next generation.
Professor Allison Jaggar, Chairperson of the Committee on the Status of Women in Philosophy of the American Philosophical Association, quoted by John Taylor in 'Are You Politically Correct?', New York, January 21st 1991.

It serves to perpetuate male clubbishness and to exclude women from the club.
In Body Politics, *1977, Nancy Henley doesn't approve of the handshake.*

The message is that women are incapable. The detachment of the acts from the concrete realities of what women need and do not need is a vehicle for the message that women's actual needs and interests are unimportant or irrelevant. . . . The message of the false helpfulness of male gallantry is female dependence, the invisibility or insignificance of women, and contempt for women.
Marilyn Frye, Oppression, *1988, doesn't like men holding doors open for her.*

Cricket legitimises the demarcation by men of yet another time and space where they can be free of women and united with other men.
Joan Smith, New Statesman, *c. 1980.*

Women must refuse to collaborate in their victimization by silence, and we cannot tolerate images of ourselves being bound and tortured for men's profit and sexual gratification.
Nikki Craft objects to . . . bathing suit tops: New York Times *(no date found).*

Mind was male . . . Nature was female, and knowledge was created as an act of aggression – a passive nature had to be interrogated, unclothed, penetrated, and compelled by man to reveal her secrets.
The findings of a New Jersey task force charged with finding ways to eliminate sex bias in Science teaching; quoted by John Taylor in 'Are You Politically Correct?', New York, January 21st 1991.

Coitus is punishment, I say. I am a feminist, not the fun kind. Coitus is the punishment for cowardice, for the fear of being alone.
Andrea Dworkin: Ice and Fire, *1986.*

All heterosexual intercourse is rape, even if women consent to it.
Andrea Dworkin, c. 1976 and often since.

Of the silent comedians, Laurel and Hardy are perhaps the most threatening to women . . . They are an aesthetic offence, with their disaster-prone bodies and their exclusive relationship that not only shuts out women but questions their very necessity. They constitute a two-man wrecking team of female – that is civilised and bourgeois – society.
Molly Haskins, From Reverence to Rape, *1987.*

Marriage is legalised prostitution. It's an insult and women shouldn't touch it.
BBC 'Women's Hour' presenter Jenni Murray allies herself with HRH Prince Philip in The Independent, *June 20th 1992.*

I am grateful to *The Official Politically Correct Handbook* (Henry Beard & Christopher Cerf, Grafton, 1992) and *The Book of Wimmin* (Compiled by Two Men, Private Eye/André Deutsch 1986) for many of the above quotations.

Possibly the most fatuous statement of all time

I think God was making a feminist and political statement when he made man and woman.
The Dean of the Cathedral of St John the Divine, New York, on the installation of a statue depicting a crucified woman.

Scientific Proof and Materia Medica

'When a distinguished but elderly scientist states that something is possible, he is almost certainly right. When he states that something is impossible, he is almost certainly wrong.'

Arthur C. Clarke

Contrary to popular belief – for which many scientists are themselves partly to blame – scientists are as susceptible as the rest of us to the weakness of pride, fear, envy, greed and sheer silliness, and every bit as likely as the average politician or music critic to get things wildly wrong. If they differ from the rest of us it is, perhaps, only in the strength and seeming irrefutability of their mistaken convictions. Anecdotal evidence would certainly seem to indicate that the average research establishment contains every bit as much screeching, unreasoning, back-stabbing bitchery as the average green room or office canteen.

There are, as every good scientist knows, no such things as 'wrong theories'; instead there are theories which, in course of time and as the result of the accumulation of experimentally or mathematically verifiable evidence, are superseded by 'better' theories: theories which explain observable phenomena more satisfactorily and more elegantly, and which are capable of a more nearly universal application. The world of Science, grounded as it is in its unquestioning acceptance of the sacred and overriding need for impersonal, dispassionate and disinterestedly rational analysis, then accepts these better theories and proceeds to apply and extend them in its ceaseless and unselfish quest for the Grail of the ultimate explanation . . .

And if you still believe that after reading this section, then presumably you'll have no trouble believing that 8 out of 10 Schroedinger's cats prefer bozon-flavoured Whiskas.

The Earth: knowing our place

It is once for all clear that the earth is in the middle of the world and all weights move towards it.

Ptolemy, 2nd century AD.

People give ear to an upstart astrologer who strove to show that the earth revolves, not the heavens or the firmament, the sun and the moon. Whoever wishes to appear clever must devise some new system, which of all systems is of course the very best. This fool wishes to reverse the entire science of astronomy.

Putting Copernicus in his place: Martin Luther in 1543.

According to poll surveys conducted in the 1980s, approximately 40% of British people still prefer Luther's version.

Animals, which move, have limbs and muscles; the earth has no limbs and muscles, hence it does not move.

Scipio Chiaramonti, Professor of Philosophy and Mathematics at the University of Pisa, proves the Earth is a cauliflower in 1633.

I, Galileo, being in my seventieth year, being a prisoner on my knees, and before your Eminences, having before my eyes the Holy Gospel, which I touch with my hands, abjure, curse and detest the error and the heresy of the movement of the earth.
Galileo Galilei confesses his way out of prison in 1634.

***Eppur si muove* (‘Yet it does move’)**
His muttered codicil to the above: probably apocryphal.
In 1994 – along with about 60% of the British population – the Vatican conceded that Galileo was right after all.

The Earth: what, when and how

The world was created on 22nd October, 4004 BC at 6 o’clock in the evening.
And why not? A perfectly irrefutable theory at the time it was written: James Ussher, Archbishop of Armagh, Annals of the World, *1650.*

Heaven and earth, centre and circumference, were created together, in the same instant, and clouds full of water. . . . This work took place and Man was created by the Trinity on the twenty-third of October, 4004 BC, at nine o’clock in the morning.
The proof of a good theory is that it should be capable of experimental exposition: Dr John Lightfoot, Vice-Chancellor of Cambridge University, has reason (but no excuse, in the year that saw publication of The Origin of Species*) to tweak Archbishop Ussher’s data a little in 1859.*

Is there anyone anywhere so foolish as to think there are Antipodeans – men who stand with their feet opposite to ours, men with their legs in the air and their heads hanging down? Can there be a place on earth where things are upside down, where the trees grow downwards, and the rain, hail and snow fall upward? The mad idea that the earth is round is the cause of this imbecile legend.
Yet it appears that in the 3rd century AD there were such mad and foolish people: Constantine the Great’s tutor, Lactantius Firmianus, made it his job to rubbish them ‘once for all’ in De opificio dei, *AD 304.*

The ‘Doctrine of Uniformity’ in Geology, as held by many of the most eminent of British Geologists, assumes that the earth’s surface and upper crust have been nearly as they are at present in temperature, and other physical qualities, during millions and millions of years. But the heat which we know from observation, to be now conducted out of the earth yearly is so great that if this action had been going on with any approach to uniformity for 20,000 million years, the amount of heat lost out of the earth . . . would be more than enough to melt a mass of surface rock equal in bulk to the whole earth. No hypothesis . . . can justify the supposition

that the earth's upper crust has remained nearly as it is, while from the whole, or from any part of the earth, so great a quantity of heat has been lost.

William Thompson – afterwards Lord Kelvin – believed the earth to be no more than 100 million years old, a theory that bothered many geologists, who had good reason to believe it was a very great deal older. He answered them in The Doctrine of Uniformity in Geology briefly refuted, *published in the* Proceedings of the Royal Society of Edinburgh, *1866.*

So much the worse for geology as at present understood by its chief authorities, for, as you will presently see, physical considerations from various independent points of view render it utterly impossible that more than ten or fifteen millions of years can be granted.

Kelvin's colleague Peter Guthrie Tait divides his friend's estimate by ten and takes a swipe at Darwin and Lyell in his Lectures on Physical Science, *1876. Current estimates put the age of the Earth at roughly 4,250,000,000 years.*

Smashing the Plate Theory

Can we call Geology a science when there exists such difference of opinion as to make it possible for such a theory as this to run wild? . . . We must either modify radically most of the present rules of the geological game or else pass the hypothesis by. If we are to believe Wegener's hypothesis we must forget everything which has been learned in the last 70 years and start all over again.

Unthinkable! Geologist R. T. Chamberlin rubbishes the Continental Drift Theory at a symposium organised by the American Association of Petroleum Geologists in 1926; its proceedings were edited and published two years later.

My principal objection to the Wegener hypothesis rests on the author's methods. This, in my opinion, is not scientific, but takes the familiar course of an initial idea, a selective search through the literature for corroborative evidence, ignoring most of the facts that are opposed to the idea, and ending in a state of auto-intoxication in which the subjective idea comes to be considered as an objective fact.

Which is, in fact, rather what Wegener's opponents got up to . . . E. Berry at the 1926 symposium.

Many hypotheses of geotectonics have caused considerable damage to geotectonics, giving non-specialists the impression that this is a field in which the most superficially conceived fantasy reigns. The clearest example is Wegener's hypothesis of continental drift . . . fantastic and nothing to do with science.

Ideologically incorrect: Soviet Academician Vladimir Vladimirovich Beloussov finds the theory lacking in dialectical materialist rigour in 1954 . . .

Something will certainly remain after the theory of plate tectonics goes. Let us keep our minds open and look for alternatives. I am sure that in the near future we shall need them.

. . . and in 1979: Beloussov again.

Plate Tectonics – the application of Wegener's despised theory – is now universally accepted as the explanation for many otherwise inexplicable phenomena of geological formation, evolution, climate change, species distribution and extinction, and volcanic activity. Explanatory diagrams of wandering continental plates are published in the newspapers every time there is a major earthquake; earthquakes like the one that devastated Kobe in January 1995 are caused by their collision and friction.

Evolution and Natural Selection: the Devil's Doctrines

If the book is true, the labours of sober induction are in vain; religion is a lie; human law is a mass of folly, and a base injustice; morality is moonshine; our labours for the black people of Africa were works of madness; and man and woman are only better beasts.

Horribile dictu! Adam Sedgewick, Woodwardian Professor of Geology at the University of Cambridge, responds to Robert Chambers' pioneering book The Vestiges of Creation *in 1844. Chambers' theory – which can be crudely summarized as 'evolution minus natural selection' – was so outrageous that the book was published anonymously. Its hostile and horrified reception was one of the reasons Darwin delayed publication of his own* Origin of Species *for several years.*

This year . . . has not, indeed, been marked by any of those striking discoveries which at once revolutionize, so to speak, the department of science in which they occur.

Small earthquake in Chile . . . Thomas Bell, President of the Linnaean Society, sums up 1858 – the year Darwin's and Wallace's background papers for The Origin of Species *were read to the Society.*

I have read your book with more pain than pleasure. Parts of it I admired greatly, parts I laughed at until my sides were almost sore; other parts I read with absolute sorrow, because I think them utterly false and grievously mischievous. You have deserted . . . the true method of induction . . .

Sedgewick again: the Woodwardian professor writes to Darwin after publication of On the Origin of Species by Means of Natural Selection*, 1859.*

Archaeological remains show no trace of any emergence from barbarism on the part of man, indeed man has gained nothing of moment from the dawn of history. Man's earliest state was his best.

Geologist Sir J. W. Dawson, Origin of the World*, 1877.*

I trust to outlive this mania.
Louis Agassiz, Professor of Geology and Zoology, Harvard University from 1847 to 1873, with a contemporaneous private reaction to 'Darwinism' in a letter published posthumously in 1893.

It shall be unlawful for any teacher in any of the universities, normals and all other public schools of the state which are supported in whole or in part by the public school funds of the state, to teach any theory that denies the story of the divine creation of man as taught in the Bible, and to teach instead that man has descended from a lower state of animals.
Setting up a really good part for Spencer Tracey, the State of Tennessee Statute of 1925 that led to the (in)famous 'Monkey Trial'. It was repealed in 1967.

In the 1980s, the Reagan-Bush administrations worked to ensure that all public schools in the USA taught 'Creation Science' [sic] as well as 'Evolutionism', for the sake of 'balance'.

In every text-book on zoology, the evidence in favour of evolution is set forth and nothing against it . . . I maintain that if the evidence were more fairly put you would not get half these young men to accept evolution. I was taught it. It took me more than twenty years of work before I discovered it was wrong.
What a waste! Douglas Dewar FRZ, ornithologist, 1944.

The Party, the Government and J. V. Stalin personally, have taken an unflagging interest in the further development of the Michurin teaching.
Trofim D. Lysenko: Report to the Lenin Academy of Agricultural Sciences, *1948. Ivan Michurin – and, more notoriously, Lysenko himself – were followers of Lamarck's doctrine of inheritance of acquired characteristics – or (as David Langford puts it in* Facts and Fallacies*) the belief that 'by pulling the wings off flies and subsequently mating them you would eventually breed wingless flies'. This was an attractive idea for Stalin & Co., since it made plausible the creation of* Homo Sovieticus, *planned and bred along strict Party lines. Lysenko's teachings were not formally abandoned in the USSR until 1964.*

Our next illustration (Fig. 11) is of a very celebrated person, the Piltdown Man, *Eoanthropus Dawsoni*, or the Man of the Dawn, so named after his finder, Mr Charles Dawson. We should be very proud of *Eoanthropus*, because he is the first known Englishman. . . . Since 1912 scientific men all over the world have written articles, indulged in friendly controversy, and found out all kinds of things about the Piltdown Man.
. . . But it wasn't until 1953 that they discovered that 'the first Englishman' had been cobbled together out of bits of human and ape skull and was thus either a crude hoax or the remains of the very first football hooligan: a disillusioning experience for the generation of tots brought up on M. & C. H. B. Quennell's Everyday Life in the Old Stone Age *(1921).*

The Sun – and other temperate, habitable places

The sun . . . appears to be nothing else than a very eminent, large and lucid planet, evidently the first, or in strictness of speaking, the only primary one of our system . . . Its similarity to other globes of the solar system . . . leads us to suppose that it is most probably inhabited . . . by beings whose organs are adapted to the peculiar circumstances of that vast globe.
Basing his case on 'astronomical principles', William Herschel publishes a paper in Philosophical Transactions of the Royal Society *in 1795. He went further, describing it in 1801 as 'a most magnificent inhabitable globe', and in 1814 he concluded that the stars were 'so many opaque, habitable, planetary globes'. He was also the discoverer of Uranus and two of its satellites, and two satellites of Saturn, and he made a catalogue of double stars. But he did have this bee in his bonnet about the sun.*

Nothing can be more certain than that the stars have not changed their declinations or latitudes one degree in the last 71 and three-quarter years.
Captain Woodley RN publishes some potentially disastrous navigational advice in 1834.

Unidentified falling objects

The stone . . . is an ordinary one, struck and altered by lightning, and showing nothing unusual in analysis.
Antoine Lavoisier and the French Academy of Sciences fail to identify a meteorite in 1772, despite eyewitness accounts of its falling from the sky.

How sad it is that the entire municipality enters folk tales upon an official record, presenting them as something actually seen, while they cannot be explained by physics nor by anything reasonable.
Mass hallucination is Academician Claude Berthollet's explanation after reading an affidavit sworn by the Mayor of Barbotan and 300 of its citizens following a meteorite strike there in 1791.

At last, a meteorite shower on the town of L'Aigle was analysed by a competent astronomer and physicist, Jean Baptiste Biot, who described them correctly in 1803.

The Planets

Jupiter's moons are invisible to the naked eye and therefore can have no influence on the earth, and therefore would be useless, and therefore do not exist.
Francisco Sizzi, Professor of Astronomy, with an elegant application of the Robust Anthropic Principle ('If it's no use to us, what's the point in it?') in 1610.

The present inhabitation of Mars by a race superior to ours is very probable.
Camille Flammarian, founder of the French Astronomical Society, La planète Mars et ses conditions d'habitabilité, *1892.*

Irrigation, unscientifically conducted, would not give us such truly wonderful mathematical fitness . . . A mind of no mean order would seem to have presided over the system we see – a mind certainly of considerably more comprehensiveness than that which presides over our own public works.

Their trains run on time, and even their drains are better. . . . Percival Lowell, founder of the Lowell Observatory, bangs the drum for Martian canals in 1908. He did redeem himself somewhat by predicting the existence of Pluto, which was finally observed in 1930.

MARTIANS BUILD TWO IMMENSE CANALS IN TWO YEARS

Vast Engineering Works Accomplished in an Incredibly Short Time by Our Planetary Neighbors.

Headline, New York Times, *August 27th 1911, after Lowell's telescope observes two previously unseen bits of straightish line on the planet.*

The final proof of the whole cosmic ice theory will be obtained when the first landing on the ice-coated surface of the Moon takes place.

The Hörbiger Institute expects never to be proved wrong in 1953. Hans Hörbiger's Cosmic Ice Theory held that all the planets – except, for inscrutably anthropocentric reasons, the Earth – are covered in layers of ice several miles thick, chunks of which break off causing hailstorms, sunspots, and lousy reception on Medium Wave. It was, for a time, official Nazi science policy.

Nuclear Physics: fraudulent and useless.

It seems almost unnecessary now to republish a book, the lesson of which is that objective force and matter have nothing whatever to do with science, and that atom and ether are merely intellectual concepts solely useful for the purpose of describing our perceptual routine.

The whole scientific world knows that atoms don't really exist, according to professor Karl Pearson in his Grammar of Science, *1892.*

X-rays will prove to be a hoax.

A turn-of-the-century prediction from Lord Kelvin, President of the Royal Society from 1890–95.

On thermodynamical grounds which I can hardly summarize shortly, I do not much believe in the commercial possibilities of induced radio-activity.

Chemist J. B. S. Haldane doesn't want to go into fiddly details: he just knows. 1923.

There is no likelihood man can ever tap the power of the atom. The glib supposition of utilizing atomic energy when our coal has run out is a completely unscientific Utopian dream, a childish bug-a-boo. Nature has

introduced a few foolproof devices into the great majority of elements that constitute the bulk of the world, and they have no energy to give up in the process of disintegration.
Atoms? Nothing in 'em, according to Nobel Prize-winning physicist Dr Robert Millikan in 1923.

There is by no means the same certainty today as a decade ago that the atoms of an element contain hidden sources of energy.
Sir Ernest Rutherford doubts the value of his work shortly before splitting the atom and locating the hidden sources of energy in 1923 . . .

The energy produced by the breaking down of the atom is a very poor kind of thing. Anyone who looks for a source of power in the transformation of the atom is talking moonshine.
Having located their energy sources, Sir Ernest Rutherford still doesn't think much of them in 1936.

The slow neutron is extraordinarily efficient in causing transmutations with a large evolution of energy, but the neutron itself can only be produced by very inefficient processes, so that there appears to be no chance of gaining more energy from the reaction than has to be supplied.
In his last lecture before his death, Sir Ernest Rutherford still considers nuclear energy to be a pretty feeble thing: 1937.

That is how the atom is split, but what does it mean? To us who think in terms of practical use, it means – nothing!
1932: Lord Ritchie Calder, educationist and science populariser.

There is not the slightest indication that energy will ever be obtainable. It would mean that the atom would have to be shattered at will.
Well, quite. Dr Albert Einstein wraps it up in 1932.
And talking of Einstein brings us to . . .

Relativity: a discredited fringe theory

I can accept the theory of relativity as little as I can accept the existence of atoms and other such dogma.
Killing two birds with one Regrettable stone: Professor Ernst Mach (of Mach Number fame) in 1913.

Worthless and misleading.
US Government Observatory Director Professor T. J. J. See sums up Einstein's theories for the benefit of the California Academy of Sciences, November 8th 1924.

We certainly cannot consider Einstein as one who shines as a scientific discoverer in the domain of Physics, but rather as one who in a fuddled

sort of way is trying to find some meaning for mathematical formulas in which he himself does not believe too strongly, but which he is hoping against hope somehow to establish.
Whereas Jeremiah J. Callahan, President of Duquesne University, is nowadays famous for . . . er . . . writing Euclid or Einstein *in 1931, of course!*

The so-called theories of Einstein are merely the ravings of a mind polluted with liberal, democratic nonsense which is utterly unacceptable to German men of science.
Jawohl! They preferred Hörbiger's Cosmic Ice Theory. Dr Walter Gross – Hitler's favourite 'Nordic Scientist' – puts the inferior racial specimen in his place.

The theory of a relativistic universe is the hostile work of the agents of Fascism. It is the revolting propaganda of a moribund, counter-revolutionary ideology.
. . . Whereas the Universe, as every good citizen knows, conforms to the Laws of Socialist Necessity. The Soviet Astronomical Journal *falls into place.*

Einstein's theory is unnecessary.
. . . But useful to Harold Aspden, presumably, or he wouldn't have been able to publish Physics Without Einstein *in 1969.*

Molecular biology

However fascinating it may be as a scholarly achievement, there is virtually nothing that has come from molecular biology that can be of any value to human living in the conventional sense of what is good, and quite tremendous possibilities of evil.
Genetic engineering of pest- and disease-resistant crops, the identification of the genes responsible for inherited diseases, DNA retrieval from fossil tissue, giant strides in the investigation of viral diseases. . . valueless? Nobel Prize-winning virologist Sir Frank MacFarlane Burnet, 1968.

A quantum hobble

Your paper . . . is too speculative and involves no new physics.
1969: the Physical Review *rejects a paper by Leo Esaki and Raphael Tsu on 'superconducting superlattices' – the little widgets that make possible such things as personal computers, compact discs, satellite television . . . .*

Ornithology

The Swallow does not migrate in winter, but hibernates each autumn in ponds and streams.
Daines Barrington, 1727–1800. His basic theories on birdsong, however, remain valid more than two centuries after their publication in 1773.

That birds can be taught to talk better than other animals is explained by the fact that their mouths are Nordic in structure.
What, even blackbirds? Professor Hermann Gauch outlines Nazi Science in The New Foundation for Research into Social Race Problems, *1933.*

Mathematics: scientifically useless.

Whatever knowledge is obtainable by means of the sense of Sight, we may hope to attain with regard to the stars, whether we at present see the method or not; and whatever knowledge requires the aid of other senses, we must at once exclude from our expectations. The mathematical terminology created by Fournier may tempt us to hope that we may in time ascertain the mean temperature of heavenly bodies; but I regard this order of facts as for ever excluded from our recognition. . . .

Every attempt to refer chemical questions to mathematical doctrines must be considered, now and always, profoundly irrational, as being contrary to the nature of the phenomena and contrary to the spirit of chemistry. If the employment of mathematical analysis should ever become so preponderant in chemistry (an aberration which is happily almost impossible) it would occasion vast and rapid retrogradation, by substituting vague conceptions for positive ideas, and an easy algebraic verbiage for a laborious investigation of facts.
So there! August Comte – the scientist who coined the word 'scientist' and the world's first Sociologist – puts algebraic verbiage firmly in its unscientific place, 1835–38.

Laboratory teaching: a worthless pastime.

We assert that if the resistance of the air be withdrawn a sovereign and a feather will fall through equal spaces in equal times. Very great credit is due to the person who first imagined the well-known experiment to illustrate this; but it is not obvious what is the special benefit now gained by seeing a lecturer repeat the process. It may be said that a boy takes more interest in the matter by seeing for himself, or by performing for himself, that is, by working the handle of the air-pump; this we admit, while we continue to doubt the educational value of the transaction. The boy would also probably take more interest in football than in a Latin grammar; but the measure of his interest is not identical with that of the importance of the subjects.

It may be said that the fact makes a stronger impression on the boy through the medium of his sight, that he believes it the more confidently. I say that this ought not to be the case. If he does not believe the statements of his tutor – probably a clergyman of mature knowledge, recognized ability and blameless character – his suspicion is irrational, and manifests a want of the power of appreciating evidence, a want fatal to his success

in that branch of science which he is supposed to be cultivating.
Listen to the Voice of Authority, my boy! Isaac Todhunter argues unsuccessfully against the building of the Cavendish Laboratory for Experimental Physics at Cambridge, 1873.

Zoology

BARNACLE, a Soland Goose; a Fowl in the Bass, an Island on the Coasts of *Scotland*, supposed by some to grow on the Trees, or by others, to be bred out of rotten Planks of Ships, *&c.*
BASILISK, a Serpent call'd a *Cockatrice*.
BAT, a small Bird resembling a Mouse.
COCKATRICE, a Serpent call'd a *Basilisk*.
DRAGON, a sort of Serpent.
INSECT, any small Living Creature that creeps or flies, either not divided into Limbs and Joints as other Creatures; but encompas'd with Rings or Divisions capable of being parted without utterly destroying Life, as Worms, *&c.*, or else divided between Head and Body, as Flies, Pismires, Bees, *&c.*
MOTH, a Fly which eats Clothes.
PHOENIX, a Bird in *Arabia*, about the bigness of an Eagle, which is reported to live 600 Years, and that there is but one of them in the World at a Time, and that she, having lived that Time, builds her a Nest of combustible Spices, which being set on Fire by the Sun, she fans it with her Wings, and burns her self in it, and that a Worm rises out of her Ashes, which comes to be a new Phoenix.
RAT, an Animal which infests Houses, *&c.*
REPTILE, a creeping Thing, any thing that crawls upon its Belly.
UNICORN, a Beast said to be as big as a Horse, having one white Horn in the middle of its Forehead, about five handfuls long, found in the Province of *Agoas* in the Kingdom of *Damotes* in *Ethiopia*, said to be a timerous Beast, residing in the Woods, yet sometimes ventures into the Plains.
WHALE, the greatest of Fishes.
WORM, a creeping Insect.
N. Bailey: A Universal Etymological English Dictionary, *1724. Its definition of 'Mermaid' carried the warning, 'if we may credit Poets and Painters.'*

Bees are generated from decomposed veal.
St Isidore of Seville, 7th century.

So when the Oxe corrupteth into Bees, or the Horse into Hornets, they come not forth in the image of their originals. So the corrupt and excrementous humours in man are corrupted into Lice. . . .
A diamond, which is the hardest of stones, not yielding unto steel, emery or any other thing, is yet made soft by the blood of a goat.
Sir Thomas Browne, Pseudodoxia Epidemica, *1646.*

When it is pursued, knowing this to be on account of the virtues of its testicles for medicinal uses, not being able to flee any further it stops and in order to be at peace with its pursuers bites off its testicles with its sharp teeth and leaves them to its enemies.
Leonardo da Vinci, 1452–1519, on a little-known habit of the beaver.

Eels are not produced from sexual intercourse . . . they originated in what are called the entrails of the earth.
But could Aristotle (4th century BC) *explain why one never sees a dead donkey?*

We have experienced also that the hairs of a horse's mane laid in the waters became serpents, and our friends have tried the same. No man denies but that serpents are easily engendered of man's flesh, especially of his marrow.
Giambattista Della Porta, Natural Magic, *early 17th century.*

Floating islands are invariably Krakens.
Bishop Erik Pontoppidan, A Natural History of Norway, *1752–54.*

There is little hope of discovering new species of large quadrupeds.
Georges Cuvier, 'the father of Paleontology', 1812.

Science, schmience.

I am tired of this sort of thing called science. We have spent millions in that sort of thing for the last few years, and it is time it should be stopped.
Senator Simon Cameron of Pennsylvania tries to cut off funding for the Smithsonian Institution in 1861.

MEDICAL SCIENCE

Knowing What's Best For You: A Chronology of Bedside Nonsense

You know, Tolstoy, like myself, wasn't taken in by superstitions like science and medicine.

George Bernard Shaw

Post hoc, ergo . . .

A young man does not take the gout until he indulges in coition.
Hippocrates, 'the Father of Medicine', c. 460–377BC.
See also: **The Perils of Sex** *(p. 178).*

Music hath charms

The sound of the flute will cure epilepsy, and a sciatic gout.
Theophrastus, c. 370–285 BC.

A Satanist writes. . ..

All diseases of Christians are to be ascribed to demons.
St Augustine, 354–430.

Jumbo cure

If the excrement of an elephant should be smeared on skin in which lice appear and left until it dries upon the skin, the lice will not remain on it but will depart immediately. . . . If an ounce of elephant bone is drunk with ten ounces of wild mountain mint from something which a leper first touched, it does the most for a headache.
The pioneer New Age healer St Albertus Magnus, c. 1250.

Hygiene in a cold climate

Damp baths are to be eschewed except by the rich . . . And this in summer only, for in winter I would advise them to abstain from ordinary baths entirely.
Bruges physician Francis Raspard, A Great and Perpetual Almanack, *1551.*

Killing with kindness

If the wound is large, the weapon with which the patient has been wounded should be anointed daily; otherwise, every two to three days. The weapon should be kept in pure linen and in a warm place but not too hot, nor squalid, lest the patient should suffer harm.
And the patient . . .? Daniel Beckher, Medicus Microcosmus, *1622.*

Aaaargh!

For epilepsy in adults I recommend spirit of human brain or a powder, to be compounded only in May, June and July, from the livers of live green frogs.
. . . Or would you rather stick with the flute? Professor Johann Hartmann, University of Marburg, Praxis chymiatrica, *1633.*

Wonder drug (1)

Among the remedies which it has pleased Almighty God to give to man to relieve his sufferings, none is so universal and so efficacious as opium.
Thomas Sydenham perfects tincture of opium in 1670.

Tastes nasty, too!

It is good not only in fevers, diseases of the lungs, cancer, scrofula, throat diseases, apoplexies, chronic diseases of all kinds, but also as a general drink for infants.
Bishop Berkely has some wonderful Further Thoughts on Tar-Water, *1752.*

Nature's way

One half of the children born die before their eighth year. This is Nature's law; why try to contradict it?

Jean-Jacques Rousseau, a fan of the Noble (and short-lived) Savage, in his child-rearing manual Emile, ou l'education, *1762.*

Sir, I'm talking nonsense.

He said, 'Macaulay, who writes the account of St Kilda, set out with a prejudice against prejudices, and wanted to be a smart modern thinker; and yet he affirms for a truth, that when a ship arrives there, all the inhabitants are seized with a cold. . . .

'The late Reverend Mr Christian, of Docking – after ruminating a little, "The cause," (says he) "is a natural one. The situation of St Kilda renders a North-West Wind indispensably necessary before a stranger can land. The wind, not the stranger, causes an epidemic cold."'

Dr Samuel Johnson – a man renowned for his common sense – spring 1768.

This may well be true

If a body could just find out the exact proper proportion and quantity that ought to be drunk every day, and keep to that, I verily trow that he might live forever . . . and that doctors and kirkyards would go out of fashion.

James Hogg seeks the perfect dose for malt whisky, c. 1820. The search goes on . . . thank goodness.

Sadists' charter

The abolishment of pain in surgery is a chimera. It is absurd to go on seeking it. Knife and pain are two words in surgery that must live forever in the consciousness of the patient. To this compulsory combination we shall have to adjust ourselves.

You've got to be cruel to be . . . cruel. Dr Alfred Velpeau, surgeon and professor at the Paris Faculty of Medicine, 1839.

Thus far, and no farther

There cannot always be fresh fields of conquest by the knife; there must be portions of the human frame that will ever remain sacred from its intrusions, at least in the surgeon's hands. That we have already, if not quite, reached these final limits, there can be little question. The abdomen, the chest, and the brain will be forever shut from the intrusion of the wise and humane surgeon.

Sir John Eric Erichsen, later to become the Royal Surgeon, 1837.

Germs? Pah!

Pasteur's theory of germs is a ridiculous fiction. How do you think that these germs in the air can be numerous enough to develop into all these

organic infusions? If that were true, they would be numerous enough to form a thick fog, as dense as iron.
Physiologist Professor Pierre Pochet, 1872.

The simplest way to kill most microbes is to throw them into an open street or river and let the sun shine on them, which explains that when great cities have recklessly thrown all their sewage into the open river the water has sometimes been cleaner twenty miles below the city than thirty miles above it. . . . In the first frenzy of microbe killing, surgical instruments were dipped in carbolic oil. Microbes are so fond of carbolic oil that they swarm in it.
George Bernard Shaw, preface to The Doctor's Dilemma, *1911.*

A genuine kiss generates so much heat it destroys germs.
Mind, it has to be genuine! Dr S. L. Katzoff of the San Franciso Institute of Human Relations [sic], April 1940.

Wonder drug (2)

Exhilaration and lasting euphoria, which in no way differs from the euphoria of the healthy person . . . You perceive an increase in self-control and possess more vitality and capacity for work. In other words, you are simply more normal, and it is soon hard to believe that you are under the influence of any drug.
Sigmund Freud notes the beneficial effect of cocaine in Über Coca, *1884.*

Cocaine can take the place of food, make the coward brave, the silent eloquent, free the victims of alcohol and opium habit from their bondage, and, as an anaesthetic, render the sufferer insensitive to pain.
Magazine advertisement, 1885.

Vaccines? Pshaw!

If we are afflicted with smallpox, it is because we had a carnival last winter, feasting the flesh, which has offended the Lord.
Anonymous Roman Catholic priest, Montreal, 1885. Most Roman Catholics regarded vaccination as contrary to the Will of God.

Cowpox . . . fails to exercise any specific power against Small Pox.
Edgar Crookshank, Professor of Comparative Pathology and Bacteriology at King's College London: History and Pathology of Vaccination, *1889.*

It was fancifully represented as an amulet or charm against smallpox, by the idle gossip of incredulous persons who listened only to the jingle of names.
Medical historian Charles Creighton, Jenner and Vaccination, *1889.*

The medical broadcasters and writers of leading articles still keep repeating like parrots that vaccination abolished smallpox, though vaccinia is now killing more children than smallpox.
George Bernard Shaw, Everybody's Political What's What, *1944.*
Thanks ultimately to Jenner and his cowpox vaccine, the entire planetary population of the smallpox virus is now confined to one laboratory. It is otherwise extinct.

Wonder drug (3)

It possesses many advantages over morphine . . . It is not hypnotic and there is no danger of acquiring the habit.
Oh good! James R. L. Daly analyses heroin in the Boston Medical and Surgical Journal, *1900.*

Smoke your way to health

The power of tobacco to sustain the system, to keep up nutrition, to maintain and increase the weight, to brace against severe exertion, and to replace ordinary food, is a matter of daily and hourly demonstration.
George Black, The Doctor at Home, *1898.*

If excessive smoking actually plays a rôle in the production of lung cancer, it seems to be a minor one.
Dr W. C. Heuper of the US National Cancer Institute, April 1954.

What do these statements have in common?
Scrofula is cured by the laying on of royal hands;
A good treatment for tuberculosis is horseback riding;
Gout is manifestly an affliction of the nervous system.
Answer:
They were all believed correct by leading members of the medical profession at one time, but were later proved to be false. To this list may be added the statement that cigarette smoking causes lung cancer.
California Medicine, *June 1963.*

For the majority of people, smoking has a beneficial effect.
Los Angeles surgeon Dr Ian MacDonald, Newsweek, *November 18th 1963.*
Well. . . .

Zen and the art of cancer cure

No illness is more simple to cure than cancer (this also applies to mental diseases and heart trouble) through a return to the most elementary natural eating and drinking: Diet No. 7.
It would be nice to think there was a special place in hell for people like George Ohsawa, whose Zen Macrobiotics *(1965) prescribed a diet consisting in its entirety of whole grain cereal and minimal liquids for these ailments.*

Some mistake, surely?

No woman should be kept on the Pill for 20 years until, in fact, a sufficient number have been kept on the Pill for 20 years.

Sir Alan Sterling Parks, 1970.

Premature congratulation

Malaria has been licked.

World Health Organisation press release on a May morning in 1973. In the afternoon the WHO Deputy General, Dr Tom Lambo, was admitted to hospital suffering from . . . malaria.

Happy talk

I have never known a drug's effect to be so global – to extend social popularity, business acumen, self-image, energy, flexibility, sexual appeal . . . [or] . . . so free of unwelcome side-effects . . . The capacity of modern medication to allow a person to experience, on a stable basis, the feelings of someone with a different temperament and history is among the most extraordinary accomplishments of modern science.

More than half a century after Aldous Huxley imagined 'soma', Dr Peter D. Kramer makes large claims for Prozac – the drug that makes you 'better than well' – in Listening to Prozac, *Fourth Estate, 1994. The 'transforming' effect of the antidepressant has been observed in, at most, 10% of users, while 15% have reported such unwelcome side-effects as nervousness, anxiety, insomnia, nausea, dizziness, asthenia, headache and skin rashes.*

THE PERILS OF SEX:

All You Didn't Want to Know About it But Were Told Anyway

(1) THE NUTS AND BOLTS OF IT

Erection is chiefly caused by scuraum, eringoes[1], cresses, crymon, parsnips, artichokes, turnips, asparagus, candied ginger, acorns bruised to powder and drank in muscatel, scallion, sea shell fish, etc.

[1] = candied roots of sea-holly. *'Scuraum' and 'crymon' do not appear in* The Shorter Oxford English Dictionary.

Aristotle: The Masterpiece, *4th century BC.*

And if, in the act of copulation, the woman earnestly look on the man, and fix her mind on him, the child will resemble its father. Nay, if a woman, even in unlawful copulation, fix her mind upon her husband, the child will resemble him even if he did not beget it.

Aristotle: Ibid. *He appears to have had little first-hand experience of real life.*

The act of coition being over, let the woman repose herself upon her right side, with her head lying low and her body declining, that by sleeping in that posture, the cani, on the right side of the matrix, may prove the place of conception; for therein is the greatest generative heat, which is the chief procuring cause of male children, and rarely fails the expectations of those that experience it.
Aristotle: Ibid. *Obviously it was the woman's fault if it turned out to be a girl.*

If it is a male, the right breast swells first, the right eye is brighter than the left, the face is high-coloured, because the colour is such as the blood is, and as the male is conceived of the purer blood and of more perfect seed than the female.
Ah, the wisdom of the Greeks! Aristotle, Ibid.

Wood pigeons check and blunt the manly powers; let him not eat the bird who wishes to be amorous.
Martial: Epigrams, *c. AD 90.*

Let no-one say that because we have these parts, that the female body is shaped this way and the male that way, the one to receive, the other to give seed, sexual intercourse is allowed by God. For if this arrangement were allowed by God, to whom we seek to attain, He would not have pronounced the eunuch blessed (Matthew 19:12).
Artificial insemination advocated by the Gnostic theologian Julius Cassianus in the 2nd century AD.

The woman ought, in the moment during coitus when the man ejaculates his sperm, to hold her breath, draw her body back a little so that the semen cannot penetrate to the Os Uteri, then immediately get up and sit down with bent knees and, in this position, provoke sneezes.
A thousand years before Durex, the Gynaecology *of Soranus recommends a method of contraception, AD 138.*

If they wish to have a male child let the man take the womb and vulva of a hare and have it dried and pulverised; blend it with wine and let him drink it. Let the woman do the same with the testicles of a hare and let her be with her husband at the end of her menstrual period and she will conceive a male.
Alternatively, have daughters: Trotula, Professor of Medicine at the University of Salerno, The Diseases of Women, *c. 1059.*

Semen descends principally from the liver.
Vincent of Beauvais, Speculum Naturalae, *1244–54.*

A great portion of semen cometh from the brain.
Ambroise Paré, De hominis generatione, *1573.*

I saw in the human sperm, two naked thighs, the legs, the breast, both arms, etc. . . . the skin being pulled up somewhat higher over the head like a cap.
The 17th-century Dutch naturalist Stephen Hamm observes a homunculus in his microscope.

Everything explained in one volume

Neglect or crossness deadens a wife's love, and thereby *shrivels her mammaries.*
You have been warned – by Professor Oswald Squire Fowler, in Sexual Science, *1870.*

Twins and triplets undoubtedly originate in second and third copulations, immediately following the first, each drawing and then impregnating an egg. The fact that twins are born as soon as possible after each other supports this view.
A parent of twins? Professor Fowler knows what you've been up to!

He believes that in coition the sperm is injected from one testicle only, the right one producing a boy, the left one a girl. If a boy is to be generated, Sixt says, the husband must lie to the right of his wife and put the right knee over first, thus producing tension, which draws up the right testicle into place. 'If,' Sixt states, 'the left testicle should somehow be drawn up towards the abdomen, it may be pushed down quite easily, during coition, and the right one pushed up to be sure of attaining the desired end.'
Ouch! Professor Fowler quotes a German authority on testicular gender-preference.

Do a pregnant mother's experiences affect the offspring? Indeed they do. The eminent Dr Napheys reports the case of a pregnant lady who saw some grapes, longed intently for them, and constantly thought of them. During her period of gestation she was attacked and much alarmed by a turkey-cock. In due time she gave birth to a child having a large cluster of globular tumours growing from the tongue and exactly resembling our common grapes. And on the child's chest there grew a red excrescence exactly resembling a turkey's wattles.
Oh well, that proves it then, obviously. Sexual Science *was a best-seller of its day.*

Sex ends at 40

After the 'change of life' with women, sexual congress while permissible, should be infrequent, no less for her sake than that of the husband, whose

advancing years should warn him of the medical maxim: 'Each time a man delivers himself to this indulgence, he casts a shovelful of earth upon his coffin.'

Naught for Dr Comfort's comfort – but it's not a bad way to go. Nicholas Francis Cooke, writing as 'A Physician', Satan in Society, *1876.*

You have been warned

Every man who has sexual relations with two women at the same time risks syphilis, even if the two women are faithful to him, for all libertine behaviour spontaneously incites this disease.

Alexandre Weill: The Laws and Mysteries of Love, *1891.*

Fun is for men

If she is normally developed mentally, and well-bred, her sexual desire is small. If this were not so, the whole world would become a brothel and marriage and family impossible.

Nice girls don't have clitorises, according to Professor Joseph Richardson MD and seventeen others in Health and Longevity, *1909.*

A strenuous cure

White sugar is the curse of civilisation – it causes fatigue and sexual apathy between husband and wife. My recipe against sexual fatigue is to take honey in large quantities; two Gev-E-Tabs, 10 vitamin E pills, four wheatgerm oil tablets, four vitamin A pills, four bonemeal tablets, six liver-plus tablets, two dessertspoonfuls of Bio-Strath Elixir, twice a day.

On second thoughts, how about separate beds and a nice book? Dame Barbara Cartland's daunting prescription for sexual regularity in marriage, 1970s.

(2) THE CURSE OF EVE

Among the whole range of animated beings, the human female is the only one that has monthly discharge . . . On the approach of a woman in this state, milk will become sour, seeds which are touched by her become sterile, grafts wither away, garden plants are parched up, and the fruit will fall from the tree beneath which she sits.

And as for P.M.T. . . . !! Pliny the Elder, Natural History, *c. AD 70. Women would, however, seem to be quite useful when it comes to harvesting apples.*

On contact with this gore, crops do not germinate, wine goes sour, grasses die, trees lose their fruit, iron is corrupted by rust, copper is blackened. Should dogs eat any of it, they go mad. Even bituminous glue, which is dissolved neither by iron nor by waters, polluted by this gore, falls apart by itself.

. . . Or so they say. St Isidore of Seville makes a trenchant case against women priests in Etymologies, Book XI: Man and His Parts, *c. 610.*

The more remote any individual state or society was placed from moral and political habits, and the various causes which are capable of interfering with the actions of nature, the less frequent would be the occurrence of the menstrual phenomenon, and in some instances, it might be wholly unknown or nearly so.

The 'Back-to-Eve' cure: Essays on the Female Economy *by Dr John Power, physician at the Westminster Lying-In Institution, 1821.*

We cannot too emphatically urge the importance of regarding these monthly returns as periods of ill-health, as days when the ordinary occupations are to be suspended . . . Long walks, dancing, shopping, riding and parties should be avoided at this time of month invariably and under all circumstances.

Without wings: Dr W. C. Taylor, A Physician's Counsels to Women in Health and Disease, *1871.*

THE SOLITARY VICE

Onanism produces seminal weaknesses, impotence, dysury, tabes dorsalis, pulmonary consumption, dyspepsia, dimness of sight, vertigo, epilepsy, hypochondriasis, loss of memory, manalgia, fatuity, and death.

Hands up all those who aren't feeling very well . . . Dr Benjamin Rush, Professor of Physic and Dean of the Medical School at the University of Pennsylvania, Medical Inquiries, *1812.*

I personally know of a young man sent to the insane asylum as a result of continuous masturbation practices since childhood. At the request of his mother, a fine woman, showing no signs of a degenerative strain, the son was castrated . . . Two years later she reported that he was earning a salary of $1,800 a year and had married an unsexed girl.

Gosh, there's hope for us all – even unsexed girls! Dr Benethia Angelina Owens-Adair, professor at the University of Michigan, 1880. She wrote the State of Oregon's Human Sterilization Bill.

Victims of self-abuse have pallid, bloodless countenances, hollow sunken and half-ghastly eyes, with a red rim about the eyelids, and black-and-blue semicircles round the eyes. Red pimples on the face, with a black spot in their middles, are a sure sign of self-pollution in males, and irregularities in females. Stance is another sign: self-polluters often stand and sit in the posture assumed during masturbation. . . .

But are not the dangers exaggerated? That would be impossible! Masturbation poisons your body, breaks down your nerves, paralyses your whole system . . .

Does it really lead to insanity? This excess causes more insanity than anything else except intemperance. Hundreds have been brought to our

lunatic asylums by this single form of vice, and some must be tied down to prevent further destruction.

Coo-er! With problems like these, no wonder they did it! Orson Squire Fowler: Sexual Science *(surely one of the most ill-named books of all time) 1870.*

Masturbation is the producer of amblyopia, retinal haemorrhage, follicular inflammation, catarrh, trachoma, retinal irritation, neuro-retinitis in young ladies, agoraphobia and, in extreme cases, total blindness.

And what's more, he could prove it! Henry Power, Relation of Ophthalmic Diseases to certain normal and psychological conditions of the sexual organs, *Presidential Address to the Ophthalmological Society of the United Kingdom, 1888.*

When the habit is discovered, it must in young children be put a stop to by such means as tying the hands, strapping the knees together with a pad between them, or some mechanical plan.

How we were brought up before Dr Spock . . . Ada Ballin, editor of Baby Magazine, *in* From Cradle to School: A Book for Mothers, *1902. Nice of her to think of the pad, but we don't much like the sound of that 'mechanical plan'.*

It is called in our schools 'beastliness', and this is about the best name for it . . . should it become a habit it quickly destroys both health and spirits; he becomes feeble in body and mind, and often ends in a lunatic asylum.

So, of course, did a lot of unmarried mothers at that time: Robert (later Lord) Baden-Powell, Scouting for Boys, *1908.*

It is often said that masturbation is a cause of insanity, epilepsy and hysteria. I believe it to be more likely that the masturbation is the first manifestation of a developing insanity.

And that he alone was sane? Dr Charles Hunter-Dunne (no relation, presumably, to John Betjeman's arousing Tennis Girl), in Pediatrics: The Hygiene and Medical Treatment of Children, *1920.*

At the worst, confinement in poroplastic armour, as for spinal caries, or severe poliomyelitis, may be necessary.

With a pad, one hopes. Hector Charles Cameron, The Nervous Child, *1930.*

Masturbation is certainly the most dangerous sexual vice that a society can be afflicted with, in the long run.

Hark who's talking! . . . D. H. Lawrence, in Pornography and Obscenity, *1930.*

. . . Cf the long, thin, almost imperceptible black hair growing out of the middle of the palm of the left hand of masturbators.

One wonders how many people the Freudian psychiatrist Rudolf Friedmann actually knew*: 1954.*

Oh my god, women do it too . . .

If practised in girlhood, does it affect married life? Yes, those girls who practise it fail to develop as women. They become flat-chested and lose the female glow which draws gentlemen around them. They develop amatory vertigo and become very nervous.

Sexual Science: *the wise Dr Fowler again, in 1870.*

No one who has realised the amount of moral evil wrought in girls by medical manipulations can deny that remedy is worse than disease. I have seen young unmarried women, of the middle class of society, reduced by the constant use of the speculum to the mental and moral condition of prostitutes; seeking to give themselves the same indulgence by the practice of solitary vice; and asking every medical practitioner to institute an examination of the sexual organs.

The male medical student's dearest fantasy: Dr Robert Brudenell Carter, 1900.

AIDS: THINK OF A NUMBER. . . .

Every time you sleep with a boy you sleep with all his old girlfriends.

Legal, decent, honest even . . . but not truthful: Government-sponsored advertisement, 1987.

There will be one million AIDS cases in Britain by the end of 1991.

Report of the UN-financed World Health Organisation, July 1989.

AIDS became a notifiable disease in Britain in 1984. By June 1993 there was a cumulative total of 7699 reported AIDS cases in Britain.

Suppose HIV doesn't equal AIDS. Then we will have witnessed the biggest medical and scientific blunder this century.

But it does and we didn't: The Sunday Times *of March 1992 gives a double-page spread to the fallacies of Professor Peter Duesberg of the University of California at Berkeley, proponent of the 'lifestyle-only theory' of AIDS infection.*

Between 30 and 40 million people worldwide will be infected with HIV by the end of the century.

Allowing itself a generous margin of error, the WHO again – which on July 2nd 1994 also 'estimated' that there had been a 60% rise in the world infection rate during the previous twelve months. Time will tell.

THE BLUNT EDGE OF TECHNOLOGY

‘The thing that hath been, it is that which shall be; and that which is done is that which shall be done; and there is no new thing under the sun.’

Ecclesiastes, Chapter 1, Verse 9.

‘Everything that can be invented has been invented.’

Charles H. Duell, Director, US Patents Office, 1899.

'If God had intended us to fly,' observed Michael Flanders, 'He would never have invented the railways.' On the other hand, if He hadn't got a sense of humour He wouldn't have invented Sir Clive Sinclair. . . .

Fortunately for us, Mr Duell failed in the attempt to persuade President MacKinley to abolish his office – and the author of Ecclesiastes was correct in his assertion that 'of making many books there is no end'.

The following pages are a tribute to all those who said it couldn't be done . . . and to one or two who said it could.

LET THERE BE LIGHT

There is a young madman proposing to light the streets of London – with what, do you suppose? – with smoke!
Sir Walter Scott fails to see the possibilities of gas in 1810.

When the Paris Exhibition closes electric light will close with it and no more will be heard of it.
Professor Erasmus Wilson of the University of Oxford, 1878.

Sub-division of the electric light is an absolute *ignis fatuus*.
Sir William Preece, Engineer-in-Chief at the Post Office, gives evidence to a British Parliamentary Committee set up to examine Mr Edison's incandescent electric lamp in 1878.

Good enough for our transatlantic friends . . . but unworthy of the attention of practical or scientific men.
The Committee reaches a conclusion.

Everyone acquainted with the subject will recognize it as a conspicuous failure.
Back in the US, Professor Henry Morton is equally unimpressed in 1879.

There is no plea which will justify the use of high-tension and alternating currents, either in a scientific or a commercial sense. . . .

My personal desire would be to prohibit entirely the use of alternating currents. They are as unnecessary as they are dangerous.
Edison himself, a low-power Direct Current man, rubbishes Tesla's rival AC system in 1889.

TRUST YOU AVOID GIGANTIC MISTAKE OF ADOPTION OF ALTERNATING CURRENT

Edison's friend and partner Lord Kelvin sends a telegram to the Niagara Falls Power Company. They ignored it.

It can be predicted with all security that in fifty years light will cost one fiftieth of its present price.

J. B. S. Haldane, February 3rd 1927.

A few decades hence, energy may be free – just like the unmetered air.

John von Neumann, winner of the Fermi Award for Science, 1956.

The Con Ed system is in the best shape in fifteen years, and there's no problem about the summer.

Charles Franklin Luce, Chairman of Consolidated Edison, New York, July 10th 1977. Three days later a massive Con Ed failure blacked out the whole of metropolitan New York for over 24 hours.

NUCLEAR POWER

Don't delay, buy a reactor today!

The basic questions of design, material and shielding, in combining a nuclear reactor with a home boiler and cooling unit, no longer are problems . . . The system would heat and cool a home, provide unlimited household hot water, and melt the snow from sidewalks and driveways. All that could be done for six years on a single charge of fissionable material costing about $300.

The US Institute of Boiler and Radiator Manufacturers hears an address from its General Manager Robert E. Ferry, June 1st 1955.

I do not hesitate to forecast that atomic batteries will be commonplace long before 1980 [and] it can be taken for granted that before 1980 ships, aircraft, locomotives and even automobiles will be atomically fuelled.

General David Sarnoff, Chairman of RCA, The Fabulous Future: America in 1980, *1955.*

Nuclear-powered vacuum cleaners will probably be a reality within ten years.

It beats as it sweeps as it irradiates . . . vacuum cleaner manufacturer Alex Lewyt, President of Lewyt Corporation, seizes the chance to steal a march on Hoover and gives a quote to the New York Times *of June 10th 1955.*

Safer than food

A nuclear power plant is infinitely safer than eating, because 300 people choke to death on food every year.

The world according to Dixy Lee Roy, who in 1977 had recently relinquished his post as Chairman of the US Atomic Energy Committee, the American public's nuclear safety watchdog. Scary, isn't it?

Safer than sex with your wife (or friends)

What do you think you get more radiation from, leaning up against an atomic reactor or your wife? I don't want to alarm you, but all human beings have radioactive potassium in their blood – and that includes your wife . . . I do not advocate a law forcing couples to sleep in twin beds [but] from the point of view of radiation safety, I must advise you against the practice of sleeping every night with two girls, because then you would get more radiation than from Dresden III.

Dr Edward Teller, 'The Father of the Atom Bomb', auditions for the remake of Dr Strangelove at the public hearing concerning the building of the Dresden III reactor in Illinois, USA, in August 1979 – and proves by implication that women are immune to radiation sickness.

Three Mile Island: perfectly normal, no need to fuss

A normal aberration.

Jack Herbein, Vice-President of Consolidated Edison, on a scare story concerning a so-called leak at the Three Mile Island nuclear reactor, March 28th 1979.

The coolant leakage is nothing – just a small amount.

At a press conference on March 28th, PR man Don Curry waves aside questions about a leak of radioactive cooling water onto the reactor's floor. It was afterwards revealed that the 'small amount' was, in fact, 250,000 gallons.

There have been no recordings of any significant levels of radiation and none are expected outside the plant. The reactor is being cooled according to design by a reactor cooling system, and should be cooled by the end of the day.

Later on March 28th, Consolidated Edison issue a clarifying statement to which Don Curry adds a soothing rider concerning the automatic shutdown equipment: 'Everything worked.' *But it didn't. In addition to the quarter of a million gallons of spilled radioactive coolant, the automatic opening of a 'safety' valve released a large amount of radioactive gas into the air outside the plant; it drifted 16 miles downwind, causing the evacuation of the whole of Three Mile Island. Inside the plant, atmospheric radiation was measured at 1000 times its normal level.*

This accident is not out of the ordinary for this kind of reactor.

It's a fair bet that Con Ed President Jack Herbein wished he hadn't said that – it might, after all, be misinterpreted. . . .

I would not call it an accident. I would call it a malfunction.
. . . but there's no misinterpreting the words of Edward Teller in a subsequent Playboy *interview. They are oddly unreassuring.*

The only accident is that this thing leaked out. You could have avoided this whole thing by not saying anything.
Perhaps Craig Faust, Three Mile Island control room operator, wished he'd taken his own advice and kept his mouth shut in April 1979.

There is no alternative!

The power of the tides may be made available to produce power on a large scale. If extensively exploited over a long period of time, however, it might result in bringing the moon too close to earth for safety.
An abnormal aberration: John P. Lockhart-Mummery, M.A., B.C., F.R.C.S., alerts the planet in After Us, *1936.*

ON COMMUNICATION

His master's nonsense

It is quite impossible that the noble organs of human speech could be replaced by ignoble senseless metal.
French Academician Jean Bouillaud: before viewing Mr Edison's phonograph on September 30th 1878.

A crude fake sustained by ventriloquism.
Jean Bouillaud, after viewing it.

It isn't of any commercial value.
Mr Edison's own view of the thing in 1880.

Mr Morse, the dotty inventor

I watched his countenance closely, to see if he was not deranged. I was assured by other Senators after we left the room that there was no future in it.
Samuel Morse demonstrates his telegraph to the US Congress in 1842: Senator Hampton Smith of Indiana delivers his verdict.

I am not satisfied that under any rate of postage that could be adopted, its revenues could be made to equal its expenditures.
The US Postmaster General turns down Morse's offer to sell the rights to his invention for $100,000: 1845.

Hello . . . hello?

Well-informed people know it is impossible to transmit the voice over wires and that were it possible to do so, the thing would be of no practical value.

Well-informed people did not read the Boston Post *in 1865, the year Joshua Coopersmith was arrested for fraud after trying to raise capital to develop a telephone.*

Hmph! Only a toy.

Alexander Graham Bell's father-in-law Gardiner Greene Hubbard inspects the prototype in 1876.

An amazing invention – but who would ever want to use one?

The year is 1876: President Rutherford B. Hayes makes a call from Washington to Philadelphia, and displays the sort of percipience that takes a US politician all the way to the top. In 1877, Western Union turned down Bell's offer of exclusive rights for $100,000.

Tuned in, turned off

Radio has no future.

Lord Kelvin, past President of the Royal Society, sworn enemy of Alternating Current and X-rays (see p. 168), on Mr Marconi's experiments in 1897.

DeForest has said in many newspapers and over his signature that it would be possible to transmit the human voice across the Atlantic before many years. Based on these absurd and deliberately misleading statements, the misguided public has been persuaded to purchase stock in his company.

. . . Whereas, of course, everything that could be invented had already been invented by 1899. A United States District Attorney outlines the case for the Prosecution in the matter of The People vs. Lee DeForest, radio pioneer, accused of fraud in 1913.

I am reported to be 'pessimistic' about broadcasting. . . . The truth is that I have anticipated its complete disappearance – confident that the unfortunate people, who must now subdue themselves to 'listening-in', will soon find a better pastime for their leisure.

Like watching TV, for instance. . . .? Popular Science guru H. G. Wells looks ahead in The Way The World Is Going, *1928.*

The idiot in the corner

For God's sake go down to reception and get rid of a lunatic who's down there. He says he's got a machine for seeing by wireless! Watch him – he may have a razor on him.

The editor of the Daily Express *sends a minion to deal with a mad inventor called*

John Logie Baird in 1925. Rejected by the paper, Baird instead organized a public demonstration of a thing he called 'television'.

While theoretically and technically television may be feasible, commercially and financially I consider it an impossibility, a development of which we need waste little time dreaming.
. . . Which just goes to show you can't get 'em all right: persecuted radio pioneer Lee DeForest doesn't rate the competition in a New York Times *interview in 1926.*

Television won't matter in your lifetime or mine.
Keep on listening-in, advises Radio Times *editor Rex Lambert in 1936.*

Video won't be able to hold on to any market it captures after the first six months. People will soon get tired of staring at a plywood box every night.
Showing his contempt for the new medium by getting its name wrong, Darryl F. Zanuck of 20th Century-Fox tries to talk it out of existence in 1946.

GETTING FROM A TO B

TRAVEL BY WATER

To listen to him you would fancy that with steam you could navigate ships, move carriages; in fact, there's no end to the miracles which, he insists upon it, could be performed.
Short shrift for Salomon de Daus from Cardinal Richelieu (founder of the French Academy in 1634), who was so unimpressed he had the hapless inventor confined in a lunatic asylum.

Even if the propeller had the power of propelling a vessel, it would be found altogether useless in practice, because the power being applied in the stern it would be absolutely impossible to make the vessel steer.
Naval surveyor Sir William Symonds explains why screw propellers won't work: 1837.

We have, as an extreme limit of a steamer's practical voyage, without receiving a relay of coals, a run of about 2000 miles . . . Men might as well project a voyage to the moon as attempt to employ steam across the stormy North Atlantic.
Professor Dionysus Lardner addresses the British Association for the Advancement of Science in 1838 – the year the Great Western *made the first Atlantic crossing by steam power.*

There is no greater fallacy than to suppose that ships can be navigated on long voyages without masts and sails.
Lieutenant (afterwards Vice Admiral Sir) George Strong Nares, The Naval Cadet's Guide: or Seaman's Companion, *1860.*

I cannot imagine any condition which would cause a ship to founder. Modern shipbuilding has gone beyond that.
Captain Edward J. Smith of the White Star Line, future commander of the Titanic, *cheerfully optimistic in 1906.*

The *Titanic* is well able to withstand almost any exterior damage and could keep afloat indefinitely after being struck.
P. A. S. Franklin, Vice President of the International Mercantile Marine Company, issues a statement on the morning of April 15th 1912 – by which time the ship and most of her passengers were at the bottom of the ocean.

TRAVEL BY CANAL

A man, a plan. . . .

To seek or make known any better route than the one from Porto Bello to Panama is forbidden under the penalty of death.
King Philip II of Spain issues an edict against civil engineers in the 1550s.

I have crossed both at the site of the Panama Railroad and at three other points more to the south. From all I could see, combined with all I have read on the subject, I cannot entertain the slightest hope that a ship canal will ever be found possible across any part of it.
Surveyor John C. Trautwine reports in the Journal of the Franklin Institute, *May 1854.*

The Panama Canal is actually a thing of the past, and Nature in her works will soon obliterate all traces of French energy and money expended on the Isthmus.
Scientific American *rejoices in the bankruptcy of the Compagnie Universelle du Canal Interoceanique in January 1891. The US Government bought the French interest out for $40 million and – after organizing a war in Colombia to assist the project – opened the canal to shipping in 1914.*

Constructing a troublespot in Suez

A most futile attempt and totally impossible to be carried out.
Chancellor of the Exchequer Benjamin Disraeli speaks in the House of Commons in 1858. As Prime Minister in 1875, he bought Britain a half share in the completed canal.

I have a very strong opinion that such a canal will not and cannot be made . . . and that steam navigation by land will and ought to be the means of transit through Egypt.
Novelist Anthony Trollope puts his government experience in Egypt to good use in The West Indies and the Spanish Main *in 1859.*

No one will ever collect a farthing in tolls from this impossible canal.
The Globe *thunders an opinion on November 30th 1859 – thirteen days after the first voyage through the Suez Canal.*

TRAVEL BY RAIL

What can be more palpably absurd and ridiculous than the prospect held out of locomotives travelling *twice as fast* as stage-coaches! We should as soon expect the people of Woolwich to suffer themselves to be fired off upon one of Congreve's ricochet rockets, as trust themselves to the mercy of such a machine going at such a rate.
The Quarterly Review *of March 1825 sets a reasonable limit to railway mania.*

The most absurd scheme that ever entered into the head of a man to conceive . . . Every part of the scheme shows that this man has applied himself to a subject of which he has no knowledge, and to which he has no science to apply.
Leading counsel Mr Alderson submits hostile evidence to the Parliamentary Inquiry into George Stephenson's proposal for a Stockton–Darlington railway in 1825.

I see no reason to suppose that these machines will ever force themselves into general use.
The Duke of Wellington doesn't see any future in steam locomotives in 1827.

As you well know, Mr President, railroad carriages are pulled at the enormous speed of 15 miles per hour . . . The Almighty certainly never intended that people should travel at such breakneck speed.
Martin van Buren, Governor of New York, writes to President Andrew Jackson in 1829.

Rail travel at high speed is not possible, because passengers, unable to breathe, would die of asphyxia.
Professor Dionysus Lardner, c. 1830.

That any general system of conveying passengers would go at a velocity exceeding ten miles an hour is extremely improbable.
Railway engineer Thomas Tredgold, Practical Treatise on Railroads and Carriages, *1835.*

I should say no railway ought to exceed 40 miles an hour on the most favourable gradient; but on a curved line the speed ought not to exceed 24 or 25 miles an hour.
Shortly after designing a locomotive capable of 80mph, George Stephenson himself has cold feet in 1841.

Railways can be of no advantage to rural areas, since agricultural products are too heavy or too voluminous to be transported by them.
F-J-B Noël publishes a pamphlet with the weighty title of The Railways Will Be Ruinous For France, And Especially For The Cities Through Which They Go, *1842.*

TRAVEL BY ROAD

If a man were to propose to convey us regularly to Edinburgh in seven days, and bring us back in seven more, should we not vote him to Bedlam?
Sir Henry Herbert MP amuses the House of Commons in 1671.

Regular travel at such a prodigious speed must surely result in death from an apoplexy.
A Doctor Writes . . . in the Bath Argus *of the late 1780s after John Palmer's mail coach service cut the journey time between London and Bath from 3 days to 17 hours.*

The discovery with which we are dealing involves forces of a nature too dangerous to fit into any of our usual concepts.
The US Congressional Record *of 1875 notes an inquiry into what it terms* 'the so-called internal combustion engine' *and does not foresee a paradigm-shift.*

The ordinary 'horseless carriage' is at present a luxury for the wealthy; and although its price will probably fall in the future, it will never, of course, come into as common use as the bicycle.
The Literary Digest, *October 14th 1899.*

The actual building of roads devoted to motor cars is not for the near future, in spite of the many rumours to that effect.
Harper's Weekly, *August 2nd 1902. Try telling that to the M11 protesters . . .*

That the automobile has practically reached the limit of its development is suggested by the fact that during the past year no improvements of a radical nature have been introduced.
Everything that can be invented. . . . Scientific American, *January 2nd 1909.*

In 15 years, more electricity will be sold for electric vehicles than for light.
Thomas Edison drums up trade for his nickel-cadmium battery, 1910.

The motor-car will never usurp the place of the horse.
A hot tip from The Economist *in 1911.*

In less than twenty-five years the motor car will be obsolete, because the aeroplane will run along the ground as well as fly over it.
Just imagine: multi-storey airports! Sir Philip Gibbs, The Day After Tomorrow: What is Going to Happen to the World, *1928.*

Next year's cars should be rolling out of Detroit with plastic bodies.
Was L. M. Bloomingdale, in The Future of Plastics, *Yale Scientific Magazine, Spring 1941, the original for Mrs Robinson's husband in* The Graduate*? Just to prove him wrong, Henry Ford made a car from crushed jojoba beans in 1942. Anita Roddick, please note. . . .*

The deluxe open-road car will probably be 20 feet long, powered by a gas turbine engine, little brother of the jet engine.
Predictions for 1965 in 1955 from Leo Cherne of the Research Institute of America.

The Wankel will eventually dwarf such major post-war technological developments as xerography, the Polaroid camera and colour television.
General Motors announces a move away from the piston engine in 1969.

The reciprocating-piston engine is as dead as a dodo.
Sports Illustrated *reads the runes the same year.*

The gas-guzzling Wankel rotary engine was killed off by the oil crises of the early 1970s.

TRAVEL BY AIR

It is entirely impossible for man to rise into the air and float there. For this you would need wings of tremendous dimensions and they would have to be moved at three feet per second. Only a fool would expect such a thing to be realised.
. . . Or a balloonist like the Montgolfier brothers, who rose into the air and floated there a year after this piece from the pen of Academician Joseph de Lalande was published in the Journal de Paris *of May 18th 1782.*

Put these three indisputable facts together:
(1) There is a low limit of weight, certainly not much beyond fifty pounds, beyond which it is impossible for an animal to fly. Nature has reached this limit, and with her utmost effort has failed to pass it.
(2) The animal machine is far more effective than any we can hope to make; therefore the limit of the weight of a successful flying machine cannot be more than fifty pounds.
(3) The weight of any machine constructed for flying, including fuel and engineer, cannot be less than three or four hundred pounds.

Is it not demonstrated that a true flying machine, self-raising, self-sustaining, self-propelling, is physically impossible?
Nature has also failed to evolve the railway locomotive – but this had evidently not occurred to Professor Joseph le Conte of the Faculty of Natural History at the University of California, writing in Popular Science Monthly, *November 1888.*

It is apparent to me that the possibilities of the aeroplane, which two or three years ago was thought to hold the solution to the problem, have been exhausted, and that we must turn elsewhere.
Thomas Edison quoted in the New York World, *November 17th 1895.*

Heavier than air flying machines are impossible. I have not the smallest molecule of faith in aerial navigation other than ballooning.
It's that man again: Lord Kelvin, 1896.

The demonstration that no possible combination of known substances, known forms of machinery and known forms of force, can be united in a practical machine by which men shall fly long distances through the air, seems to the writer as complete as it is possible for the demonstration to be.
Simon Newcomb – professor at Johns Hopkins University, author of Elements of Astronomy *and discoverer of the planet Neptune – ends speculation in 1900 . . .*

Flight by machines heavier than air is unpractical and insignificant, if not utterly impossible.
. . . and in 1902 . . .

Aerial flight is one of that class of problems with which man will never have to cope.
. . . and in 1903.

On December 17th 1903 Orville and Wilbur Wright successfully flew a heavier-than-air machine. In 1901 Wilbur had told Orville: 'Man will not fly for fifty years.' *But then he found he'd nothing better to do anyway. . . .*

This machine may even carry mail in special cases. But the useful load will be very small. The machines will eventually be fast, they will be used in sport, but they are not to be thought of as commercial carriers.
Octave Chanute, engineer and author of Progress in Flying Machines, *1904. One of the first passenger airfields was named after him.*

I do not think that a flight across the Atlantic will be made in our time, and in our time I include the youngest readers.
Charles Stewart Rolls, co-founder of Rolls-Royce Ltd., 1908. Charles Lindbergh flew the Altantic non-stop on May 21st 1927.

A popular fallacy is to expect enormous speed to be obtained . . . there is no hope of competing for racing speed with either our locomotives or our automobiles.

A pity British Rail never studied Aeronautics *(1908) by Harvard astronomer William Pickering – the man who also found evidence of plant and insect life on the moon.*

The popular mind often pictures gigantic flying machines speeding across the Atlantic and carrying innumerable passengers in a way analogous to our modern steamships . . . It seems safe to say that such ideas are wholly visionary, and even if a machine could get across with one or two passengers the expense would be prohibitive to any but the capitalist who could own his own yacht.

The popular mind knew better than William Pickering in 1910. Fortunately, Robert Maxwell never got round to trading up his yacht for a Boeing 747.

With the possible exception of having more pleasing lines to the eye while in flight, the monoplane possesses no material advantage over the biplane.

Glenn H. Curtiss, patron and founder of the Curtiss Award, speaks to The New York Times *of December 31st 1911.*

Over cities, the aerial sentry or policeman will be found. A thousand aeroplanes flying to the opera must be kept in line and each allowed to alight upon the roof of the auditorium in its proper turn.

Waldemar Kaempfert, Managing Editor of Scientific American, *June 28th 1913.*

The first real air-liner, carrying some five or six hundred passengers, will probably appear after or towards the end of the battle between fixed and moving-wing machines. And it will be a flying boat.

Oliver Stewart: Aeolus, or the Future of the Flying Machine, *1927.*

People are always asking me to give a name to R101. I hope it will make its reputation with that name.

Lord Thompson of Cardington, 1929. The R101 airship made its name a year later when it crashed and burst into flames, killing all on board.

We follow with interest any work that is being done in other countries on jet propulsion, but scientific investigation into the possibilities has given no indication that this method can be a serious competitor to the air-screw combination engine. We do not consider we should be justified in spending any time or money on it ourselves.

1934: The Ministry of Supply replies to a letter from the newly-formed British Interplanetary Society drawing the Government's attention to German developments in liquid-fuel rocketry – which were to lead (under the direction of the unprosecuted Nazi war criminal Werner von Braun) to the V-2 rocket bomb ten years later and to NASA's Apollo program.

In its present state, and even considering the improvements possible . . . the gas turbine engine could hardly be considered a feasible application to airframes.

Report of the The National Academy of Sciences Committee on Gas Turbines, June 1940. In 1941 the gas turbine or 'jet' engine was successfully tested on a Gloster; 1942 saw the advent of the jet-propelled Messerschmitt Me 262. Sir Frank Whittle, who invented the jet engine and fought a ten-year battle to have it taken seriously, inscribed his copy of this report with the annotation: 'Good thing I was too stupid to know this – FW.'

A very friendly boom, like a pair of gleeful handclaps.

But whose hands? UK Government scientific adviser Sir James Lighthill allays fears that the supersonic Concorde might be noisy, 1971. Ear-witnesses described the prototype's breaking of the 'sound barrier' as 'like flying bombs landing half a mile away'.

The new engines are far quieter than the prototypes. People living near the airports will hardly notice the aircraft.

Mr Henry Marking of British Airways, June 1975. Concorde's production model was even noisier – 'equivalent to thirty of the noisiest subsonic aircraft all taking off together' *according to air noise expert Geoffrey Holmes. People living near Heathrow made similar, though more colourful, observations.*

Russia's TU 144 supersonic airliner, drastically altered in design and now performing extremely well, is likely to win the race to get into airline service before the Concorde.

Air Commodore E. M. Donaldson, air correspondent of the Daily Telegraph, *1973. That year, the drastically altered Tupolev TU 144 fell out of the sky over the Paris Air Show, killing everyone on board – and the Soviet project.*

SPACE – THE IMPOSSIBLE FRONTIER

If we are thinking within our system, then it is certain that no-one has ever been on the moon. Not merely is nothing of the sort ever seriously reported to us by reliable people, but our whole system of physics forbids us to believe it. For this demands answers to the questions, 'How did he overcome the force of gravity?', 'How could he live without an atmosphere?' and a thousand others which could not be answered.

The philosopher Ludwig Wittgenstein (1889–1951) – who trained as an aeronau-

tical engineer and, in 1911, designed a reaction jet propeller – applies a little logic in On Certainty, *a collection of notes and essays published posthumously in 1969.*

Still, to be filled with uneasy wonder and to express it will be enough, for after the rocket quits our air and really starts on its longer journey, its flight would be neither accelerated nor maintained by the explosion of the charges it might then have left. To claim that it would be is to deny a fundamental law of dynamics, and only Dr Einstein and his chosen dozen, so few and fit, are licensed to do that.

That Professor Goddard, with his chair in Clark College and the countenancing of the Smithsonian Institution, does not know the relation of action to reaction, and of the need to have something better than a vacuum against which to react – to say that would be absurd. Of course he only *seems* to lack the knowledge ladled out daily in high schools.

An editorial in The New York Times *of 1921 authoritatively ridicules Dr Robert Hutchings Goddard, inventor of the bazooka, who was conducting experiments in rocketry on his aunt's farm and had proposed that rockets could be manoeuvred in space. The 'fundamental law of dynamics' does indeed require something for a force to 'react against' – in the case of rocket fuel fired in the vacuum of space, that 'something' is the rocket itself, a fact the* Times *editor (despite his presumably impeccable High School education) somehow overlooked.*

Following the successful voyage of Apollo 11 in July 1969 The New York Times, *to its eternal credit, printed an apology to the late Dr Goddard.*

This foolish idea of shooting at the Moon is an example of the absurd length to which vicious specialisation will carry scientists working in thought-tight compartments. Let us critically examine the proposal. For a projectile entirely to escape the gravitation of the Earth, it needs a velocity of 7 miles a second. The thermal energy of a gramme at this speed is 15,180 calories . . . The energy of our most violent explosive – nitroglycerine – is less than 1,500 calories per gramme. Consequently, even had this explosive nothing to carry, it has only one-tenth of the energy necessary to escape the Earth . . . Hence the proposition appears to be basically impossible.

Working in a thought-free compartment: Professor A. W. Bickerton of Christchurch, New Zealand, 1926. An absurd piece of reasoning, for two reasons which a professor of Physics and Chemistry – of all people – should have known: first, because liquid fuels (such as the kerosene-liquid oxygen mixture proposed by the people Bickerton was ridiculing) contain much more energy, gramme for gramme, than nitroglycerine; and secondly, because (of course) a rocket does not need to carry its own fuel into space – it burns nearly all of it whilst getting there.

Professor Bickerton was the author of a book called Perils of the Pioneer. *As Arthur C. Clarke commented in 1979, 'Of the perils that all pioneers must face, few are more disheartening than the Bickertons.'*

The whole procedure presents difficulties of so fundamental a nature, that we are forced to dismiss the notion as essentially impractical, in spite of the author's insistent appeal to put aside prejudice and to recollect the supposed impossibility of heavier-than-air flight before it was actually accomplished. An analogy such as this may be misleading, and we believe it to be so in this case.
Clinging to prejudice: astronomer Richard van der Riet Woolley gives a hostile peer-group review to P. E. Cleator's Rockets in Space *in the March 14th 1936 issue of* Nature.

The acceleration which must result from the use of rockets . . . inevitably would damage the brain beyond repair.
One small step for a cabbage. . . . A touch of the Dionysus Lardners from John P. Lockhart-Mummery, MA, BC, FRCS, in After Us, *1936.*

While it is always dangerous to make a negative prediction, it would appear that the statement that rocket flight to the Moon does not seem so remote as television did less than one hundred years ago is over-optimistic.
Professor J. W. Campbell of the University of Alberta with a mathematical demonstration of the near-impossibility of space travel in Rocket Flight to the Moon, *1941. Professor Campbell stated that it would need one million tons of fuel to propel one pound of cargo into space: the actual amount of fuel required (at present) is one ton per pound. Again, the answers to Campbell's objections were already published – in a paper by that well-known scientific ignoramus Professor Robert Hutchings Goddard,* A Method of Reaching Extreme Altitudes, *published by the equally well-known Looney Tunes organisation, the Smithsonian Institution.*

Space travel is utter bilge.
The considered scientific opinion of the Astronomer Royal in January 1956 – none other than Dr Richard van der Riet Woolley, still debunking space travel twenty years on. The USSR launched Sputnik I the following year – and got mixed reviews. . . .

Reds over the head. . . .

The USA has lost a battle more important and greater than Pearl Harbor.
The end of Kup Kakes as we know them: Dr Edward Teller assesses the military significance of Sputnik I in a CBS TV commentary, October 1957.

A lump of iron almost anybody could launch.
Rear Admiral Rawson Bennett, on NBC, begs to disagree.

No matter what we do now, the Russians will beat us to the moon . . . I would not be surprised if the Russians reached the moon within a week.
. . . with snow on their retro-thrusters. The Smithsonian's John Rinehart takes a gloomy view, October 1957.

Few predictions seem more certain than this: Russia is going to surpass us in mathematics and the social sciences . . . In short, unless we depart utterly from our present behaviour, it is reasonable to expect that by no later than 1975 the United States will be a member of the Union of Soviet Socialist Republics.
Even with a Republican in the White House! George R. Price, Fellow of the American Association for the Advancement of Science and a veteran of the Manhatten Project, dons sackcloth and ashes and books himself a passage to the Gulag in the November 18th 1957 issue of Life.

But to place a man in a multi-stage rocket and project him into the controlling gravitational field of the moon, where the passenger can make scientific observations, perhaps land alive, and return to earth – all that constitutes a wild dream worthy of Jules Verne.
Having accepted television and heard the signals from Sputnik I, Lee DeForest gags on manned space flight: Reader's Digest, *1957.*

Racing certainties . . . .

We stand on the threshold of rocket mail.
Arthur E. Summerfield, US Postmaster General, predicts same-day delivery by guided missile on January 23rd 1959.

The odds are now that the United States will not be able to honour the 1970 manned-lunar-landing date set by Mr Kennedy.
New Scientist, *April 30th 1964.*

I'll have my first Zambian astronaut on the Moon by 1965, using my own firing system, derived from the catapault. . . . I'm getting them acclimatised to space travel by placing them in my space capsule every day. It's a 40-gallon oil drum in which they sit, and then I roll them down a hill. This gives them the feeling of rushing through space. I also make them swing from the end of a long rope. When they reach the highest point, I cut the rope – this produces the feeling of free fall.
Edward Mukaka Nkoloso, Director-General of the Zambia National Academy of Space Research, takes a leaf out of Evelyn Waugh's Black Mischief *on November 3rd 1964.*

THE COMPUTER: GARBAGE IN, GARBAGE OUT

This extraordinary monument of theoretical genius accordingly remains, and doubtless will forever remain, a theoretical possibility.
1884: a biographer's epitaph for the 'Analytical Engine' – the forerunner of all computers – which was conceived and designed by Charles Babbage (1791–1871) from the 1830s onward. Babbage's first brainchild, the 'Difference Engine', was the prototype for all calculating machines.

Where a calculator on the ENIAC is equipped with 18,000 vacuum tubes and weighs 30 tons, computers in the future may have only 1000 vacuum tubes and perhaps only weigh 1 ton.
Popular Mechanics *takes a long look ahead in March 1949.*

What the hell is it good for?
An engineer's reaction to the microprocessor: Robert Lloyd of IBM's Advance Computing Systems Division, 1968.

For expert opinions on the commercial possibilities of the computer, see **Muck & Brass** *(p. 110).*

MILITARY TECHNOLOGY
A Regrettable Collection of Civilian Expertise

Railways

Transport by railroad car would result in the emasculation of our troops and would deprive them of the great marches which have played such an important rôle in the triumph of our armies.
Vive la Gloire aux pieds! François Arago, French scientist and politician, has the best interests of the common soldier at heart in 1836. In 1848 he was made Minister of War.

Submarines

My imagination refuses to see any sort of submarine doing anything but suffocate its crew and founder at sea.
Invisible men and time machines, yes; submarines, no. H. G. Wells writes Anticipations *in 1902.*

Aircraft

Another popular fallacy is to suppose that flying machines could be used to drop dynamite on an enemy in time of war.
Astronomer William H. Pickering – already encountered as a debunker of 'the popular mind' – in Aeronautics, *1908.*

To affirm that the aeroplane is going to 'revolutionize' naval warfare of the future is to be guilty of the wildest exaggeration.
Scientific American, *July 16th 1910.*

The position of our enemies will be hopeless. We will be able to put down a vast army, anywhere in the world, within a single week . . . the whole world will be our front yard. And our enemies will be beaten to their knees.
Shipbuilding engineer Henry J. Kaiser seeks funding to develop a fleet of giant cargo planes in 1942. He got backing from reclusive millionaire Howard Hughes, and the US Reconstruction Finance Corporation.

Now, whatever you do, Henry, do not interfere with Howard. He is thorough and he is a genius and do not interfere with him.
Reconstruction Finance Corporation boss Jesse Jones reassures Henry Nelson, head of the War Productions Board, who had doubts about the project after seeing the first prototype, a 200-ton wooden seaplane with a wingspan that exceeded the length of a football pitch.

The project was completed in 1947. The largest aircraft ever built, the 'Spruce Goose', flew for half a mile, low over Long Beach, with Hughes at the helm. Then it was mothballed forever.

The plane is the greatest single step forward in combat aircraft in several decades.
US Secretary of Defense Robert McNamara hails the F-111 'Swing Wing' fighter-bomber on October 15th 1964.

The F-111 will be superior in its class to any other tactical weapons system in the world.
US Defense Department expert witness to Congress, September 1966.

The F-111 in a Nixon Administration will be made into one of the foundations of our air supremacy.
Richard Nixon at El Paso, Texas, on November 2nd 1968.

In December 1970 a Senate Committee report found that the F-111 project had been 'a fiscal blunder of the worst magnitude'. Of 500 built, fewer than 100 came 'reasonably close' to performing as per specifications. Thirteen of them had fallen out of the sky.

The Sheridan Tank–Shillelagh Missile System

The Sheridan Weapons System, with the Shillelagh, will provide the Army with a major advancement in tank-like weapons systems and a significant improvement in fire power.

Colonel Paul A. Simpson, manager of the Sheridan project, 1966. First tests of the tank revealed a problem: its shells exploded prematurely and blew the gun turret off.

I really don't know what the Russians have, but I'd like to place a bet for a month's pay that this is better.

Major General Edward H. Burba, senior Tank Development Officer, US Army, at a 1967 public demonstration which was abandoned when the tank filled with smoke and had to be evacuated.

Although the cost of the programme has risen substantially above the original estimates, it is believed that the tank will meet or surpass nearly all of its performance objectives.

US Secretary of State Robert McNamara announces the deployment of the tank in Vietnam, January 1968.

The first 54 Sheridans sent to Vietnam logged 446 'failure incidents' between them, including weapon misfires (41) and complete engine replacements (25). The recoil mechanism of the 152mm gun was considered too unreliable for it to be used in a 'combat situation'.

These problems now are solved.

The US Army announces the shipment of another 171 Sheridans in 1969.

The Sheridan–Shillelagh Weapons System was scrapped in 1970. It had cost the US taxpayer over $1,000,000,000.

Inter-continental ballistics

There has been a great deal said about a 3000-mile high-angle rocket. The people who have been writing these things that annoy me, have been talking about a 3000-mile high-angle rocket shot from one continent to another, carrying an atomic bomb and so directed as to be a precise weapon which would land exactly on a certain target, such as a city.

I say, technically, I don't think anyone in the world knows how to do such a thing, and I feel confident that it will not be done for a very long period to come. I think we can leave that out of our thinking. I wish the American public would leave that out of their thinking.

Dr Vannevar Bush, President of the Carnegie Institution of Washington, December 1945.

Cold feet on the atom bomb

I'm not sure that the miserable thing will work, nor that it can be gotten to its target except by oxcart. That we become committed to it as a way to save the country and the peace seems to me to be full of dangers.
He didn't mean that in quite the same way CND do. Robert Oppenheimer, Director of the Manhattan Project, on the eve of Hiroshima, 1946.

Nuclear testing

We have not conducted tests in a way which is hazardous to health.
Dr Willard Libby of the US Atomic Energy Commission, May 17th 1957.

In February 1995 it was officially revealed that, throughout the 1940s and 50s, the USAEC had carried out involuntary radiation tests on over 9000 US citizens. Prisoners, mental patients and seriously ill babies had been injected with radioactive isotopes to see what would happen to them.

POSTSCRIPT: perpetual motion

***Kwiatowski and Stefanski's Improved Water Power Engine* is operated by a waterwheel which, via cranks and lazy tongs, pumps water to itself.**
British Patent No 5723/1904.

Regrettable Dip

A BRAN TUB OF OTHERWISE
UNCLASSIFIABLE
BALDERDASH

CRYSTAL BALLS

**Prediction is very difficult,
especially about the future.**

Neils Bohr

POPULATION TRENDS

In all probability the next doubling of the people of England will be in about six hundred years to come, or by the Year of Our Lord 2300, at which time it will have eleven millions of people. The next doubling after that will be, in all probability, in less than twelve or thirteen hundred years, or by the Year of Our Lord 3500 or 3600. At which time the Kingdom will have 22 millions of souls.
Gregory King: Observations on the State of England, *1696.*

After performing the most exact calculation possible . . . I have found that there is scarcely one tenth as many people on earth as in ancient times. What is surprising is that the population of the earth decreases every day, and if this continues, in another ten centuries the earth will be nothing but a desert.
Charles, Baron Montesquieu, Lettres persanes, *1721.*

Population is constant in size and will remain so right up to the end of mankind.
L'Encyclopédie, *1756.*

It may be safely asserted . . . that population, when unchecked, increases in geometrical progression of such a nature as to double itself every twenty-five years.
Thomas Robert Malthus would have made a good WHO statistician: A Summary View of the Principle of Population, *1830, paints a gloomy future for any nation deprived of war, famine or pestilence.*

In 1993 there should be a population within the present area of the United States of 580,000,000 . . . Lives of 120 years will be as frequent as now are those of 90.
Van Buren Denslow, lawyer, contributes a prediction to the 1893 Chicago World's Fair. The US population is now c. 220,000,000. Only one person now living is known to be 120 years old; she is French.

Hardly anyone believes that the birth rate, which has been falling rapidly in recent years, will rise much in the near future, even if it does not fall further still. It is, to say the least, highly probable that in twenty years' time the [UK] population will not exceed 40,000,000.

G. D. H. Cole and Raymond Postgate, The Common People *1746–1946, Second Edition 1946, corrected 1956. In 1966 the UK population was c. 54,500,000; in 1976 it was c. 55,928,000. It stands now (1995) at c. 60,000,000.*

TOMORROW'S WORLD

T. Baron Russell: a regrettable tribute

In 1905 Mr Russell published A Hundred Years Hence. *The following predictions may or may not be proved correct in ten years' time.*

Sky bikes: **As a means of amusement, the idea of aerial travel has great promise. Small one-man flying machines or the aerial counterpart of tandem bicycles, will no doubt be common enough.**

Down the tubes: **The process of making up van loads of mail matter for despatch to remote centres, and redistribution there, is far too clumsy for what commerce will demand a hundred years hence. No doubt the soil of every civilised country will be permeated by vast networks of pneumatic tubes: and all letters and parcels will be thus distributed at a speed hardly credible today.**

Clause Four fulfilled: **What will happen a hundred years hence is that trade disputes will have disappeared because all the workers will be practically their own employers . . . the workers in every industry being paid, not by fixed wages, but by a share in the produce of their labour.**

Energy on tap: **Most likely the universal source of power, then, before the middle of the century, will be the recomposition of water – in other words, we shall get all the power we want by splitting up water into oxygen and hydrogen, and then allowing these gases to recombine, thereby returning to us energy we have employed in the analysis.**

What about chess? **The growing gentleness of mankind will abolish, as barbarous, games which take the form of modified assault, as football, boxing, wrestling, fencing and the like.**

Machines for living: **Square corners and rectangular junctions of wall and floor, wall and ceiling, will certainly before long be replaced everywhere by curves.**

Miserable health: **Such a wasteful food as animal flesh cannot survive: and even apart from the moral necessity which will compel mankind, for**

its own preservation, to abandon the use of alcohol, the direct and indirect wastefulness of alcohol will make it impossible for beverages containing it to be tolerated. Very likely tobacco will follow it.
A forecast yet to be fulfilled . . .?

Another tribute: John Langdon-Davies, FRAI

Mr Langdon-Davies published A Short History of the Future *in 1936.*

Daily Express leader: **There will be no war in western Europe for the next five years.**

Not quite, not yet: **Democracy will be dead by 1950.**

We never had it so good: **By 1960 work will be limited to three hours a day . . . food, clothing and shelter will cost as little as air.**

Sex without strings: **By 1975 parents will have ceased to bring up their children in private family units . . . sexual feeling and marriage will have nothing to do with each other.**

Still a lot of it about: **Crime will be considered a disease after 1985 and will cease to exist by AD 2000.**
Disease, however, is coming to be considered as something of a crime. . . .

American psycho

When we get piled upon one another in large cities, we shall become as corrupt as in Europe, and go to eating one another as they do there.
I say, old chap, steady on! Thomas Jefferson, 1787.

National curriculum

Crime will be virtually abolished by transferring to the preventive process of school and education the problems of conduct which police, courts, and prisons now seek to remedy when it is too late.
So we can all blame the teachers after all! The US National Education Association makes a contribution to What Shall We Be Like In 1950? *in the January 10th 1931 edition of* The Literary Digest.

National heritage

Executions are so much a part of British history that it is almost impossible for many excellent people to think of the future without them.
Twelve Excellent Men? Viscount Templewood, In the Shadow of the Gallows, *1951.*

Chicken McTechnological

50 years hence . . . we shall escape the absurdity of growing a whole chicken in order to eat the breast or wing, by growing those parts separately under a suitable medium.

Winston Churchill MP, Popular Mechanics *magazine, 1932.*

Just one of those guys

He had principles all his life. All he ever tried to do was to keep boys out of trouble.

March 1995: Charles Kray puts the record straight about his tragically misunderstood younger brother Ronnie, who died while serving a life sentence for a murder committed while he and his twin brother Reggie were gangland bosses in London's East End. Ex-fellow villain John MacVicar, however, reported that 'He sliced up more people than most normal people slice up Sunday joints.'

THE COURSE OF TRUE LOVE

Two Tales of Bumpy Rides

(1) Barbara Hutton

I've found happiness. I know this is safe and true.

The $45 million Woolworth heiress marries her second husband, Count Kurt Heinrich Haughwitz-Hardenberg-Reventlow, 1933.

I will never marry again.

She divorces the Count three years later.

It's sheer heaven.

After the 'Cash-and-Cary' marriage to Cary Grant, 1939.

I will never marry again. You cannot go on being a fool for ever.

She divorces Cary Grant in 1942.

It makes me sad to think of all the silly things I've done.

Getting it right at last: marriage to number five, Porfirio Rubirosa, December 1952.

Don't call me Mrs Rubirosa.

Another mistake, apparently: February 1953.

I ought to have married him eighteen months ago, but at that time I was married. This is positively my final marriage.
Husband number six is Baron Gottfried von Cramm, November 1955.

I'm in no hurry to go through all that crazy routine again.
After divorcing Baron Gottfried von Cramm in 1959.

He's a composite of all my previous husbands' best qualities without any of the bad qualities.
Welcome aboard, number seven: Prince Doan Vinh de Champacak, 1964.
In 1966 she left her husband a cheque for $1 million and checked out of the hotel where they were staying. Afterwards she remained single.

(2) Mickey Rooney

If I don't make this one last, there's something wrong with me.
The Hollywood star marries his third wife, 1949.

Tell the girls I'm still in the running.
Divorcing his third wife in 1951.

This one is for keeps. We're really in love.
November 1952: marriage to Elaine Melinken.

I guess I'm just an excitable guy.
1957: trial separation from Elaine Melinken. She divorced him in 1958.

The perfect end to an imperfect journey.
Marriage to his fifth wife, Barbara Thomasson, 1959. In 1966 they divorced.

It's unimportant how many times a person is married. We don't think in chronological numbers. Margie's my wife and we're sure this is a good one.
Wedding number six, September 1966. In December Margie Rooney sought a divorce on the grounds of mental cruelty.

I am my own man for the first time.
Mr Rooney finds Jesus, and his seventh wife, in April 1972. She filed for divorce in October 1974.

At last I've found the real one. Love can conquer anything.
Marriage to 25-year-old Jan Chamberlain, 1975.

His previous wives just didn't understand him.
Mrs Rooney VIII, 1975.

Out of the question!

We can tell you with comparative assurance that Aristotle Onassis is not likely to be marrying Jackie Kennedy or anyone else . . . His friends are a little offended that columnists keep on harping on his friendship with Jackie, trying to make a romance out of it; their family friendship goes back several years.

Earl Wilson, syndicated Hollywood columnist, September 1968. Two weeks later their engagement was officially announced.

Nothing will ever separate us. We'll probably be married another ten years.

Ten years feels like forever for Elizabeth Taylor, telling the Chicago Daily News *about her marriage to Richard Burton on July 21st 1974. On July 26th they announced their divorce.*

THE VOLSTEAD ACT

Thirteen years of prohibition

In 1920 the Eighteenth Amendment to the US Constitution came into effect, prohibiting the manufacture, distribution and sale of alcoholic beverages.

There will not be any violations to speak of.

Colonel Daniel Porter, Supervising Revenue Agent in charge of the Volstead Act's enforcement, January 16th 1920.

Thirteen states with a population less than that of New York State alone can prevent repeal until Halley's Comet returns. One might as well talk about his summer vacation on Mars.

Lawyer Clarence Darrow, January 1921.

In a generation, those who are now children will have lost their taste for alcohol.

John Fuller, Atlantis: America and the Future, *1925.*

The abolition of the commercialized liquor trade in this country is as final as the abolition of slavery.

. . . . Which, as we all know, is a part of History that is not bunk. Henry Ford, My Philosophy of Industry, *1929.*

There is as much chance of repealing the 18th Amendment as there is for a humming-bird to fly to the planet Mars with the Washington Monument tied to its tail.
Senator Morris Shephard of Texas, September 1930.

America's first great experiment in mass social engineering came to an end in 1933 with the ratification of the Twenty-First Amendment to the Constitution, which repealed the Volstead Act. Some US commentators now forecast that an Act to outlaw the manufacture, distribution and sale of tobacco products is not very far off.

DEADLY IRONIES

A Collection of Regrettable Exit Lines

I think I could eat one of Bellamy's veal pies.
But he couldn't: William Pitt the Younger, 1806.

Boys, boys, you wouldn't hang your sheriff, would you?
Yes, they would. Tired of being robbed and intimidated by Sheriff Henry Plummer's own 200-strong gang, nicknamed 'The Innocents', the citizens of Bannock, Washington, string him up on January 10th 1864.

The bullet hasn't been made that could kill me.
Possibly not, but there were still two years to go . . . Chicago gangster Jack 'Legs' Diamond, architect of the St Valentine's Day Massacre, speaks in 1929. He was gunned down in 1931.

– Hey, where are the parachutes?
– What's the matter, Miller, you wanna live forever?
December 15th 1944: an exchange between bandleader Glenn Miller and USAF pilot Major Norman Basell. The plane left Britain for Paris, and disappeared without trace.

Well, Mr President, you can't say that the people of Dallas haven't given you a nice welcome!
Mrs John Connally, wife of the Governor of Texas, makes in-car conversation with President John F. Kennedy on November 22nd 1963.

I'm going because I want to avoid all the violence in the streets.
1970: Ulsterwoman Mrs Elizabeth McClelland, 78, tells the Belfast Telegraph

why she is emigrating to New Zealand. She died in a Christchurch, NZ, hospital in February 1972 after being hit over the head with a placard demanding Civil Rights in Ulster.

I don't need bodyguards.
. . . Teamsters' Union boss Jimmy Hoffa tells Playboy *magazine in June 1975. He disappeared on July 30th and was never seen again.*

What would they want with an old man like me?
1978: Earl Mountbatten of Burma pooh-poohs suggestions that he might be a target for the IRA while on holiday in Ireland. On August 27th 1979, while on holiday in Ireland, he was killed by an IRA bomb.

No-one knows more about this mountain than Harry. And it don't dare blow up on him! This goddamned mountain won't blow. Scientists don't know shit from apple butter!
1980: mountain man Harry Truman, 83, refuses to leave his home on the slopes of Mount St Helens in Washington, USA. He was killed when it erupted.

THIS IS THE END

The world will end by a giant flood on February 20th 1524.
Johannes Stoeffler, Tubingen University. The world certainly ended for hundreds who took to the Rhine on the appointed day and were drowned when storms capsized their boats.

The world will be destroyed by fire on April 3rd 1843.
New England, 1833: having mistakenly predicted the end of everything that year, former atheist William Miller announces he was a decade out. The appearance of a comet towards the end of March 1843 fuelled a certain amount of hysteria; the New York Herald *published the prediction, and 'Millerites' began killing their families – and then themselves – in order to get to heaven early. On April 3rd thousands gathered on the hilltop overlooking Miller's home . . . and waited. . . .*

On April 4th Miller recalculated; July 7th was the new correct date. Followers dug themselves mass graves and had coffins made, and Miller sold them special white robes to wait in . . . He sold a few more to the faithful who waited on the next appointed day, March 21st 1844 . . . and the next one, October 22nd.

This time, they had had enough. The 100,000-strong Millerite Brethren split up – thereby giving birth to the Church of Seventh Day Adventists, among other things.

The world then to an end shall come
In Eighteen Hundred and Eighty-One.
Life & Prophecies of Ursula Sontheil (Mother Shipton), *1881.*

The world then at an end we'll view
In Eighteen Hundred and Eighty-Two.
Life & Prophecies of Ursula Sontheil (Mother Shipton), *1882.*

My figures coincide in fixing 1950 as the year when the world must go smash.
US historian Henry Adams, Letters, *March 22nd 1903.*

The deliverance of the saints must take place some time before 1914.
Jehovah's Witnesses founder Charles Taze Russell, Studies in the Scripture, *Volume III, edition of 1910.*

The deliverance of the saints must take place some time after 1914.
Charles Taze Russell, Studies in the Scripture, *Volume III, edition of 1923.*

If Christ does not appear to meet his 144,000 faithful shortly after midnight on February 6th or 7th, it means that my calculations, based on the Bible, must be revised.
He didn't, so presumably they were: Margaret Rowen, leader of the Church of Advanced Adventists, who foretold that the Messiah would come to Hollywood in 1925. Perhaps He never made it past the screen test.

The Pyramid symbolism, when considered in conjunction with biblical prophecy, indicates that its message is addressed to the present era, and that the final Time of Tribulation, so often prophesied in the Bible, is now upon us.
D. Davidson and H. Aldersmith, in The Great Pyramid: Its Divine Message, *1924, calculated that the world would end on September 6th 1936.*

A very real problem was, and still is, to ascertain the literal significance and character of the epoch whose crisis date was September 6th 1936.
How true. George F. Riffert, Great Pyramid Proof of God, *post-1936 editions. Many pyramidologists subsequently decided the epochal event must have been the abdication of King Edward VIII. The 1940 edition of* The Great Pyramid: Its Divine Message *fixed August 20th 1953 as the date of the Second Coming.*

I think the world is going to blow up in seven years. The public is entitled to a good time during those seven years.
Henry Luce, publisher of Life, Time *and* Fortune, *justifies his decision to publish* Sports Illustrated *in 1960. He died seven years later.*

Moses made mistakes, Abraham made mistakes, David made mistakes, Elijah made mistakes. . . .
Herbert W. Armstrong, publisher of The Plain Truth, *explains why the world didn't end in 1972, as foretold by him.*

The world then to an end shall come
In Nineteen Hundred and Ninety-One.
Life & Prophecies of Ursula Sontheil (Mother Shipton), *post-1882 editions.*

A great king of terror will descend from the skies
The year 1999, seventh month,
To resuscitate the great king of Angolmois,
Around this time Mars will reign for the good cause.
Quatrain from the Centuries *of Nostradamus. If the great king of Angolmois has reason to believe this is* not *a Regrettable prophecy, he may care to contact the publishers . . . nicely.*

How to use the index
Roman numerals indicate that the person, event or theme listed is the *subject of the quotation.*
Bold numerals indicate that the person, newspaper, periodical etc. listed is the *source of the quotation.*